CRIMSON DESERT

CRIMSON DESERT

Indian Wars of the American Southwest

ODIE B. FAULK

New York
OXFORD UNIVERSITY PRESS
1974

For LAURA
Who reads all of them first

PREFACE

The land mass that now constitutes the American Southwest has endured successive waves of migration and invasion. More than 20,000 years ago the Paleo-Indians came in nomadic tribes to establish their homes, hunt food, and seek perfection for some afterlife. Centuries and tens of centuries passed, each era bringing some newcomer to the region, some new tribe to contest with the old for ownership of the better land. Wars of epic proportion were fought, each tribe facing its own Armageddon, some definitive contest that saw it annihilated or so enslaved that it was swallowed by its conqueror or else driven onto land so marginal and undesirable that its neighbors left it alone. By the sixteenth century this cycle had been repeated dozens of times: wandering tribes were supplanted by cave dwellers, who, in turn, gave way to basket makers and cliff dwellers and hunters and farmers.

Suddenly, however, the tribes were confronted by new and different invaders, the Europeans who gradually came to the land in ever-increasing numbers. Although these newcomers arrived by a different route—by ship across the Atlantic rather than over some land bridge from Asia—they too contested for the best land and drove the others onto the marginal acres. By the last half of the nineteenth century, the newcomers, usually called the white race, and the older owners, referred to as the red race, had arrived at a time of total confrontation. Together these two races, red and white, sowed hatred and distrust, and they reaped mutilation, death, and destruction. They left an enduring legacy of recrimination and antipathy.

The wars were marked by the anguished screams of children seeking parents no longer able to hear; by the moans of teen-agers enslaved, even mutilated, by an alien race; and by the cries of soldiers and warriors whose life blood was draining away to crimson the land. Each race had its heroes and its villains—and no monopoly on truth and right. Both performed deeds of daring and dishonor, of valor and cowardice, of magnanimity as well as meanness of spirit. And, as always in war, one side won and the other lost.

Herein is a history of the wars of the Southwest, a summary and a synthesis of the bloody confrontation between white and red. The emphasis is on the years following 1846, when the Stars and Stripes began to fly over the land. There were battles fought other than the ones covered in this volume, for a total coverage is impossible, short of a multi-volume effort and the study of several lifetimes. I chose to concentrate on the Apache, Comanche, and Navajo tribes, for most of the remaining groups in the Southwest were placed on reservations early and posed no real impediment to white domination. The result is a chronicle of man's inhumanity to man.

In drafting this volume I have incurred numerous debts. The staff of the Library at Oklahoma State University, as always, provided great help, as in years past did the staffs of the Texas State Library and Archives, the Library of the University of New Mexico, the Library at the University of Arizona, and the Arizona Historical Society. Each of these repositories contains original and secondary sources difficult to find elsewhere, and their librarians and directors have been most generous. The source of each photograph in the book is identified beneath it; to those who generously hunted for these and who made them available, I offer my thanks, as I also do to Aaron and Ruth Cohen for the aid and encouragement they have given me over the years. And I acknowledge with gratitude the help of the editorial staff at Oxford University Press, particularly that of Sheldon Meyer, who has done much to improve this work.

Finally, I dedicate this book to my wife Laura, who over the years has proofread my manuscripts first, catching my mistakes of spelling, grammar, and syntax, and offering criticism in the finest sense of the word. My debts to her grow with each passing year, as do my appreciation and love.

O.B.F.

Stillwater, Oklahoma
Spring 1974

CONTENTS

CRIMSON DESERT

1
A LAND TO LOVE, A LAND TO HATE

Mount Tsikomo in northern New Mexico rises from the desert below to thrust a barren and windswept summit almost 12,000 feet toward the heavens. From it can be seen the Jemez Mountains to the west and south, the Rocky Mountains to the north, and to the east a plateau that drops away toward the Rio Grande Valley. On the eastern slope of this mountain the waters drain into the Gulf of Mexico and the Atlantic, while on the western side the moisture moves toward the Gulf of California and the Pacific. This is a mid-place, a continental divide, a place where the weary traveler realizes that he is halfway across the Southwest.

Most early Americans crossing the Southwest found the Continental Divide a welcome sight, for to them the region was strange and foreign. As they moved west, either from Missouri down the Santa Fe Trail or from towns in Texas to El Paso, they left the Mississippi Valley behind, along with everything familiar. They traveled across the Great Plains on this trip, a treeless region where there was increasingly less rainfall the farther west they went. Zebulon Montgomery Pike in 1806 summed up the reaction of most Americans when he stated that the Great Plains constituted a "Great American Desert," one forever unfit for farming and a place habitable only for wandering Indians.

As weary pilgrims approached New Mexico they became more

aware of the mountains. Nothing east could have prepared them for such mighty peaks. In New Mexico they came upon the southern Rockies, a chain that extended down from Colorado and west into central Arizona. And in California, within sight of the Pacific Ocean, was the Coastal Range, also known as the Sierra Nevada. Between these two systems was the Sierra Madre Occidental (the Mexican Rockies), which extended northward into southern Arizona. On the sides of all the mountains grew piñon pines, Douglas fir, and Englemann spruce, and some of their summits were so high that no trees could withstand the extreme cold and gale-blast winds that swirled around them.

These mountains are the source of water for the four major river systems of the Southwest: the Pecos, the Rio Grande, the Colorado, and the Gila. They are born high in the mountains from the snow which falls each winter; moreover, occasional cloudbursts give off large amounts of water, which likewise runs into the rivers. The streams, for the most part, flow through lands of barren plateaus, sheer cliffs, and wide deserts, and all are major movers of silt. Rarely along their courses are the streams tree-lined and stately; rather they roar between granite cliffs hundreds of feet high, throwing white water against imprisoning walls. Where they are wide and turgid, their neighbors are cactus, Spanish daggers, yucca, and mesquite, and jack rabbits, lizards, wild hogs, and deer drink from them.

The American pioneers, as they crossed the Southwest, wended their way around the mountains and, where possible, along the rivers. Elsewhere they tried to carry enough water to get from one stream or waterhole to the next. The mountains were never out of sight or out of mind. However, it was the desert which occupied their attention most. Perhaps the most memorable plant of all to them was the Saguaro cactus, which was fitting, for it is indeed the king of cacti. Growing occasionally to fifty and more feet in height and ten tons and more in weight, the Saguaro cacti throw out branches that gracefully curve until they have the appearance of a candelabrum. In the shadow of these desert giants are a rich variety of plants, shrubs, and trees: sagebrush, saltbush, cholla, palo verde, ocotillo, mesquite—most prickly with thorns and spines and all with deep root systems. Even the animal life was strange to the early pioneers: the rock squirrel, which lives on the ground; snakes of a dozen and more varieties, many of them poisonous; lizards, among them the famed gila monster; birds, most notorious of which is the road runner, but equally strange the cactus wren, which makes its home among the thorns of the cacti; spiders, including the tarantula; and mammals, such as the skunk, the coyote, the bobcat, the deer, and the javelina (wild hog). Most of these animals are night foragers or come out only in the early morning or late afternoon to hunt, for in summer at midday or early afternoon the temperature rises to 125° and more at ground level. During the heat of the day they seek shade or go underground. Only the birds can escape the heat by flying up to cooler temperatures, and thus they alone roam during the heat of the day.

To the American newcomers the desert seemed a harsh, cruel place where animals and insects were involved in a vicious chain of eat-or-be-eaten, where almost everything was simultaneously hunter and hunted. Plants, animals, geography—all were alien to the travelers. Most Americans wanted to cross this region as rapidly as possible. Their object was to get to the California coast where the land was more similar to what they knew and where they saw economic opportunity. Yet in crossing the Southwest—and later, when some of them came to recognize the beauty and even the economic potential of the area—they came into conflict with the inhabitants who saw the Southwest as home.

Just as Mount Tsikomo is a geographical landmark, so also it was a spiritual place for one major group of Southwestern Indians. At the exact center of the top of this mountain, there is a mound of stones eleven feet in diameter and five feet in height. From inside the mound rises a spruce tree without bark. The Indians of the vicinity, generally known as the Pueblo tribes, regarded this as the exact center of the earth, the mid-point between all directions of the compass as well as everything above and below. South of the mound and slightly lower in elevation was the "shrine of the middle," consisting of an oval ring of rock; from it a number of short, stone-bordered paths ran, each leading in the direction of one of the principal pueblos of Indians. To the east was Taos and Sia; to

The Zuñi pueblo. *Courtesy Western History Collections, University of Oklahoma Library.*

the south was Laguna, Ácoma, and Zuñi; and to the west was the Hopi. Inside the ring of stones at the shrine of the middle was a pool of water, and from it, these Indians thought, came all the water so essential to them in their desert homeland.

The major pueblos in this region numbered about twenty at the time of the arrival of the first Spaniards in 1540. The tribes lived in permanent villages, their stone houses built around a central plaza. Many of the structures were several stories in height and contained living quarters for many families. They were the first apartment houses in North America. At the center of each village was the "kiva," a round house partly underground in which religious ceremonials were held, the sacred masks and robes were kept, and the elders of the tribe convened to make major decisions.

The land surrounding the pueblo was owned by the tribe in common, although each family was allotted its own plot. On this land the tribal members grew their food: corn, beans, pumpkins, squash, peppers, and other vegetables. On the common pasture lands they herded their animals (most of which were introduced by the Spaniards): sheep, goats, burros, and horses. Each day the men went out to work in the fields or to tend the animals, returning every afternoon to the safety and protection of the pueblo walls. Sometimes the fields were as far as ten miles away, for the farming had to be done where water was available—which meant that the distance had to be covered on foot twice a day by the farmer. To get water to these fields, the Pueblo Indians built diversion dams of brush and stones and conveyed the water to the fields in ditches that were—and are—marvels of engineering (modern irrigation experts have learned that the best rate of flow for irrigation water is a two-foot drop per one hundred feet of distance covered, and this is exactly the way the Indian ditches were dug). The tribes also made pottery and baskets, spun and wove cloth, gathered piñon nuts and

A Zuñi Indian weaving. *Courtesy Western History Collections, University of Oklahoma Library.*

Hopi Indians in traditional dress. *Courtesy Western History Collections, University of Oklahoma Library.*

wild berries, raised orchards of peaches, plums, grapes, apricots, and melons, hunted, and fished.

They were a kind and hospitable people. Their lives were dominated by their religious beliefs. Much of their worship consisted of trying to persuade their gods to make it rain more often so there would be water for their crops, for such was their only means of controlling nature; other than through religion they accepted their weather and geography. In years when the harvest was bountiful, they stored excess food for use in years when the rains failed them. Theirs was a life of hard work, thrift, and industry.[1]

To the west, across the present state boundary separating Arizona and New Mexico, the Hopi lived. They were cousins of the

The interior of a Hopi dwelling in the pueblo. *Courtesy Western History Collections, University of Oklahoma Library.*

Pueblo tribes and made their homes on three great mesas in northeastern Arizona. From the great Kaibab Plateau are three ridges, much like fingers, which extend south into the desert country. These huge fingers are broken at the tips to form three high mesas with flat tops; the Hopi referred to them as the First, Second, and Third Mesas. Originally there were many Hopi villages, but by 1846 and the American conquest only three were still in existence.

They, like the Pueblo Indians, followed a schedule of heavy work and prayer. Growing sufficient food to feed themselves was difficult, for they did not dig irrigation ditches; rather they depended on the rainfall, which they tried to influence with their annual rain dance. With the water that did fall from the sky they raised corn, beans, and squash. They never adopted Christianity from the Spaniards, and they resisted the use of the Spanish language; rather they

Pima and Maricopa Indians meeting with soldiers in the 1850s. *Courtesy Western History Collections, University of Oklahoma Library.*

held to their ancient language and gods. The animals they acquired were herded on the deserts below their mesas; the women carried up water in jars on their heads, and the timber for firewood and for building the Hopi cut in canyons, some of which were miles away.

To the southwest of the Hopi were the desert tribes of Arizona: the Pima, the Maricopa, and the Papago. The Pima occupied the valley of the Gila River, the Maricopa that of the Salt River, and the Papago the desert country of southwestern Arizona. They were principally agricultural Indians who built their homes of cactus ribs and thatch. The most prosperous of the three were the Pima, who practiced irrigation, cultivated extensive fields of corn, wheat, and vegetables, and made fine pottery and baskets. The Maricopa were agricultural and not as industrious as their Pima neighbors. John Russell Bartlett, who visited the Pima in 1852, noted, "In these communities, there are men who labor in the fields, while others lounge about the villages doing nothing. They seem to have their dandies and gentlemen of leisure, as well as their more civilized brethren. The women, too, were carrying water on their heads, or transporting other things in the sprawling frames upon their backs."

The Papago were less prosperous yet, for they did not practice irrigation. Rather they planted small fields at the base of hills, where the runoff of rain water would occasionally wet their crops; a small earthen wall on the downhill side would hold what little moisture came down, and in this muddy ground the Papago would plant corn in the spring. They constructed small artificial lakes from which to water their animals and to get their own drinking water; such lakes naturally attracted game animals, which were

A Pima Indian village in central Arizona. From J. Ross Brown, *A Tour Through Arizona* (1864).

Papago Indians. *Courtesy Western History Collections, University of Oklahoma Library.*

killed for food. Other than these animals the Papago depended on
cactus fruit as a principal source of food. They, like the Pima and
Maricopa, were a frugal and peaceful people.

Of the three desert tribes, the Papago were the most influenced
by Spanish missionaries. They adopted Spanish to the extent that
almost all the tribe could converse in the ancient tongue of Castille
and Léon, and most paid lip service to the Catholic religion. Those
who lived close to missions began dressing in the same style of
clothing as was worn by the lower classes of Mexico, so that in
most ways they resembled Mexicans more than Indians. Yet under-
neath their surface changes, they retained their old religious beliefs

Yuma Indians in ceremonial dress. *Courtesy Western History Collections,
University of Oklahoma Library.*

—as well as a tendency to celebrate in the desert when the cactus fruit ripened. And when all else failed, they gathered mesquite beans and ate them.[2]

To the west of this desert country, along the banks of the Colorado River, lived the Quechan tribes, whose homeland stretched from the Gulf of California north to the Grand Canyon area. Most numerous were the Yuma. Early Spanish explorers commented that the Yuma were noteworthy for their handsome features, tall men, and beautiful women. Father Francisco Garcés, who worked among them in 1780-1781, wrote, "They bathe at all seasons, and arrange the hair, which they always wear long, in diverse figures, utilizing for this purpose a kind of gum or sticky mud. Always are they painted, some with black, others with red, and many other colors."

The Yuma secured most of their food through farming. Because of the warm climate, they planted their melons, corn, beans, and pumpkins in March; then, when the snow melted in the mountains, the Colorado River would flood their region, thereby irrigating their crops. Moreover, they knew how to store some of their food so that it would not spoil; Captain Juan Bautista de Anza, when he crossed this area in 1776, wrote that he and his party were given melons which the Indians had preserved by burying in the sand.

Although the Yuma lived along the Colorado River, they ate fish only on rare occasions. When the river failed to flood and irrigate their crops, they preferred to subsist on mesquite beans, piñon nuts, roots, and seeds. They did not build boats on which to travel the river. When they had to cross the river, they used rude rafts made of bundles of reeds and twigs; whatever goods they had were piled on the rafts, and the people held on with their hands and moved the rafts by kicking their feet. Along the river they constructed their homes of cottonwood branches, with walls and roofs of thatch. The huts were grouped together into villages of families, from which they rarely moved. When danger threatened, they fought and fought hard—they were more warlike than the Pima and Papago; they did not seek out war, however, for their economy was not based on booty taken in raids.

Upriver from the Yuma lived their cousins, the Mohave. Joseph

Soldiers visiting a Mojave Indian village in the 1850s. *Courtesy Western History Collections, University of Oklahoma Library.*

C. Ives, who visited this region in 1858, said the Mohave were as fine a people physically as he had ever seen; the men were strong and athletic, the women beautiful. The one feature which distinguished them from the Yuma was their practice of tattooing themselves, generally their faces. And they loved to paint their bodies in artistic ways. They, like the Yuma, depended on the annual flooding of the Colorado to irrigate their crops of beans, corn, melons, and pumpkins; they supplemented this food with mesquite beans, piñon nuts, and, to a limited extent, fish. The Mohave had also learned to store their grain by building round mud structures with flat roofs, in which they kept a year's supply of food.

Their homes were made for comfort in their hot desert environment, not for protection. The walls were constructed up to a height of three feet, either of earth or of thatch held upright by cottonwood sticks; posts at the four corners supported a flat roof made of

Mohave Indians. Note the ceremonial tatooing. *Courtesy Western History Collections, University of Oklahoma Library.*

brush covered with sand. Homes were rarely grouped together to form a village; rather they were scattered. But the Mohave were not a nomadic people. They lived in peace; the river, their source of livelihood in a vast desert of heat and drought, protected them from invasion.[3]

The natives of southern California were similar in appearance to the Indians along the Colorado River, yet their level of civilization was extremely low. Pottery was practically unknown to them, most of their homes were of grass or brush, and they did not farm. In fact, their civilization was still at the hunting and gathering stage; the warriors hunted deer and small game and fished, while the women gathered acorns, seed, roots, and berries. Theirs was a simple life with little open warfare, for the pursuit of food was always so time-consuming that they had little time or inclination for warfare.

All of these tribes—Pueblo, Hopi, Pima, Maricopa, Papago, Yuma, Mohave, and California Indians—were more passive than active in their relations with other natives. They were not out to

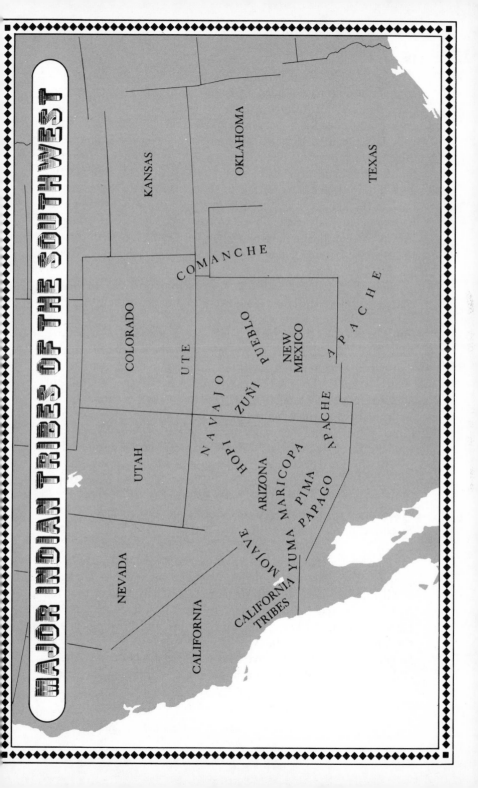

MAJOR INDIAN TRIBES OF THE SOUTHWEST

KANSAS

OKLAHOMA

TEXAS

COMANCHE

COLORADO

UTE

PUEBLO

NEW
MEXICO

APACHE

NAVAJO

ZUÑI

HOPI

UTAH

APACHE

ARIZONA

MARICOPA

PIMA

PAPAGO

MOJAVE

YUMA

NEVADA

CALIFORNIA
TRIBES

CALIFORNIA

conquer or dominate other people, just as they did not try to conquer, dominate, or change nature. To them the land was as their gods had intended it to be, and who were they to change it? Their gods had provided game to be hunted and wild fruits and vegetables to be harvested. The elders of some tribes told how the gods had taught them to plant, harvest, and store food. Sometimes the gods did not make the rain fall in sufficient quantity or the rivers flood at the right season, but these they tried to remedy through religious ceremonials. Basically they were defensive tribes trying to live in harmony with nature—and to withstand the incursions of the aggressive Indians living in the area: the Apache, the Navajo, and the Comanche.

These three tribes likewise accepted nature and did not try to change it. They and their gods were in harmony on this point. However, the men were warriors who were determined to conquer sufficient food to supplement what nature provided. In all three tribes there were hereditary chieftains, but their heredity entitled them to only token power; anything more had to be earned through ability. In short, the tribal chief who inherited his position did not lose it through incompetence, but became merely a titular leader. To gain anything more he had to compete with the war chiefs, who came to their position through success on the warpath. When raids were organized, the warriors followed whatever leader inspired their confidence, and a chief who failed would find his following melting away until he had no following at all. Leadership—real leadership— among these Indians was pure democracy in action.

Most numerous of the three tribes were the Apache. To the sedentary, passive tribes of the Southwest, the Apache indeed were the enemy—the word "Apache" was a Zuñi word meaning "enemy." The Apache called themselves "Nde," which meant "the people." The exact origin of the Apache is unknown, as are those of all Indians; however, anthropologists generally believe that the Apache migrated from northwestern Canada into the Southwest between 900 and 1200 A.D. and drove out the Indians who occupied the land they wanted. The Apache are members of the Athapascan language group and still have cousins in western Canada, Alaska, and the coast of Washington and Oregon. According to Apache folklore, they are descended from a time when the world was covered with darkness.

"Among the few human beings that were yet alive," the Apache war chief Geronimo stated about their origins, "was a woman who had been blessed with many children, but these had always been destroyed by the beasts," particularly a dragon. At last a "son of the rainstorm" was born to her; him she hid in a deep cave, denying to the dragon that she had any more children for him to eat. One day, when the boy was older, he decided to hunt with his bow and arrows in the mountains. He killed a deer. Suddenly the dragon appeared; he took the meat from the boy and said, "Boy, you are nice and fat, so when I have eaten this venison I shall eat you." But the boy shot an arrow "with true aim, and it pierced the dragon's heart."

According to Geronimo, the boy grew to manhood with the name Apache: "Usen [the Apache word for God] taught him how to prepare herbs for medicine, how to hunt and how to fight. He was the first chief of the Indians and wore the eagle's feathers as the sign of justice, wisdom, and power. To him, and to his people, as they were created, Usen gave homes in the land of the west."

At the time the Apache arrived in the Southwest, they were hunters and gatherers, living on small game, which they killed with their bows and arrows, and on wild plants. In their new homeland, the eastern Apache became buffalo hunters—the meat of these shaggy beasts provided their major supply of food; from the hides they made clothing, and from the bones, utensils. Although fish and bear could be had, they were taboo. On the plains their shelters were called tepees, conical homes made of poles and buffalo hides. With the arrival of the horse, the eastern Apache became mobile, nomadic raiders.

In the desert Southwest, the western Apache lived in brush shelters, called wickiups which the women made easily and quickly from poles, mud, and brush; such a dwelling was necessary for wandering and nomadic tribesmen. Although they too acquired horses, they never really became "horse Indians" as did their eastern cousins; rather they prided themselves on their ability to travel quickly on foot through their mountain-and-desert homeland.

The ribs of an Apache wickiup showing general shape of this dwelling. *Courtesy Western History Collections, University of Oklahoma Library.*

All Apache, western and eastern, adopted basket making from their neighbors, and they made some pottery. In physical appearance they were slightly taller than average for Indians, and they were noted orators. But principally they were skilled warriors. Because of the nature of the land on which they lived, a region that was hard and which had little forgiveness in it for human mistakes, and perhaps in part because they had made enemies of the Indians who previously lived in the area, the Apache became hard and cruel to anyone except themselves—remorseless warriors and guerrilla fighters. They traveled in very small bands because the land would not support large numbers at once, each subtribe with hereditary chiefs to whom they gave allegiance. But on the warpath the men followed whichever leader inspired their confidence by his success as thief and murderer. They came in sudden raids, swooping down on unsuspecting villages of other Indians (and later on the Spaniards and Mexicans); they drove off all possible livestock, seized all available corn, beans, and food, and enslaved women and children (whom they adopted into the tribe in a way that eventually brought equality). They were noted for their cruel and warlike nature, their strength and endurance, and their ability to spread terror among other tribes.[4]

One band of Apache eventually became so largé that gradually it assumed the status of a separate tribe, the Navajo. Their homeland was northwestern New Mexico and northeastern Arizona, an enormous area that even spilled over into parts of Colorado and Utah. Normally they drifted in small bands seeking pasture for their herds of animals, but Canyon de Chelly in northeastern Arizona was their great stronghold. There, they cultivated fields of corn, melons, and other vegetables. They had no central government in the form of one chief; rather each band had its own chief, and the chiefs would come together at Canyon de Chelly to form a tribal council that settled issues of importance to the entire tribe.

As with their Apache cousins, the Navajo obtained their livelihood in part from hunting deer and small animals and from gathering piñon nuts and other local plants. However, their principal source of food—and wealth—was livestock: sheep, cattle, and horses. They stole them from the Spaniards, who moved into New Mexico beginning in 1598. Generation after generation of Navajo lived from birth to death on mutton stolen from the haciendas of Spanish grandees, supplemented by whatever else they could take on their raids. Moreover, the Navajo believed in slavery, and on their forays into Spanish (and later Mexican) territory they captured people to work for them, just as they enslaved Indians from other tribes.

Because theirs was an economy based in large measure on the herding of sheep, the Navajo became expert weavers. Their women gained widespread fame—which persists to this day—for their exceptional blankets, because of their beauty and their utility. According to Navajo legend, their ancestors did not know the use of the loom, but learned it from Pueblo Indian women who were enslaved. From captives taken from the Ute Indians (of southern Colorado), they learned the art of basket weaving.

The outstanding feature of Navajo life was the home—or *hogán*. Usually built in conical form, it was constructed by setting poles in

A Navajo hogan. *Courtesy Western History Collections, University of Oklahoma Library.*

the ground and then covering them with branches, grass, and earth (some were made of logs and others of stone). Such structures had to be of simple construction, for the superstitious Navajo would not live in a house where anyone had died (probably no other Indians have such a dread of ghosts), and so when death occurred in a hogán, the house was deserted or destroyed.

The Navajo varied greatly in physical appearance. Some towered more than six feet in height, and others were as short as five feet, two inches. This, along with their variety of coloring and facial features, was probably a result of their intermarrying with the women they captured from other tribes and adopted. Yet, overall, they were closest in appearance to Apache. Also notable about the Navajo was their sense of humor; when no strangers were present, they laughed much and were given to jokes and banter. Moreover, they were an industrious people; even the proudest among them did not disdain hard work. And, although they were fierce in battle, they did not kill for sport or torture their captives.[5]

The Apache and the Navajo were gentle in comparison to the Comanche, who rightfully saw themselves as "Lords of the Plains." Cousins of the Cheyenne, they originally lived in the mountains. With the arrival of the Spaniards and the spread of wild horses onto the plains, the Comanche captured these beasts and adapted to a horse culture, becoming in a short time the world's greatest mounted warriors. Emerging from the central Rockies, they gradually moved south in search of a warmer climate and richer booty. They were first reported at Santa Fe in 1706, but rarely did they raid this town; rather they came to New Mexico to trade for weapons, ammunition, and European goods. As they moved south they came into contact and conflict with the eastern Apache, who had

Navajo Indians in traditional dress. *Courtesy Western History Collections, University of Oklahoma Library.*

ruled the southern Great Plains for centuries. The two tribes soon became deadly enemies—with the Comanche almost always winning when battles occurred. By 1743 the Comanche were at San Antonio, and thereafter they would raid regularly as far south as the Gulf of Mexico, on occasion even riding deep into Mexico on their forays. So frequently did they slip into the Mexican state of Chihuahua that a regular road, known as the Comanche War Trail, ran from the Panhandle region of Texas through the Big Bend country and south.

As a plains tribe living on horseback, the Comanche were nomadic buffalo hunters, rarely bothering to plant or harvest crops. Their homes were tepees made of buffalo hides and lodge poles cut in the mountains; these could be erected easily, taken down quickly, and moved with little difficulty from place to place. The Comanche roamed in small bands, following whatever war chief they pleased, going north during the summer and south in the winter—and taking what they needed from anyone they encountered. Their domain was from western Texas north to Kansas and from the Rocky Mountains east to the edge of the timbered country. Within this vast domain they were divided into a number of bands held together only by a common language and set of beliefs, which meant that during negotiations the Comanche could not be represented by just one chief and that even if all the chiefs signed some agreement any warrior was free to break it. The most important subtribes among them were the Yamparika, or Root-eaters, who ranged in the vicinity of the Arkansas River; the Kotsoteka, or Buffalo-eaters, who lived to the south of the Arkansas; the Nokoni, or Wanderers, who occupied the land along the Red River; the Quahadi, or Antelope People, whose domain was the High Plains; and the Penateka, or Honey-eaters, who were in western Texas (and who would be most associated with the wars in that state).

The Comanche saw themselves as the children of the sun, superior to all other Indians and infinitely better than Spaniards and other Europeans. Yet the Comanche's word for himself was "snake"; in fact, in their sign language they indicated "Comanche" by clinching the right fist over the left breast and withdrawing it with a slithery motion to indicate stealth. This was the greatest virtue, for the measure of a Comanche's social, political, and economic stature was the number of horses he owned, which he usually obtained by theft. Thus the man who would be a political chief among the Comanche, the one who would be wealthy, the one who would have high social standing had to be as stealthy as a snake in stealing the beasts. Their entire economy was based on booty taken on raids. Prior to the arrival of the Spaniards, the raids were undertaken against other tribes; afterward, the raids were against Indian and white alike.

Shooting an enemy from a distance brought no great prestige—or "coup" as it was called—to a Comanche warrior. Rather coup, which every young man needed to "count" in order to consider himself a warrior, came from something more, something involving physical bravery as well as that indefinable something which might be called style. One story on this subject involved two Comanche who set out to see who was the better warrior. Arriving on the outskirts of a Ute village, one of them disguised himself with a blanket, entered the enemy village, went into a lodge to mingle, and touched every enemy there—the touching of a live enemy involved great coup and the touching of a dead one very little. A Comanche telling of this exploit exclaimed, "He had counted coup on twenty enemies at one time. It was a great deed."

The other warrior traveled on until late the next day when he came upon a ranch house. At night he slipped into the house where the rancher and his wife were asleep; without waking them, the warrior slipped the woman from the bed and took her away to the main camp of the Comanche. It was he who won the contest, for this was considered the greatest coup anyone in that village had ever achieved—it had never been done before.

However, the Comanche warrior out to count coup had no wish to die in battle, for he had to guard his immortal soul. He wanted horses, he desired plunder, and he would take women and children captive if he could, but he did not want to die. To die in battle was to risk scalping, and a scalped warrior could not enter heaven, which he thought was located in the eastern skies. Courage was the highest virtue among the Comanche, and they exhibited extraordinary courage when they carried off the bodies of their

Indians attacking a wagon train. From *Harper's Weekly* (1868).

dead; but once a dead warrior's scalp had been taken, not even the
bravest Comanche would touch the corpse. Their concept of bravery was completely different from that of the Europeans who came
to live in the region. The Comanche thought it stupid to stand and
fight when there was no chance of winning anything save honor;
instead they would slink away from such a contest, to return another day to steal horses, booty, and captives.

In appearance they tended to be tall, but given to fat. They did
not believe in individual ownership of land or buffalo or wild
horses. All these were free to all, and one took what he needed.
Horses and women were the only things of value, and a warrior
could claim ownership of however many of either he could capture
from outsiders; the only requirement was that he had to be able to
provide sufficient food for all his wives and children. Overseeing
each band of warriors was a chief. Leadership did not always de-
scend to the chief's oldest son; it went to the nearest male relative
of the chief who seemed best suited to lead the people. Anyone
unhappy with the chief could leave to join the band of another
chief in whom he had trust.

Because the Comanche were a warlike people who considered
themselves superior to all non-Comanche and because theirs was
an economy based on continual warfare, they became hardened.
Torture was the lot of any adult male they captured. In fact, the
torturing of prisoners was a prime source of entertainment for a village. The only exception to their disdain for non-Comanche was
their acceptance of the Kiowa and Kiowa-Apache as allies. This
relationship meant that the Kiowa and Kiowa-Apache, plains Indians who had a horse-buffalo-raiding culture, could live in relative
peace in the same area as the implacable Comanche; in return, they
supplied warriors whenever the Comanche were engaged in some
campaign that demanded large numbers of men.[6]

These tribes—offensive and defensive, settled and nomadic, agricultural and plundering—passed quiet centuries prior to the arrival
of Europeans in their land. The years succeeded each other with
quiet, if bloody, monotony as they contended with each other and
with nature for food. Their daily lives were almost exactly the same
as those of their ancestors for innumerable generations, giving them
a feeling of being at one with nature and with their ancestors.
Theirs was not altogether a bleak, brutish existence, for there was
the pleasure of the hunt, the generosity of nature, and the satisfaction of geographical beauty. Yet life was uncertain for these pioneers of the Southwest; crops occasionally failed, game grew scarce,
the rains did not fall, and battles sometimes went against them.
They suffered from disease, from periodic famine, and from man's
cruelty to man. Such an existence was all they had ever known,
however, and they found reason within it for hope, for laughter, for
dreams.[7]

The arrival of Spaniards in the first quarter of the sixteenth century did little to change the pattern of Indian life. In 1598 New
Mexico was colonized, and a century later missionaries, soldiers,
and civilians penetrated Texas and Arizona, followed in 1769 by
the colonization of California. Spaniards never really owned the
land, although within their European context they thought they
did; in reality the masters of the Southwest were, as always, the Indians. Spaniards did bring animals—horses, cattle, sheep—and they
introduced animal power to agriculture, several new crops, such as

wheat and fruit orchards, and a work ethic. Moreover, they brought the Christian religion, making converts among some of the sedentary, passive Indians, such as the Pueblo tribes of New Mexico and the Pima and Papago of Arizona. However, even the normally peaceful natives rose in rebellion; in 1680 the Pueblo tribes of New Mexico attempted extermination of all Spaniards, as did the Pima in Arizona in 1751. The lordly Comanche and Apache were never reduced to missions; the Spanish soldiers who tried to win submission failed disastrously; and the civilians who moved to the northern frontier did so at the sufferance of the Indians. Similarly, when Mexico achieved independence in 1821, its citizens only tenuously occupied the Southwest; few of them lived in western Texas, some 30,000 in New Mexico (including Christian Indians), 600 in Arizona, and 5,000 in California.[8]

During the Mexican years in the Southwest, yet another nationality appeared: the American. These were roily, restless frontiersmen, sons and grandsons and great-grandsons of English, Scot, and Irish settlers along the Eastern Seaboard. Almost from the date of the first English settlement in America, these pioneers had moved westward in search of free land and distance from the restraint of sheriffs and neighbors. They had crossed beyond the tidewater plantations of Virginia into Kentucky and Tennessee, and when these filled up they moved still farther west. In the process they would find a suitable plot of ground, cut trees to build a log cabin, split logs to erect a rail fence, clear land to plant a crop, kill game to secure meat, and distill a little corn to make sipping whiskey. Any Indian who contested the pioneers' right to whatever land struck their fancy had to be prepared to fight.

Over and over this process was repeated, each generation moving farther west than its parents. Distance was the universal cure for whatever bothered a man; distance removed him from the plague of tax collectors, creditors, and sheriffs, all of whom seemed to flower in the sunshine created by crowds. When he began to feel hemmed in, the pioneer would load his wagon, gather his family, and set out toward the setting sun. West, ever west, marched the tide of American empire.

The frontiersmen soon crossed the Mississippi River to settle in

Louisiana, purchased by their government in 1803 from France. But the west bank of the Mississippi filled rapidly, and then the pioneer faced a startling new phenomenon: the Great Plains. This was a land on which there were no trees to build log cabins and erect split rail fences, a land where the rainfall was less than twenty inches a year and thus cotton and corn would not grow, a land where the rivers narrowed to mere streams that did not always flow year round. In short, the Great Plains was a region where all the pioneering techniques that they had been perfecting for two hundred years were of no benefit. In their search for suitable unoccupied land, these frontiersmen cast covetous eyes toward Texas. They liked what they saw there. On the far side of the Sabine River were the same towering pines so familiar across Louisiana, Mississippi, Alabama, Georgia, and much of the Atlantic region. In eastern Texas the rainfall totalled forty inches a year and more. And the soil was similar to that east of the Mississippi. Moreover, this was a land thinly populated by Indians and Spaniards only. Neither nationality disturbed the American frontiersman; he had long since decided that the Indian should be driven west or exterminated, and the Spaniard was contemptible, a member of a weak, barbarous race of timorous cowards unable to conquer and populate an extremely promising land.

At the invitation of the Mexican government, which knew it had to populate Texas or lose it, Americans after 1820 began to immigrate legally to Texas. By the mid-1830s the province had 30,000 pioneers—and they were unhappy that the Mexican system provided for no trial by jury, no freedom of religion, and no system of free, public education. However, it was the overthrow of the Mexican constitution by the would-be dictator Antonio López de Santa Anna in the summer of 1835 that drove them first to rebellion and then to revolution. On April 21, 1836, at the Battle of San Jacinto, they won their independence from Mexico and established the Republic of Texas. A tumultuous decade later they were annexed to the United States at their own request.

While these events were transpiring in Texas, other Americans were seeking fortune and adventure in other parts of the Southwest. Traders had opened the Santa Fe Trail from Missouri to the capital of New Mexico, and down this road every year came caravans of wagons loaded with goods for trade and barter. Other Americans, known as mountain men, had come southwest looking for beaver pelts; they had headquartered at the little oasis towns of Santa Fe and Taos, going out in the summer to trap their furry quarry in icy mountain streams in order to supply the raw material for the type of hat then in demand. Other Americans had been lured to California to participate in the hide and tallow trade or else to receive huge land grants on the Pacific slope. Few of them made this journey overland, however, for the desert was new, strange, alien, forbidding; instead they went around the tip of South America by ship, a slow journey of six months.

Relations between the United States and Mexico deteriorated until, in the spring of 1846, war began. On April 24 that year Mexican troops crossed the Rio Grande, following a secret declaration of "defensive war" against the United States by the Mexican Congress the day before, and attacked soldiers under the command of Brigadier General Zachary Taylor. The war that followed would bring a change in the ownership of the Southwest. Thousands of dollars would be spent, along with thousands of lives, before peace was restored in 1848 by the Treaty of Guadalupe Hidalgo. This drew a new boundary that, when supplemented in 1853 by the Gadsden Purchase, brought a new owner to the land—in the European legal sense. However, this new owner would find a previous tenant on the land, one as proud as the American frontiersman, one as contentious, one as certain of his place in the sun.

Wars of tragic proportions followed. For the Indians, raising an army was no problem. Their men, young and old, were warriors trained to believe in the glories of the warpath, and they fought for those things people everywhere have held most dear: for their homes and religion and way of life. To them the encroaching American settlers posed a physical and psychological threat, one to be eliminated.

The whites, on the other hand, thought they owned the land by right of conquest. They saw the Indians as little better than wild animals, an impediment to civilization not making productive use of the land. Those Indians who did not oppose American entry or contest American passage across the land—that is, the passive tribes such as the Pueblo natives of New Mexico, the Pima, Papago, and Maricopa of Arizona, the Yuma and Mohave of California—were allowed to live in peace; in fact, the early American frontiersmen saw little economic potential in the desert and mountainous land of the Southwest and did not contest for ownership of the homeland of these tribes. The passive Indians were quickly given reservations that encompassed the acres on which they had always lived. Except for the Indian agents who cheated them on occasion, the tribes were left in peace. The others—Comanche, Navajo, and Apache—could not be ignored, however. They made their presence known early because of their habit of raiding and of capturing women and children, along with mules, horses, and other property. When these two races came into conflict, the Americans turned to their army and demanded victory; that word meant either annihilation or confinement for the enemy. Such was the demand placed on the soldiers by most frontiersmen.

Yet Congress and the President did not always provide an army capable of performing the task demanded of it. In fact, the federal government during the four decades following the end of the Mexican War never gave the army total authority to oversee the Indian problem. Instead this responsibility was divided between the army and the Department of the Interior, which was created in 1849. The Indian Bureau (later to be called the Bureau of Indian Affairs) was attached to it. Thereafter every territory in the Southwest had its superintendent of Indian affairs, and each reservation its agent. These civilians were assigned the responsibility for nonmilitary phases of Indian management; once the Indians surrendered and were placed on a reservation, the army had no control over them in any way. The agent could be corrupt or honest, inefficient or capable, but army officers in the area could do nothing. Only when renegades fled the reservation and the agent clearly assigned jurisdiction to the army could it take the field.

And the soldiers who took the field found little sympathy or support from officials in Washington. During the Mexican War the army had grown from 7,200 to huge proportions with the enlistment of 50,000 and more volunteers. When the war came to an end an economy-minded Congress reduced the army to near its pre-war size. However, arguments were advanced that this number should be increased, for the nation's domain had almost doubled between 1845 and 1848. Therefore in 1850 Congress authorized a legal strength of some 14,000; five years later Congress again proved generous, allowing the creation of four new regiments which brought the army to some 18,000 men. Such was the size of the army called upon not only to contend with frontier Indian problems and to man all army posts, but also to try to keep the peace in "Bleeding Kansas" in the mid-1850s.

The outbreak of Civil War saw the army increasing to over a million—only to be reduced quickly at the end of that tragic conflict. In 1866 it was reduced to 54,302 men, in 1869 to 45,000, in 1870 to 30,000, and in 1874 to 25,000. These were the troops manning all army garrisons and enforcing reconstruction in the South, as well as fighting the Indians of the American West. The soldiers went West in numbers insufficient to accomplish the goals set for them. Moreover, in the period prior to the Civil War, Congressmen preferred to send infantry to fight the Indians, for a regiment of cavalry cost some $1,200,000 more annually than did a like number of foot soldiers. This meant that infantrymen frequently found themselves trying to contend with some of the best cavalrymen in the world, the Plains Indians. Both prior to and after the Civil War, the soldiers were called upon to fight with antiquated weapons and equipment, their Indian adversaries often having more modern firearms. Congress in 1866 decreed that the army had to exhaust war surpluses before ordering new materials, which meant that for the next ten years almost all weapons and equipment were obsolete.

All of the men in the Indian-fighting army were volunteers, both officers and enlistees. The average age of the soldiers was twenty-three, many of whom were recent immigrants. Some enlistees were attracted to the life by the steady employment offered and by the pride and challenge of soldiering. They received seven dollars a month in the infantry and eight dollars a month in the cavalry; this was increased by four dollars a month in 1854 and after the Civil War to thirteen dollars a month for cavalry and infantry. In addition, they also received regular rations, free medical care, and some other benefits. Other volunteers joined to "see the elephant," lured by tales of adventure in the West. Also, the military life attracted criminals and other undesirables who found it expedient to travel and who knew they could not be traced in that era before fingerprints and photographs were part of a man's service file.

Once a man was assigned to a regiment, he rarely transferred out of it, no matter how long he remained in the army. In fact, he usually did not transfer out of the company to which he was sent. Even at small posts consisting of only two companies, a man had little contact with anyone other than the men of his own outfit. In this company he found himself almost completely at the mercy of his noncommissioned officers. He could not even speak to an officer without the permission of his first sergeant, who actually ran the company. And an ability with fists was one of the first requisites for promotion to noncommissioned officer status. The men, along with the officers, could be brutal and sadistic or humane and gentle, depending more on personal temperament than on regulations. Because of isolation and ignorance, few soldiers knew how to go about complaining of injustices and unkindnesses, and few court martials were ever held to punish officers and noncommissioned officers for brutality. Punishments ranged from marching double-time around the parade ground to the branding of deserters with a D and thieves with a T. Men were suspended by their thumbs, wrists, or arms in the guardhouse for as long as a full day at a time. Harsh and unusual punishments could be given with relative impunity.

The food was not good. A typical daily menu started with a breakfast of salt pork, fried mush, and strong black coffee; lunch usually consisted of dry bread and "slumgullion stew," a concoction of debatable ancestry; and the evening meal normally was more dry bread and more coffee, occasionally with three prunes for dessert. Men at the frontier forts often tried to supplement their diet with buffalo, deer, wild turkey, and fish; they purchased fresh vegetables from local farmers where possible. In the Southwest this generally meant beans—and yet more beans.

The medical service to the soldiers was primitive, to say the least. The army at that time had no medical branch. Rather it made contracts with civilian physicians to serve at the post, usually doctors incapable of sustaining themselves in private practice. The death rate among their patients at the Western posts was appallingly high. Cholera, dysentery, fevers, even scurvy were commonplace according to medical reports forwarded to Washington, while venereal disease was epidemic. Little wonder, then, that the average annual desertion rate of enlisted men between 1848 and 1861 was 28 per cent, and from 1867 to 1891 inclusive was 33 per cent.

Almost three-quarters of the officer corps prior to the Civil War —73 per cent—were graduates of West Point, men whose names would fill the command ranks during the War Between the States. Principally they were young, competent, energetic, and proud of their recent records against the Mexicans; however, many in the upper ranks were political hacks, martinets, petty tyrants, even downright incompetents.

Soldiering was difficult for the officers, just as for the enlisted men. Isolated from polite society, the officer could associate only with his fellow officers, as fraternization with enlisted men was forbidden. He thus had a very limited circle from which to draw his friendships. His pay was small, a lieutenant after the Civil War drawing only forty dollars a month; out of this he had to pay for his mount, his equipment, and his clothing, and support his family, if he had one. After the Civil War there were too many high-ranking officers, owing to the necessities of that conflict with its huge armies; therefore promotion became intolerably slow. For the officer promotion came within the regiment, as it did for enlisted men within the company. Only through the death or retirement of senior officers was promotion open, and then it came from seniority rather than merit; this system crippled the army with old, even ancient officers whose ambitions were severely limited.

Only at the upper ranks of the army, lieutenant colonel and above, were transfers between regiments common. Prior to the Civil War the commander of the various military departments usually were colonels; afterward the departmental commanders tended to be brigadier generals. Here the competition for promotion was keen. Few such high-ranking officers hesitated to use their relatives, their in-laws, their friends, even their friends-of-friends in gaining a rung up the ladder; jealousies, intrigues, politics, and "wire-pulling" were normal.

It was the departmental commanders who set the level of morale within their units, just as they made the decisions that affected the lives—and deaths—of the soldiers under them. Some of the departmental commanders indulged themselves as petty tyrants, while others strove to improve the lot of their men. The officers and men under them, unlike the Apache, Navajo, and Comanche warriors, had no say in who commanded them or what their fate would be, for they had no vote in the matter. Commanders were assigned by the War Department, and the soldiers of civilized armies obeyed.

The relationship between the commanding officers and the troops was a shifting, mysterious one. There was occasionally an officer who managed a mystical marriage of romantic proportions wherein both parties were happy, the commanding officer dominating and the troops following with a devotion bordering on love. Such an officer had to be a man with a sense of history and humor, of timing and drama, of patience, and probity, yet of impatience with stupidity—and of ability to admit his own mistakes. In achieving such a relationship, it often helped if he was a man of small flaws; his mistakes, however, had to be minor, preferably of a humorous nature, not major ones involving a loss of lives or battles. He had to be able to endure as much as he demanded of his men, to laugh at his own foibles and discomforts, and to tolerate the minor pecadillos of his troops when they did not involve a loss of discipline.

Other commanding officers achieved a marriage of sorts with their troops, not a happy, romantic one, but a marriage that was stormy and demanded reconciliation time and again. They were men of ability but with major flaws—impatience, no sense of humor, a rigid and unbending nature. Yet the troops would forgive such a commanding officer if he was a superb tactician whose genius won campaigns.

Finally, there were commanding officers who made no marriage at all with their troops, who commanded through the raw, brute force of army regulations, rigid discipline, and an imperious attitude. The troops had little choice but to obey such a man, but from

him they withheld their respect, loyalty, love, even their enthusiasm.

Under one or another such commanding officer, however, the
troops went into battle in understrength numbers and often with
obsolete equipment. General John Pope, who well understood the
conditions under which the Indian-fighting army was operating,
stated their attitude about the wars against the native Americans
in his report of November 22, 1875: "It is with painful reluctance
that the military forces take the field against Indians who only
leave their reservations because they are starved there, and who
must hunt food for themselves and their families or see them perish
with hunger. . . . I desire to say with all emphasis, what every
Army officer on the frontier will corroborate, that there is no class
of men in this country who are so disinclined to war with the Indians as the army stationed among them. The Army has nothing to
gain by war with Indians; on the contrary it has everything to lose.
In such a war it suffers all the hardship and privation; and, exposed
as it is to the charge of assassination if Indians are killed; to the
charge of inefficiency if they are not. . . ."[9]

Yet there would be many such battles in the thirty-eight years between 1848 and 1886, for the two civilizations, red and white, were
in direct conflict. Both sides saw themselves as totally right and the
other totally wrong. Tragically they looked to the field of combat
for a settlement. The years would see war and death, torture and
murder, theft, and exile as the bases of negotiation. This was one
situation in which the vaunted American "melting pot" failed to
work, and in which there could be no compromise short of total
surrender on one side or the other.

2

THE NAVAJO CONFRONTED

"A certain people are going to come to us," declared a Ute brave who married a Navajo woman and in 1845 came to live with her people. "From below where the sun constantly rises, they are going to come to us," he predicted; "Their ears are wider than anything. They extend down to their ankles. And these people at night, covering themselves with those ears of theirs, lie down to sleep." In addition, he concluded, one of those newcomers from the east could build "a fire on his knees," yet lie down with "his back toward it."[1]

Alexander W. Doniphan, the first American to negotiate a treaty with the Navajo, would have been astonished to learn that this prophecy apparently described him. He was tall, standing six feet, four inches, and had a large frame and erect bearing. One admirer described him as "well proportioned, altogether dignified in appearance, and gentle in his manners. . . . His bright hazel eye [is] discerning, keen and expressive. . . ."[2] However, his ears were never described as unusually large, certainly not long enough to be used as a blanket at night, nor did those who followed him from Missouri to Mexico and back during the Mexican War ever claim he could make a fire on his knees.

Doniphan, born in Kentucky in 1808, was a lawyer by profession, a politician on occasion, and a Missourian by choice. He moved there in 1830 and rose steadily through the militia ranks, so that when the Mexican War began his fellow volunteers elected him colonel and he became commander of the Missouri Mounted Volunteers. That summer they marched down the road to Santa Fe as part of the Army of the West, led by Colonel (later General) Stephen Watts Kearny. Capturing the province without firing a shot, Kearny on August 18, 1846, and again the following day told the inhabitants that, among other things, the United States would protect the local citizens from Indian attack. Ominously, however, Navajo chiefs were not among the Indian leaders who came to Santa Fe to swear allegiance to the new regime.

On September 25 Kearny departed the New Mexican capital with three hundred dragoons; he was bound for California which he intended to conquer and govern. The horses his men rode were starving and gaunt, while his men in their tattered uniforms were little more impressive. Possibly this emboldened the Navajo, for less than two weeks later they were raiding along his line of march; possibly the Indians wanted to test the might of these invaders from the east. Kearny responded on October 2 by sending Doniphan an order to "march with his regiment into the Navajo country. He will cause all the prisoners, and all the [stolen] property they hold, which may have been stolen from the inhabitants of the territory of New Mexico, to be given up." Moreover, Doniphan was to "require of them such security for their future good conduct, as he may think ample and sufficient, by taking hostages or otherwise."[3]

The following day at noon a rider dashed into Kearny's camp to tell that one hundred Navajo raiders had struck the town of Polvadera that morning and had stolen their horses and cattle. Kearny responded by dispatching Captain Benjamin D. Moore and a company of dragoons to pursue the Navajo; Moore returned later to report that pursuing New Mexicans had recovered the cattle but not the horses, and that the American soldiers had arrived too late to help. On October 5 Kearny issued an order that would be of lingering significance; in this he stated: "In consequence of the frequent and almost daily outrages committed by the Navajoes . . . , I . . . hereby authorize all the Inhabitants (Mexicans & Pueblos) . . . to form War Parties, to march into the Country of their enemies, the Navajoes, to recover their Property, to make reprisals and obtain redress for the many insults received from them." His only restriction was that "The Old, the Women and the Children of the Navajoes, must not be injured."[4]

Doniphan, sitting in Santa Fe enjoying the autumn weather, received Kearny's order on October 6. He realized that his diplomatic foray into the Navajo country would have to be quick and decisive, for winter would come early in the mountains. His was not a military campaign; rather he was to secure a release of Mexicans held captive by the Indians, along with stolen livestock, and he was to negotiate a peace treaty between the United States and the Navajo. Three of his companies were at Santa Fe, another two were at Abiquiu, and the other three were near Cebolleta. Immediately he sent word to Lieutenant Colonel Congreve Jackson, who was in command of the troops near Cebolleta, to seek out the Navajo and ask them to attend a peace council. This order reached Jackson on October 10. By coincidence a Navajo chief named Sandoval was then at Jackson's camp, and he had informed the American that "most of the chiefs were inclined toward peace [with the Americans] but that they would prefer to have the white men come into their country to discuss the terms of an agreement."[5]

Jackson therefore sent Captain John W. Reid with ten volunteers to meet with the Navajo leaders. Reid and his party slowly and painfully made their way to the Northwest, gasping in the thin air of the 8,500-foot altitude, shivering in the early autumn snow, finally arriving at the camp of the aging Navajo chieftain, Narbona. The Americans were treated well, the Navajo bartering with the Americans for items strange to them, then allowing them to see Navajo games, gambling, and dancing. At last Narbona, seventy years old, arthritic, and peaceful, agreed that he and his headmen would come to Santa Fe for a peace conference. Reid then returned to meet Jackson, his food running out before the trip was completed and his men suffering terribly.

Doniphan, meanwhile, had left Santa Fe on October 26. He and three companies marched downriver to Albuquerque. His troops were decidedly unhappy. They had not been paid since enlisting the previous summer in Missouri, and all they had was summer clothing. Nor were they able to bring wagons with them; even most of their tents had been left behind. He reached Jackson's camp without incident—although he did continue to hear of numerous Navajo raids on New Mexicans—on November 5. There he found little that was encouraging, for Jackson had run out of fresh food; they had been living on parched corn and pumpkins, most of them were sick (possibly with scurvy), and some had died.

Doniphan chose to wait there for the Navajo who had promised to follow Reid toward Santa Fe. However, the only one who came was Sandoval, and he arrived only to tell the Americans that the Navajo chiefs preferred the Americans to meet with them at Ojo del Oso (Bear Spring), which is near the present Gallup, New Mexico—far to the west. Doniphan sent word to Major William Gilpin, who commanded companies A and E of the Missouri Mounted Volunteers, to proceed to Ojo del Oso by November 20 and to bring with him any Navajo leaders he might encounter. This Gilpin did, skirting Canyon de Chelly and meeting many Navajo along the way. Doniphan himself set out on November 15 accompanied by Lieutenant Colonel Jackson and 150 troops. The next night the Americans were covered by thirteen inches of snow; they awakened to find ice in their whiskers, for they were without tents—and overcoats. Some of the men declared that their trek into Navajo country was equal to that of Hannibal or at least of Napoleon. And on November 17 these men had to move through snow waist deep, but such was Doniphan's determination that they arrived at Ojo del Oso on November 21. Major Gilpin was waiting for them, as were more than five hundred Navajo, including all the important chiefs of the subtribes, lesser tribal officials, and many warriors. The elevation was 6,500 feet, snow was on the ground, and it was intensely cold, yet the talks began that first day.

Through an interpreter identified only as T. Caldwell, Doniphan explained briefly his reasons for coming and then everyone retired for the night. The next day the American colonel spoke again. John Taylor Hughes, a member of Doniphan's party who in 1848 would publish a book,[6] recorded these conversations. Doniphan told the Navajo that

> the United States had taken military possession of New Mexico; that her laws were now extended over that territory; that the New

Mexicans would be protected against violence and invasion; and that their rights would be amply preserved to them; that the United States was also anxious to enter into a treaty of peace and lasting friendship with her red children, the Navajos; that the same protection would be given them against encroachments, and usurpation of their rights, as had been guaranteed the New Mexicans; that the United States claimed all the country by the right of conquest and both they and the New Mexicans were now become equally her children. . . .

He assured the Navajo that he had come with ample powers to "negotiate a permanent treaty between the Navajos, the Americans, New Mexicans." Finally, after extending the olive branch of peace, he threatened the alternative: a war. He warned them that they should enter into no treaty they did not intend to observe "strictly, and in good faith." The alternative, he concluded, was "powder, bullet, and the steel."

Zarcillos (also spelled Sarcilla) Largos served as spokesman for the Navajo. At this time he was middle aged, and his logic was fresh; quickly he explained to Doniphan the inconsistencies which his people detected in what had just been spoken:

Americans! you have a strange cause of war against the Navajos. We have waged war against the New Mexicans for several years. We have plundered their villages and killed many of their people, and made many prisoners. We had just cause for all this. You have lately commenced a war against the same people. You are powerful. You have great guns and many brave soldiers. You have therefore conquered them, the very thing we have been attempting to do for so many years.

You now turn upon us for attempting to do what you have done yourselves. We cannot see why you have cause of quarrel with us for fighting the New Mexicans on the west, while you do the same thing on the east.

Look how matters stand. This is our war. We have more right to complain of you for interfering in our war, than you have to quarrel with us for continuing a war we had begun long before you got here. If you will act justly, you will allow us to settle our differences.

The other Navajo chiefs could well nod their heads in agreement with these words.

Doniphan could not, however, for he had his orders—if not his own point of view. The New Mexicans had surrendered, he explained, and it was the "custom with the Americans when a people gave up, to treat them as friends thenceforward." The whole country "and everything in it" had become American by right of conquest. Therefore, when the Navajo stole something, they no longer were stealing only from New Mexicans but from Americans; when they killed, they were killing Americans. Moreover, continued Doniphan, it would be to the Navajo advantage for peace to settle upon the land. Then Americans would come to settle New Mexico, Americans who would "open a valuable trade [with the Indians] by which means they could obtain everything they needed to eat and wear in exchange for their furs and peltries."

Doniphan even invited young Navajo to journey to the United States, where they might be taught a trade. He said he saw that the Navajo were intelligent and capable of learning skills that would help their people. Apparently this prospect sounded promising to some young Navajo, for they volunteered to leave with Doniphan; he had to explain that before returning to Missouri he was on his way to Chihuahua to fight the Mexicans. That cooled the ardor of the Navajo, for the young warriors were certain the Mexicans would kill them if possible.

Doniphan apparently impressed the Navajo, for at the end of his speech to the young warriors, Zarcillos Largos indicated an Indian willingness to sign a treaty. He stated that his people did not want war with a nation that was so powerful. There followed the signing of a treaty consisting of five articles. The first of these asserted that "A firm and lasting peace and amity shall henceforth exist between the American people and the Navajo tribe of Indians." Article 2 clearly specified that both New Mexicans and Pueblo Indians were "included in the term American people." Article 3 stated that trade would be carried on between Navajo, Americans, and New Mexicans, and that all were free to visit any part of the geographical area "without molestation." Article 4 provided for a return of all prisoners "each for each" and the rest redeemed by purchase. Finally, Article 5 provided that all property taken by either party "since the 18th day of August last, shall be restored."[7]

When the treaty had been signed by Doniphan, Jackson, and Gilpin, on behalf of the United States, and by the fourteen Navajo chiefs, the Missouri colonel distributed presents which he had brought from Santa Fe. He stated that he had waited until after the treaty was signed to give them because he did not want the gifts to be misinterpreted as an attempt to buy friendship; the United States, he said, did not purchase friendship. The Navajo responded by giving him some of their blankets (Doniphan later forwarded these to the War Department as an example of what Indian industry could produce).

At the end of this conference, Doniphan was eager to get about his task of invading Mexico. However, one other task remained to be completed: peace between the Navajo and the Zuñi. If peace was to come to New Mexico, these two enemy peoples had to be persuaded to come to terms. He sent most of his troops back to the Rio Grande under the command of Monroe M. Parsons; his task was to care for the sick and then to move all able-bodied men to Valverde to await Doniphan. The colonel kept Major Gilpin and Lieutenant Colonel Jackson with him. These three, along with three Navajo chiefs and a few American troops, marched south some sixty miles to Zuñi, a pueblo containing an estimated 6,000 Indians. Doniphan, his aides, and the Navajo chiefs were housed inside the pueblo, while Gilpin and the troops bivouacked nearby. The next day, November 26, after lengthy quarrels between Zuñi and Navajo, a treaty was signed. However, the three Navajo so feared for their lives inside a Zuñi camp that they never left Doniphan's protection. Doniphan then departed for the Rio Grande and his invasion of Mexico, no doubt feeling that his negotiations had produced the "permanent peace" about which he wrote the adjutant general, Roger Jones.

That same day of November 26 near Socorro, New Mexico, Indian raiders drove off seventeen government mules and approximately eight hundred sheep (which had been purchased to feed the Missouri Mounted Volunteers). Two soldiers, Privates James Stewart and Robert Spears, were told to recover the sheep. Their bodies were found later just six miles from the river—filled with Navajo arrows.[8] Already the treaty was a dead letter. An editor in

Santa Fe referred to Doniphan's effort as "not likely to effect any very substantial peace," for "the Nabajoes [sic], it is here thought, will continue to steal sheep and commit other outrages, until they are well whipped a few times."[9]

The Navajo did in fact continue to raid the New Mexicans as had been their custom for more than two centuries. Moreover, they were not especially frightened of the Americans, for they as yet had no way of knowing their fighting capacity or their numbers. Nor did the Americans have any way of demonstrating this capacity, for they were too involved with the Mexican counter-revolution in New Mexico. The American soldiers who had been left behind at Santa Fe as an army of occupation had fallen to drinking, gambling, courting the local girls, and fighting with the local men. On January 19, 1847, the Mexicans rose at Taos, killed Governor Charles Bent, the sheriff, an army captain, and a district attorney. Colonel Sterling Price, the local military commander, was hard pressed in the next month to suppress this uprising, leaving the Navajo free to continue their theft of animals and slaves.

Not until September 2, 1847, did an expedition take the field, an informal sort of army commanded by Major Robert Walker. According to one account the volunteers of the "Santa Fe Battalion" were a "very wild and reckless set. Nearly every man left drunk."[10] Walker apparently held the Navajo in low repute, for he believed he could bring them to bay within thirty days. The 140 men in this party were described in the Santa Fe *Republican* of September 10, 1847, as "hardened and inured to the service and are determined upon giving this set of marauders a chastizing which they will not soon forget." An unusual feature of the expedition was that it contained artillery.

Moving down the Rio Grande to a point south of Albuquerque, Walker ordered a turn to the west toward Ojo del Oso. West of Ácoma, Walker left his wagons, with their two months' rations, and proceeded with pack animals laden with ten days' provisions. Arriving at last at Laguna Colorado (Red Lake), Walker split his command into three detachments to scour the surrounding countryside. Only one of these parties, that commanded by Lieutenant Thomas H. Coats, made contact with the Navajo; he was fired upon in Pueblo Colorado Wash by some twenty Navajo warriors. However, none of his men were killed. He then led a charge against the Navajo, killing one of them and wounding others. Walker, his command reunited, marched into the east entrance of Cañon de Chelly for six miles—before he realized the danger he was in and withdrew. Moreover, he realized his mistake in leaving his supplies behind. He had arrived in the Navajo country too late to live off the land; the fields had already been harvested, and no sheep were to be had for butchering. As the army retreated in haste—and hunger—toward their base camp, they killed their pack mules and ate them. When they were gone, dogs went into the dinner pot. As winter set in the battalion was assigned to duty at Socorro.

Late in November a delegation of Navajo chiefs came to Santa Fe to ask for a peace council. Walker had not forced them to come in begging; however, the expedition doubtless caused the chiefs to consider that peace might be more beneficial than war. The army officer with whom they spoke, probably Colonel Edward W. B. Newby, the commander of the Ninth Military Department of New Mexico, told the Indians that they should return with a larger delegation of Navajo chiefs, along with all their prisoners and stolen livestock, and that a treaty then could be negotiated. The chiefs promised on their departure to return within a month. G. K. Gibson, owner and editor of the Santa Fe *Republican*, commented that he had no faith in the promise, nor did he believe that peace with the Navajo would come until the government sent an army into the Navajo country to lay it waste. He proved correct. The Navajo did not return, although there was a lull in the raiding until the following spring.

Colonel Edward Newby noted the renewal of Navajo raiding in the spring of 1848 when on March 27 he issued Orders No. 22 at Santa Fe; he noted his disappointment at the reports "he daily receives of frequent outrages, committed upon the persons and property of the peaceful inhabitants of the Territory. . . ." He noted that three-fourths of his command consisted of infantry which was "powerless against the rapid movements" of the mounted Indians, "who are familiar with every inch of the country, and that, in consequence, his garrisons are compelled to sit still while murder and robbery is committed under their very eyes." His only alternative was to authorize the "Mexican inhabitants" of the territory "to arm and equip themselves—organize in parties or bands" and hold themselves ready "to repel all incursions and to recover the property that may have been taken from them by the Indians."[11]

These volunteer forays apparently inflamed rather than calmed the situation, for on May 1, 1848, Newby departed Santa Fe with two hundred mounted soldiers. Five days later he saw dust rising in the distance, indicating that the Navajo were gathering their horses and sheep and driving them into the mountains away from him. He therefore sent Captain David D. Stockton and fifty troops to pursue the Navajo; according to one account, Stockton was ordered to follow the Indians "night and day," to "overtake them—to secure their stock and scour their country."[12] However, just five miles away he made camp for the night. The next morning he found himself in the midst of many Navajo driving their animals into the mountains. Some of the soldiers, without orders, captured eleven Navajo prisoners, but Stockton made no move to have them disarmed or even to unhorse them. Apparently the captain was overcome with fright, but he did send word to Newby of his situation.

When the colonel came up, he found only half the captured Indians still in camp—and still armed and mounted; the others had been allowed to leave. Moreover, other Navajo were in the hills nearby, but Captain Stockton had allowed his troops to sit about at ease. When Newby tried to disarm the prisoners, the camp was fired on and the prisoners escaped. The troops returned the Indians' fire, killing four and wounding others. Newby then formed a pursuit party, but soon changed his mind and ordered it halted. The next day a few Navajo chiefs went to make peace; to them Newby issued his ultimatum: they were to return in three days with all the other chiefs for purposes of making a treaty. Nine days later eight chiefs did arrive, and Newby signed a treaty with them. It declared a "firm and lasting peace" and repeated the clauses of the Doniphan treaty. Newby did promise to protect the Navajo from raids by New Mexicans—a rash promise, for he could not keep it. Finally, the agreement called for the Indians to deliver three hundred sheep and one hundred mules to the Americans to help defray the cost of Newby's expedition.[13] This done, Newby returned to Santa Fe. Yet within a month New Mexicans were raiding in Navajo country, although there was an exchange of prisoners between the Indians and the settlers which caused the Santa Fe *Republican* to say that "all hostilities will cease."

Several months of peace followed, months during which news of the Treaty of Guadalupe Hidalgo spread. This agreement, concluded on February 2, 1848, between the United States and Mexico, transferred New Mexico to American ownership and stipulated that the United States would protect Mexico from raids by Indians living in the United States. Colonel John Macrae Washington, a fifty-year-old veteran of Indian wars and the conflict in Mexico, arrived as civil and military governor of New Mexico. He had only five hundred soldiers with which to enforce the provisions of the Treaty of Guadalupe Hidalgo, as well as to keep Navajo and New Mexicans from raiding one another. During the winter of 1848-1849 Washington was kept busy by raiding Jicarilla Apache; then, in February 1849, just as the Apache came to terms, the Navajo struck, driving off more than 6,000 sheep. Other raids followed, and the Jicarilla and Ute joined in, causing Colonel Washington to raise volunteer companies. By the summer New Mexico was a mass of marching men, raiding Indians, confusion, theft, and murder.

On July 22, 1849, the reinforcements Colonel Washington had been requesting finally arrived, but they were weak and gaunt from a cholera epidemic, hard marching, and insufficient food and water. He allowed them to rest and eat, then on August 16 he set out to punish the Navajo. They were good troops armed with good weapons, including a six-pound field cannon and three twelve-pound mountain howitzers. They carried rations for five hundred men for thirty days, while a wagon train brought their baggage.

After marching through the hot August sun and pulling cannon through sand, the column encamped on the north fork of Tunicha Creek. The Navajo came up and partially encircled the Americans, while a delegation of their headmen came riding into camp. Washington told them that he had come to punish them for their

raids, whereupon the Navajo, seeing the strength of the army, said
the murders and raids were the work of uncontrollable Indians;
however, they said, they wanted peace and therefore would bring
in livestock in equal number to those stolen, return all captives,
and attempt to deliver any murderers of New Mexicans in their
midst.

Washington then determined to lead his troops to Canyon de
Chelly, for the Indians with whom he first treated swore they had
no connection with Navajo from west of the mountains. The route
of march proved difficult, and there were occasional skirmishes;
one chief killed was Narbona, brought down by the six-pound
cannon. This was unfortunate, for Narbona had been described as
peaceful for more than a decade and a half. Washington finally arrived at the entrance to Canyon de Chelly on September 6. The
next day two chiefs came in, Sandoval and Mariano; Washington
told them that if they wanted peace they would have to comply
with the terms of Newby's treaty. This meant they would have to
repay all animals stolen since that agreement was signed, a total
that came to 1,070 sheep, 78 cattle, 34 mules, and 19 horses. When
the Navajo agreed to this—and made a token surrender of animals
—Washington proceeded to negotiate yet another treaty with
them.

This new document stipulated that the United States could
regulate all trade with the Navajo. Moreover, it stated that the
Navajo land was part of New Mexico (the first indication of such
a move), and provided that the United States would adjust and
designate the Navajo boundaries as soon as was convenient. Finally, the agreement said that the United States would establish
whatever laws were most conducive to the Indians' prosperity
and happiness. In return for such considerations, Washington
promised that his government would give the Navajo presents and
donations, as well as adopt "liberal and humane" measures to help
the natives. And the Navajo were told that if an American murdered an Indian he would be punished according to law.[14] (Congress later would honor this agreement by voting $18,000 for the
Navajo in 1853 and $5000 in 1854.) Washington then marched
his expedition back to Santa Fe by way of the Zuñi pueblo. There

he wrote a report estimating the number of Navajo at 7,000 to 10,000, of whom he thought 2,000 to 3,000 were warriors.

Accompanying Washington on this trek into the Navajo country was James S. Calhoun, who had just been appointed the first Indian agent to New Mexico. A staunch Whig and an admirer of Zachary Taylor, the forty-seven-year-old Calhoun had been a lieutenant colonel and commander of a regiment of Georgia volunteers during the recent war with Mexico. When Taylor came into office as president, Calhoun was appointed to the post in New Mexico by Commissioner of Indian Affairs William Medill although he had no knowledge or experience in such a post. However, he accepted it and its $1,500-per-annum salary, plus $2,300 for expenses and incidentals. His orders, waiting for him in Santa Fe when he arrived there on July 22, 1849, in company with the army reinforcements for Colonel Washington, were to gather statistical data and other information which would make it possible to understand the natives of the region.[15]

Returning from the treaty-making effort with Washington, Calhoun showed how little he knew or had learned by writing, "The Navajos commit their wrongs from a pure love of rapine and plunder." He did concede that the natives were "hardy and intelligent," but felt it was "natural for them to war against all men, and to take the property of others as it is for the sun to give light by day." He estimated the number of the tribe at not more than 5,000, and argued that the Navajo should be confined to a reservation with clearly designated boundaries; there they should be kept under strict military surveillance by troops at nearby army posts.

What he—and Washington—failed to realize was that the Navajo had made a treaty with them only to satisfy the need of the moment. Moreover, the chiefs who signed the document did not and could not speak for the whole tribe, for the Navajo had no one chief and no one government. Thus by the time Washington and Calhoun had returned to Santa Fe, new raids had broken out. New Mexicans were killed and sheep stolen, for even the Navajo who intended to live up to that and earlier treaties did not see the Mexicans of New Mexico and the newly arrived Americans as the same people. The Navajo raiders made no war on Americans, but the New Mexicans were the enemies of several centuries. Thus in October and November of 1849 they raided at Zuñi, San Ilde-fonso, Santo Domingo, Santa Ana, Cebolleta, Abiquiu, Cubero, La Pugarita, and Corrales. Animals were stolen, and people were carried off into slavery.

The new military governor of New Mexico, as well as com-mander of the Ninth Military District, was Brevet Colonel John Munroe. While in New York City on June 26, 1849, he received orders to proceed to New Mexico with fresh troops; he arrived in Santa Fe, by way of Fort Leavenworth, on October 22 and assumed command the following day. Once described as "the ugliest look-ing man" in the United States Army, Munroe was a Whig of Scot descent who would take his first drink of toddy at noon "after which hour he would not attend to any official business."[16]

His decision was to establish a post at Cebolleta. For this pur-pose he sent Company K of the Second Dragoons, and it did estab-lish itself at this mountain village. Another detachment was sent to San Ysidro. The purpose of these two outposts was to contain Navajo raiders to their own country. And Colonel Munroe au-thorized Indian Agent Calhoun to begin licensing traders to go among the Navajo; this was an attempt to halt illegal trade with the Navajo, particularly by the New Mexicans involved in the pur-chase and sale of Navajo to be used as slaves. At this time Navajo children were sold for as much as $200; New Mexicans purchased them for use as servants and household menials. In this traffic the slavers were aided and abetted by Sandoval, chief of the *Diné'and'ih* (enemy Navajo) who lived on the west side of Mount Taylor. For this reason, he was hated by his own tribesmen, but he continued to come into New Mexican settlements to sell Navajo whom he had captured from other bands.

This slave trading, as well as the death of Narbona during Colo-nel Washington's expedition, caused Navajo raids, unrest, and con-fusion during the remainder of 1849 and the early months of 1850. The Zuñi were attacked for their friendliness with the Americans, and no pueblo or Mexican village west of the Rio Grande was safe because the Navajo sought revenge for the death of their chief and indemnification for the loss of people captured by the slavers.

Munroe tried to give relief to the Zuñi by sending a company of dragoons to their pueblo from Cebolleta and by shipping fifty muskets to them. Yet such measures could not bring relief to the province. Sheep disappeared, as did people; people were also murdered or else forced to flee from their homes in panic. Newspaper editors grumbled in their editorials of military ineptitude and inefficiency, knowing full well that six hundred troops could not police the entire area.

Just at this time came news that New Mexico had been created a Territory and that James S. Calhoun had been named its governor by President Millard Fillmore. Installed in office on March 3, 1851, Calhoun was also Superintendent of Indian Affairs for the Territory—and he acted swiftly to halt the Navajo raids. Fifteen days later, he issued a proclamation in which he stated, "The savage Indians who are daily murdering and robbing the people of New Mexico . . . must be exterminated or so chastised as to prevent their coming into your Pueblo. For this purpose you are . . . authorized to make war upon them, and to take their animals and such property as they may have with them, and to make divisions of the same according to your laws and customs."[17] In short, he authorized the forming of volunteer militia companies to make war on the Navajo; their reward would be all the booty they could take from the Indians—including women and children. Such volunteers were not subject to orders from army commanders, but only to those of the governor—and he was a known friend of the volunteers.

When Colonel Munroe refused to place arms in the hands of these volunteers, arms which he as military commander controlled, Governor Calhoun wrote directly to President Fillmore and to Secretary of the Interior Alexander H. H. Stuart; he complained of the territory's bankrupt treasury and of its desperate need for arms; if the arms were furnished, he assured his superiors, he could win a just and lasting peace within months.[18] Deeply stung, Colonel Munroe prepared an expedition to penetrate the heart of Navajo country in the spring of 1851. He planned to take some four hundred men and march just as soon as the grass was up sufficient to support the horses. Word of this projected expedition leaked out, spread through all the Navajo subtribes, and produced the usual

Brigadier General Edwin V. Sumner. *Courtesy U.S. Signal Corps, Brady Collection, National Archives.*

move for peace; on April 19 several Navajo came to Cebolleta to ask for terms, stating that all their tribesmen who had wanted war during the previous spring now desired peace. However, Munroe changed his mind about the expedition because he learned that the Jicarilla Apache and possibly even some Comanche planned raids into New Mexico once he was occupied to the west. The result was renewed raiding by the Navajo.

On July 19, 1851, Lieutenant Colonel Edwin Vose Sumner arrived to assume command of the Ninth Military Department. Sumner had earned the nickname "Bull-head" when a musket ball reportedly had struck him full in the head but had bounced off;

this described both the hardness of his skull and his personality, for he was stubborn to a fault. A Bostonian by birth, he entered the service without benefit of an education at West Point; commissioned a second lieutenant of infantry in 1818, he transferred to the dragoons in 1833, fought through the Indian wars, served with General Winfield Scott during the Mexican War, and rose on merit. His Yankee background made him believe that God's will should be done in all things. He arrived in New Mexico at age fifty-five, a sound believer in infantry, the correctness of his own judgment, and an unbending desire to do right. He came with orders from Secretary of War Charles M. Conrad to enforce economy, to move his troops nearer to the Indians, and to chastise the Indians in a major campaign.[19]

Sumner quickly removed the soldiers from the towns, not only to comply with his orders but also from conviction. One of his first orders was to pull the soldiers out of what he termed "that sink of vice and extravagance," Santa Fe, as well as from Albuquerque, Cebolleta, Socorro, Las Vegas, Rayado, Doña Ana, San Elizario, and El Paso. Some of them were sent to a new location halfway between El Paso and Doña Ana to establish a post named Fort Fillmore; the function of this post was to contain the Apache raiding into Mexico. Another group of soldiers were sent to Valverde

A general view of Fort Union, New Mexico, in 1875. *Courtesy U.S. Signal Corps, National Archives.*

(near Socorro) to garrison a post he named Fort Conrad in honor of Secretary of War C. M. Conrad; later this post would be renamed Fort Thorn. A third post was established near Mora in northeastern New Mexico; named Fort Union, its function was to protect the Santa Fe Traders, serve as the departmental headquarters, and act as a supply depot for the Department. Merchants in the various towns, particularly Santa Fe, protested the movement of the soldiers away from their stores and businesses, but Colonel Sumner had little sympathy for them.

Next he organized an expedition into the Navajo country—and a large one it was: four companies of cavalry, two of infantry, one of artillery, and a caravan of forty wagons to carry supplies and ammunition. Departing from Santo Domingo on August 17, the expedition marched west to Laguna and Zuñi. Once the Indians there swore friendship, Sumner continued on to a site known by the Navajo as *Tséhootsoh*, or Meadow in the Rocks (or Green Place in the Rocks). Prior to the arrival of Americans, this had been a favorite rendezvous point for the Navajo, for it contained bubbling springs always filled with fresh water. Sumner regarded this as a good site for a fort, and ordered Major Electus Backus to begin the construction of a log fort.

Just as Sumner departed with most of the troops, a warrior came in, no doubt on orders from the chiefs to learn Sumner's intentions. The colonel instructed the Navajo to tell the headmen in the vicinity to come in for a talk. When none came, Sumner instructed his men to fire on every Navajo they saw. This they did, wounding some and killing others. During the day the Navajo therefore stayed out of sight, but at night they would close in and fire on the Americans. Sumner's goal was Canyon de Chelly, and he penetrated it for more than twelve miles, destroying corn and melon fields along the way. The night of August 29, a thousand small fires could be seen on the rims of the canyon walls, and the air buzzed with an occasional enemy bullet fired at them. Sumner called a council of his officers, who voted that since the enemy so outnumbered the Americans a withdrawal was in order. Accordingly, at ten that night the soldiers saddled their mounts and cautiously moved out to retreat to Canyon Bonito, their name for the point where Major Backus was building his log fort.

Engraving by Seth Eastman, from a sketch by Lieutenant Colonel J. H. Easton, Fort Defiance, New Mexico. *Courtesy U.S. Signal Corps, National Archives.*

At that point on September 18, 1851, Sumner issued his Special Order No. 29, which officially established the building of the post he named—appropriately—Fort Defiance. His hope was that the fort would restrain Navajo raids into New Mexico. The site was beautiful, the land fertile and water plentiful. However, it was hemmed in on three sides by rock walls from atop which the Navajo could—and did—fire into the post, and it was 210 miles west of the Rio Grande and thus difficult to supply. Officers quarters, five barracks, kitchens, messrooms, storerooms, a hospital, and a guardhouse were erected to provide a home for five companies of troops, but Fort Defiance, despite its proud name, did not halt Navajo raids. In fact, while Sumner was marching on Canyon de Chelly and ordering the fort built, the Indians were raiding along the Rio Grande.[20]

Sumner's failure to chastise the Navajo caused Governor Calhoun to authorize yet more volunteer companies to raid the Indians, a move which greatly angered Colonel Sumner. He was unalterably opposed to civilians rushing about in the Indian country and refused to issue weapons and ammunition to them. Nor would Sumner comply with his orders to allow the governor to accompany him on his expeditions; in fact, he refused even to authorize a military escort when the governor, acting in his capacity of Superintendent of Indian Affairs, wanted to go west to treat with the Navajo. Calhoun bitterly wrote Secretary of State Daniel Webster that either he or Sumner "should be relieved from duty." Yet it was Sumner and his efforts that brought peace in the fall of 1851, not the volunteer companies authorized by Governor Calhoun. By the end of 1851 Fort Defiance was hampering Navajo raids, and on December 25 a conference was held at Jemez with both Calhoun and Sumner present. The Navajo, after a severe verbal chastisement from Sumner, pledged peace, whereupon the governor, over Sumner's objections, gave them several thousand dollars worth of presents, including agricultural implements.[21]

And there was peace for a time despite Sumner's stated desire for a six-month probationary period. Navajo began trading openly in the towns of New Mexico, and journeyed to the capital. Calhoun, hoping to consolidate the peace, named Samuel M. Baird the Special Agent to the Navajos on February 1, 1852; his headquarters were to be at Jemez, long a center for the illegal trade with the Navajo. Also, the governor licensed traders to go among the Navajo, while Colonel Sumner ordered the distribution from government stores of five hundred sheep, seeds, and agricultural implements.

Unfortunately for the peace, Governor Calhoun became hopelessly ill, and on April 1, 1852, named John Greiner Acting Superintendent of Indian Affairs. On May 5 Calhoun left Santa Fe to go home, but died crossing the plains toward Missouri. Sumner assumed the role of acting governor, moving his office to Santa Fe, an action without any legal sanction. Meanwhile, Greiner was without funds with which to assist the Navajo, who complained of horses stolen by New Mexicans and of land taken illegally by Pueblo Indians in the west.

Peace prevailed that summer of 1852, and late in August the new civil governor arrived to be sworn into office in September. He was William Carr Lane, who had been born in Pennsylvania in 1789; after serving as a surgeon with the army, he had resigned in 1818 and had moved to St. Louis where, among other offices, he served as first mayor of the city. He was a firm believer that "it is better to feed the Indians, than to fight them," and he acted on this, especially with the Jicarilla Apache whom he persuaded to settle on farms along the Rio Puerco (west of the Rio Grande). However, Congress refused to vote the $20,000 needed for the treaties which Lane signed, and the disappointed Apache began raiding worse than ever.

The Navajo did occasionally have one of their number steal sheep or even murder a New Mexican, but thanks to the swift actions of Governor Lane and Colonel Sumner, the peace extended into 1853. In June 1853, Lane was replaced as governor by David Meriwether, and Colonel Sumner departed for the States, his successor Lieutenant Colonel Dixon Stansbury Miles; Special Agent to the Navajo Samuel Baird was replaced in August by Henry Linn Dodge. Still the peace continued, although marred by an occasional bad incident. Councils were held occasionally, either at Santa Fe by Governor Meriwether or at Fort Defiance by Agent Dodge, who had moved his headquarters there. In the winter of 1853-1854 the federal district court at Santa Fe ruled incredibly that under the laws passed by Congress the Indians owned no land in New Mexico; the court probably issued this ruling under pressure from New Mexican ranchers who were anxious to gain access to more land on which to graze their flocks. This ruling officially opened Navajo lands to settlement, and a few New Mexican *rancheros* did order their shepherds to take flocks west to graze; when animals were stolen, the ranchers simply filed a claim with the government for payment. Despite this provocation, however, the period of peace extended into the year 1855.

In this interlude of quiet on the New Mexican frontier, Agent Henry L. Dodge was introducing changes into Navajo life—and in the process was being changed himself. His father, also named Henry, was a senator from Wisconsin, and his brother Augustus

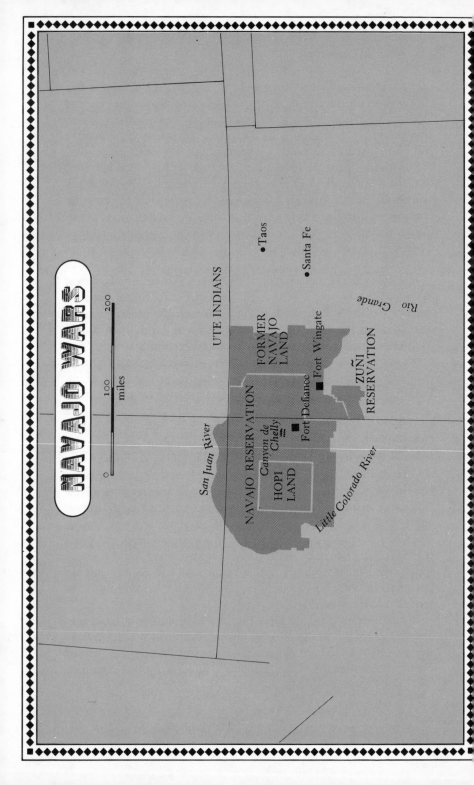

was a senator from Missouri. Dodge had gone west to explore in the Rocky Mountains and had escorted traders on the Santa Fe Trail. His first trip to the Navajo country was in 1849 when he accompanied Colonel Washington and future governor Calhoun on their treaty-making trek. The following year he was a commissary agent to the troops at Cebolleta. Finally in 1853 he was appointed agent to the Navajo by President Franklin Pierce. He quickly came to admire the Navajo. He constructed a home at Sheep Springs near Fort Defiance, eventually married a Navajo girl, and became as one with the people under him.[22]

To the Fort Defiance agency Dodge brought George Carter, an American, to teach the silversmithing art to the Navajo. One of them, Herrero (who eventually would become a chief), learned to make bridle parts, bits, even knife blades. Dodge also persuaded Juan Anea, a Mexican silversmith, to come to Fort Defiance as an assistant to Carter; there Anea taught his craft to the Navajo (a craft closely associated with this tribe today; one rarely sees a picture of a Navajo where the Indian does not have silver-and-turquoise jewelry on his person). Eventually the Navajo would learn to blacksmith all the iron parts of their horse trappings and decorate their bridles and saddles, as well as themselves, with silver jewelry.[23]

Early in 1855 a band of Ute Indians came to the Navajo to ask for an alliance against the whites. A few individual Navajo joined this scheme to rid New Mexico of all whites, but the majority chose to remain on their traditional land and to plant their spring crops. And that summer Governor Meriwether came to negotiate a new treaty with the *Diné*. Late in April 1855, he was notified that in July of the previous year Congress had appropriated approximately $25,000 with which to negotiate treaties with the Ute, the Mescalero and Mimbreño Apache, and the Navajo. His instructions were to get each of these tribes to agree to set boundaries for themselves—a nice way of saying reservations—and money was to be used to provide presents for those tribes. Thereby the tribes signed away lands which they had always claimed as their own.

Word went out to Dodge to assemble as many Navajo as possible for a conference near Fort Defiance. This convened on July

14, 1855, at the west entrance to Washington Pass (fourteen miles north of the fort), a place then known as Laguna Negra. General John Garland, then commander of the Ninth Military Department, was also present. Meriwether noted as he spoke to the Navajo that few women and children were present; rumors had spread among the Indians that the conference was a trap and that cannons would be used to kill them as had been the case with Narbona. At one that afternoon Meriwether addressed the headmen: "I have come to see you and agree upon a country the Navajos and whites may each have; that they may not pasture their flocks on each other's lands. If we have a dividing line so that we know what each other's country is, it will keep us at peace." He then outlined the treaty he proposed that they make; the Indians were to agree to a reservation, in return for which they would receive protection from white encroachment and annual presents (called annuities). He concluded by asking the headmen to discuss among themselves that evening all that he had said. The evening of that first day was marred by some scuffles between Indians and whites, and by muttered threats on the part of Indians who feared an ambush. However, the rumor gradually died.

The next day there was another difficulty. Zarcillos Largos, who had been acting as chief Navajo spokesman, sent to Meriwether his staff of office and the medal given him by the governor with the explanation that because he was too old to negotiate and he no longer could control his people, he was resigning. Meriwether accepted his resignation and requested that the headmen meet to select a new spokesman. They selected Manuelito, who, after Meriwether gave him a new cane and put a new ribbon on the medal, agreed to accept the responsibility. The conference then continued.

Meriwether spoke before an assembly of an estimated 2,000 warriors. The twenty chiefs said they agreed in principle with what the governor had said to them the day before. The governor thereupon had the treaty reduced to writing and then explained it article by article. The difficult part was Article III which specified the boundaries of the Navajo reservation; they were to receive approximately 7,000 square miles, thereby reducing their homeland by more than two-thirds (Meriwether estimated that the Navajo traditionally had some 25,000 square miles). Manuelito grumbled at this, for it would deprive the Navajo of many of their sacred places. Meriwether soothed their feelings by pointing out that the reservation did include most of their holy places, and he traced the tribal limits on a map for them to see. He also promised that they could go outside the reservation to gather salt, and he said they would be paid $102,000 over the next twenty-one years (however, the President of the United States could at his discretion use part of this money for education and moral improvement and he could deduct from it to pay for damages resulting from raids committed by Navajo). Finally, the treaty called for the Navajo to surrender any one of their tribesmen accused of a crime. After more grumbling Manuelito and the headmen came forward and signed the document, as did Meriwether. Then the governor distributed the presents he had brought.

The Treaty of Laguna Negra, as it was known, was never ratified by the United States Senate, but it was regarded as binding by New Mexicans who quickly began moving herds of sheep onto grazing land formerly regarded as Navajo. Meriwether himself was delighted with the agreement, for it had been signed by every major faction of the Navajo nation except the *Diné Aná'aih* and their leader, Sandoval. In all, the treaty was probably a good one; the Navajo were somewhat unhappy, but withall satisfied, while the New Mexicans said the treaty was too generous to the Indians. Yet in 1855 few people wanted the land set aside for the Navajo; little of it could be farmed, for it was mountainous desert. Only the Indians wanted it, and it was theirs by treaty—or so everyone thought.[24]

Peace prevailed through the remainder of 1855, but in the spring of 1856 there came a gradual renewal of raiding. General Garland demanded that all thieves be turned over to civil authorities for trial as the Treaty of Laguna Negra provided, else he would have to invade in force and arrest the culprits. The Navajo responded that New Mexicans had killed Navajo, stolen Navajo sheep, and encroached on Navajo lands; they would surrender no one until such actions ended. Unfortunately, Dodge, who might have prevented the later bloodshed, was killed on November 19, 1856, by a party of Coyotero and Mogollon Apache; "Red Shirt," as he was called, had become almost as much a Navajo as the Navajo, and he suffered the fate of those tribesmen when caught by Apache. During 1857 the army in New Mexico was busy campaigning against the Apache, but New Mexicans were not content. The Santa Fe *Weekly Gazette* on October 18, 1856, had outlined the attitude of many whites in the area when its editor demanded that a new treaty should be made restricting the Navajo to yet less land, thereby opening more grazing lands to whites. Some New Mexicans were not waiting for such a treaty. Instead they were driving their herds farther and farther west, encroaching until a few of their sheep were stolen; then they demanded military reprisals. To add to this provocation were raids by Ute into Navajoland during 1857, raids that left young Navajo warriors crying out for retaliation. And then came the summer of 1857, a particularly dry one that brought hunger to the Navajo during the following winter. The result was raiding and theft—just when the number of troops at Fort Defiance had been reduced by the campaign against the Apache.

In the spring of 1858 came a brief argument between troops and Navajo. The soldiers at Fort Defiance had been grazing their horses at a point known as Ewell's Camp, located twelve miles to the north of the post. It was land claimed by Manuelito, and that summer he turned his own livestock onto this land because pasturage was scant owing to little rainfall. Major Thomas H. Brooks, then commanding the post, ordered his soldiers to slaughter almost sixty animals belonging to Manuelito as a warning that the fort's hay camp was not subject to encroachment. Tension increased when the Indians shot volleys of arrows into the camp of a squad of soldiers on the night of July 7. Five days later a Navajo warrior at Fort Defiance brutally murdered Jim, Major Brooks' black servant. Brooks the Navajo twenty days to produce the murderer and began organizing a punitive expedition. Moreover, Brooks wrote the adjutant general of the army to suggest that the Ute be authorized to raid the Navajo and that New Mexican volunteers be used as guides to seek out the Navajo. To all of this General John Garland, commander of the Ninth Military Department, agreed readily. In fact, he sent Lieutenant Colonel Dixon S. Miles to Fort Defiance to take charge of the expected operation in the field.

Miles arrived at the post and almost immediately summoned the Navajo leader Sandoval. Miles informed the chief that unless the murderer of Jim was produced by 8:00 A.M. on September 9 the war would commence. Sandoval returned on September 6 to say that the murderer had been captured and would be brought in; however, the following day he returned to say that the murderer had died of wounds sustained during his capture. And on September 8 they brought in a body. However, an examination showed that the corpse was a young lad of about eighteen years, while the murderer was known to be about forty; and the corpse was freshly dead, not four days dead as the Navajo claimed. Thereupon the new agent to the Navajo, Samuel M. Yost, a former editor of the Santa Fe *Gazette*, informed the Navajo that he would no longer deal with them; the army would. And Major Brooks told them that a state of war existed between the Navajo and the United States.

Miles, who had refused to speak with the Navajo while they were at the post, set out with three companies of mounted rifles and two companies of infantry on September 9. Guiding the column were New Mexican scouts recruited from Albuquerque. Miles marched the column through Canyon de Chelly to its mouth near the present Chinle, Arizona; there they burned fields of corn and orchards of peaches. Then they turned north, returning to Fort Defiance on September 15. The expedition had killed six Indians, captured seven, and appropriated 6,000 sheep.

Less than a month later a new military commander succeeded General Garland in New Mexico, the legendary Colonel Benjamin L. E. de Bonneville. Born in France in 1796, he was a graduate of West Point, class of 1815. His explorations in the West made him famous, thanks to the literary talents of Washington Irving (who rewrote Bonneville's journals into readable prose and popularized them). He was a tired old man looking for retirement and did not want a war with the Navajo.[25]

War would be forced on him, however, for the final alienation of the Navajo already was far advanced, perhaps too far to be reversed. Before the end of September, Colonel Miles heard that Zarcillos Largos was encamped somewhere nearby and sent troops out to destroy the headman's home and to kill him if possible. Captain John P. Hatch, who commanded this effort, succeeded in catching Zarcillos Largos and some forty Navajos; three times the chief was wounded, and he was seen to fall from his horse. However, when the Navajo fled the field, his body was not among the six Indians found dead there. All articles found in the vicinity were burned, and Captain Hatch returned to Fort Defiance that September 24 confident that he had killed Zarcillos Largos. The following week other raiding parties probed the lower Chusca Valley. The Navajo were soon raiding in reprisal and even attacked Fort Defiance.

At this juncture Colonel Bonneville decided to mount a major two-pronged attack on the Navajo, one commanded by Miles from Fort Defiance and the other by Major Electus Baccus consisting mainly of raw recruits from the other garrisons in New Mexico. Baccus was to organize at Jemez and then march west to coordinate his efforts with those of Miles. On October 18 Miles and the troops from Fort Defiance managed to burn what was believed to be the village of Manuelito, although the chief, if he had been there, escaped unharmed. This expedition—both parts together—accomplished little other than showing American resolve in its march through Navajo country. Apparently it had the desired effect, for early in November the Indians sent emissaries saying the headmen of their nation wished to talk peace.

On November 20 a conference occurred at Fort Defiance, ironically against the wishes of Colonel Bonneville and New Mexican Superintendent of Indian Affairs James L. Collins, a Democratic appointee filled with self-importance and a former editor of the Santa Fe *Weekly Gazette*, long a mouthpiece for anti-Navajo statements. The two had decided the wars should continue until the Navajo were punished severely, but instructions to this effect for Miles at Fort Defiance were delayed and he proceeded to hold a peace conference. At the meeting Miles and Navajo agent Samuel M. Yost met with Zarcillos Largos, who proved to be very much alive, and nine other headmen. An agreement followed, one providing for a thirty-day armistice, a return by the Indians of all stolen livestock, a mutual exchange of captives, the delivery of the murderer of Jim, should he be caught, and a meeting at Fort Defiance at the end of thirty days for the drafting of a treaty.

Photograph of Fort Defiance, New Mexico. *Courtesy U.S. Signal Corps, National Archives.*

Collins was extremely unhappy when in early December he learned of what had transpired. He strongly believed that the Navajo should be moved farther west with hard, fixed boundaries on their reservation. However, both he and Bonneville had no alternative but to proceed to Fort Defiance and meet with the Navajo to make a treaty. The meeting began on Christmas Day 1858. More than a thousand troops were huddled inside and outside the fort seeking warmth from the bitterly cold weather—and all waited anxiously to learn if the future was to hold peace or war. Fifteen headmen represented the Navajo, a young nephew of Manuelito named Huero (or Herrero) the stipulated Navajo spokesman and leader. However, there were no negotiations, no give and take; rather the session opened with the Americans reading a draft of the treaty, which stipulated Navajo blame for all that had occurred. It set an eastern boundary line much farther west than the one drawn in 1855, and clearly stated that the Navajo were not to cross this for any reason; in fact, American soldiers were authorized to destroy any crops or livestock east of this boundary. Other articles provided that the Navajo must pay the New Mexicans an indemnity amounting to $14,000 for livestock losses, all captives would be released, the murderer of Jim was not to be harbored by the tribe, the United States could send troops through Navajo country at any time and build military posts there, the entire Navajo nation was to be held responsible for the actions of any of its individual members, and Huero thereafter would be the chief spokesman for the tribe. The treaty was obviously intended more as punishment of the Navajo rather than something that would bring a permanent solution. It would be called the Bonneville Treaty, and it reflected the thinking of Superintendent Collins, a bitter foe of the Indians. Agent Yost more correctly saw its consequences, for he noted that this treaty took from the Navajo their traditional grazing lands and their farmlands; said he, the treaty will force them "either to violate the agreement . . . or compel them to abandon cultivating the soil and stock raising or becoming pensioners on the government, or plunderers."

Yet during the first four months of 1859 the Navajo attempted to comply. They sent token numbers of livestock to begin payment of the $14,000 indemnity to New Mexicans, along with some captives they held. Superintendent Collins thereupon, in April, issued the annuities promised the Navajo, and peace seemed to be returning. However, Ute Indians began raiding into Navajo country, and the Navajo naturally retaliated. Soon a few young warriors were stealing a few sheep from New Mexicans as they returned from Ute territory. Superintendent Collins therefore concluded that the Navajo must be punished; he wrote that "their chastisement must be more severe, they must be well punished and thoroughly humbled." Colonel Bonneville began preparing a summer offensive, and seven hundred men marched. This brought yet another conference, on July 5-14, in which the Americans demanded a return of all stolen livestock. Huero refused to sign, however, for he believed that the Americans thought these pieces of paper bound only Indians, not the whites. Further talks proved useless, and on October 25, 1859, the new agent to the Navajo, Silas Kendrick, told the commanding officer at Fort Defiance, Major Oliver L. Shepherd, that the Navajo were delinquent and that it was the duty of the army to enforce the treaty obligations of the Indians; in short, he was to use military coercion to make the Navajo abide by the Bonneville Treaty.

By the first of the year 1860 the Navajo were again attacking in the vicinity of Fort Defiance. On January 17 they attacked a cattle herd pastured nearby and, as they retreated, killed three soldiers on a wood detail. Moreover, they harassed the quartermaster wagons going west from Albuquerque with food for the soldiers. Then on January 20 a friendly Navajo chief, Agua Chiquito, came into the post to talk with Agent Kendrick. Major Shepherd was enraged, insisting that, as he was in charge of relations with the Navajo, the headman was to talk only in his presence. When Agua Chiquito refused to speak with Shepherd, the soldier ordered him to go and then told his sentries to shoot at the chief. Agua Chiquito made his way to safety to become a bitter foe of the Americans. Moreover, Kendrick saw no reason to stay and departed for Santa Fe.

Thereafter, Navajo relations were to be an army matter, but the soldiers were unable to halt the raids. Every day came news of yet more raids, of sheep stolen and men killed. And the army could do nothing. In fact, it also was in retreat. On April 30 an estimated 1,000 Navajos attacked the post, almost overrunning it in a day-long battle. On May 4 the post was ordered abandoned in what was said by the adjutant general to be a temporary measure.[26] Preparations then began for "active operations" against the Navajo. Thereafter no peace would return until one side or the other was totally conquered. Both were ready to admit that the first fourteen years of Navajo-American relations had not been fruitful. Treaties had been made—and both sides had broken them. Both Redman and white had coveted property belonging to the other. Both were guilty of crimes. The resolution would come on the field of battle.

3

THE NAVAJO CONFINED

The Santa Fe *Gazette* on November 10, 1860, estimated that the Navajo in the first six months of that year had killed three hundred persons and had destroyed or stolen property valued at $1,500,000. Although these figures doubtless were inflated, they do reflect the consequences of the wars that became widespread that year. No one was safe from the Hopi and Zuñi villages to the Rio Grande; northwestern New Mexico was Navajo country, and the United States Army seemed powerless to halt it. In fact, Colonel Thomas T. Fauntleroy, who had replaced Bonneville as commander of the Ninth Military District, had received orders from Washington in the spring of the year that operations against the Comanche and Kiowa were more pressing, for they were raiding the mail routes; consequently he was to hold tight. Governor Abraham Rencher in some desperation turned to the use of volunteer companies of New Mexicans to combat the raiders. However, their success was minimal at best.

Again it was the pages of the Santa Fe *Gazette* that reflected the anger and frustration of local citizens. On August 13, 1860, an "Address to the People of New Mexico" was printed under the signatures of four prominent citizens. The four declared that the Navajo were responsible for many "slaughtered citizens [whose] mangled corpses [have] been crowding your graveyards." The an-

General E. R. S. Canby. *Courtesy U.S. Signal Corps, National Archives.*

swer, according to the address, was a volunteer force of 1,000 New Mexicans which would take the field.

Before such a volunteer army could be assembled, however, Colonel Fauntleroy received reinforcements and announced that he would mount a full expedition to punish the Navajo. Slowly he began preparing. Troops were gathered at Fort Defiance under the command of Lieutenant Colonel Edward R. S. Canby, a West Pointer (class of 1839) who had fought the Seminoles in Florida

and who was a veteran of the Mexican War. Canby was commanding Fort Garland when he received orders to proceed to Fort Defiance and prepare to punish the Navajo. He left Garland on September 9, taking 138 men with him.

Meanwhile, Colonel Fauntleroy had decided to use Ute Indians
as guides and scouts for the expedition. On September 4 he wrote
Superintendent of Indian Affairs James L. Collins to ask for the
assistance of the two Ute agents, Christopher "Kit" Carson and
A. W. Pheiffer. Collins replied the next day that he favored the
expedition, stating his belief that the Navajo were "the common
enemy of both Indians and white men and it seems proper that
they should make common cause against them." Ute scouts were
enlisted in the army for the expedition, and they too began marching for Fort Defiance.

Another part of the expedition left Albuquerque on September
14 led by Major Henry H. Sibley. He took his troops west through
the Wingate Valley and on to Ojo del Oso (Bear Spring), where
a new post named Fort Fauntleroy was under construction. From
there he traveled to Laguna Negra with his five companies of cavalry and infantry. There the column was approached by Agua
Chiquita, the Navajo headman, who said he wished to speak to the
commanding officer; however, Agua Chiquita grew fearful and
turned to flee; he was severely wounded before he could escape.
Sibley ordered him put to death.

On September 28 Sibley arrived at Fort Defiance. Canby followed on October 4, and less than a week later the expedition began. Canby divided his command into two parts, one numbering
270 men under Major Sibley to move to Pueblo Colorado (near
the present Ganado, Arizona) and then sweep to the mouth of
Canyon de Chelly at Chinle; Canby would take an equal number
of soldiers and march to the north rim of Canyon de Chelly and
join with Sibley at Chinle. Both groups would then sweep the region clear of hostile Navajo, while Captain Lafayette McLaws and
a third force would operate along the west base of the Chusca
Mountains to intercept any hostiles fleeing from the other two
columns. Simultaneously five companies of volunteer civilians had
rendezvoused at San Ysidro; these numbered 470 men and officers

plus forty warriors from the pueblo of Jemez, the combined command led by Manuel Chaves.

Sibley's command had little success in the campaign that followed. It returned to Fort Defiance on November 6, the cavalry horses exhausted and the men described as unfit for further service. However, the New Mexican volunteers, with the aid of Ute trackers led by Agent Pheiffer, had some success. A diary kept by Marquis Lafayette Cotton, along with a letter he wrote while in the field, was published in the Santa Fe *Gazette* on November 24, 1860; these noted that "We have captured four Indians, killed five, and wounded another badly, who was apparently a chief. We are informed by one of the prisoners that the celebrated Navajo chief, Sarcillo Largo, was amongst the killed." He was referring, of course, to Zarcillos Largos, the headman who earlier had signed treaties with the Americans and who was a known Navajo spokesman for peace. Before the expedition could return to settlements on the Rio Grande, it was "forced to eat ten of our captured horses and four Navajo dogs" for want of supplies. It was this expedition which greatly damaged the hostile Navajo, for it burned thousands of acres of corn fields and captured hundreds of head of livestock.

As always, the Navajo soon came in seeking peace. Before the end of December 1860, delegations of the Indians were at Fort Fauntleroy seeking terms, and January 12, 1861, was set as a time for a general council. Canby, taking no chances, was also making plans for continuing his sweep operations through Navajoland should the Indians refuse to accept his terms. On the appointed day a small delegation of headmen appeared at the fort, and Canby stated his terms: an armistice west of Fort Fauntleroy, war to the east; no thieves to be permitted to live among the tribes; and no more raids. The chiefs, including Manuelito, the rising spokesman for the Navajo, agreed. Canby thereupon set February 5 as the date for a full council, which was to meet at Ojo del Oso.

On February 5 there were 2,000 Navajos encamped at the spring —but only a handful of headmen, less than half those Canby wanted present. Therefore the colonel postponed the meeting for ten days to allow the other headmen to reach the council. The weather was extremely cold, dropping below zero several times, and some of the Navajo were reported to be starving. On the appointed day, twenty-four headmen awaited Canby's comments. He presented his proposals: no further Navajo aggression; all chiefs signing the document to accept the authority of the United States and to be responsible for the actions of their followers; no *ladrones* (a Spanish word meaning thieves, but here intended to mean raiders) to be permitted in their midst; all losses from Navajo theft to be indemnified; all Navajo to reside west of Fort Fauntleroy; and in return the United States would give aid and assistance to the Navajo.

The Canby Treaty was signed on February 18.[1] Eventually it would carry the signatures of fifty-four headmen, the most ever to sign such an agreement with the United States. Canby reported to Colonel Fauntleroy that the chiefs were honestly desirous of peace and they tried to exact no promises from him. Yet Canby in stating that the Navajo were to live west of Fort Fauntleroy had taken two of their four sacred mountains along with one-third of their traditional homeland. The colonel did not realize that the Navajo signed the treaty to gain breathing room, that during the autumn and early winter of 1860 they had been hounded by soldiers and civilians to the point that their crops were destroyed and they were without food. Their greatest need that winter was peace, and thus they signed the treaty without comment or question. However, Canby's Treaty was never ratified by the United States Senate, for in the spring of 1861 it had matters of greater moment with which to occupy itself. Shots had been fired at Fort Sumter; civil war had begun.

Simultaneously the New Mexicans, hearing that peace had been established with the Navajo, set out on slave raids. Other volunteer companies departed westward intent on raiding the Navajo for booty in the form of sheep and horses. Colonel Canby was aware of the raids, but could not stop them as he wished, for during that spring and summer the number of United States soldiers in the territory was gradually diminished. Some were transferred east, while others, such as Major Sibley, resigned to enter the Confederate service. Canby soon was too busy preparing for a rumored invasion of New Mexico from Texas to worry about volunteer raids on the Navajo or Navajo raids on New Mexico. He was relieved to find the vast majority of New Mexicans were loyal to the Union, and he quickly moved to muster the young men into service. The First Regiment of New Mexican Volunteers was organized late in July at Fort Union, and the Second Regiment in August at Albuquerque. Commanding the Second Regiment was Colonel Miguel E. Piño, with Lieutenant Colonel Manuel Chaves as second in command. Chaves, who had been fighting the Navajo for years, was assigned to Fort Fauntleroy at Ojo del Oso.

Chaves assumed command at the fort on August 9, his detachment consisting of 210 men and officers. The next day he began dispensing rations to the Navajo in the vicinity as provided in the Canby Treaty. On August 20 a conference was held at the post involving 2,000 Navajo, Colonel Chaves, and Agent John Ward. The Navajo indicated their peaceful intent that day, even surrendering four New Mexican captives. Ward then departed after agreeing to meet with the Indians again in forty days.

Chaves, after Ward left, liberally gave food to the Navajo in the vicinity, some 500 of them. The post sutler was permitted by the colonel to dispense liquor to the Navajo, gambling was widespread, and a carnival atmosphere prevailed. On September 13, according to later testimony, a series of horse races culminated in a disputed race. Large sums apparently had been bet on the outcome, and a quarrel started. Suddenly a shot rang out, followed quickly by volleys. The New Mexican volunteers, apparently by prearrangement, fired into the Navajo, killing some thirty or forty of them. The rest fled.[2]

Canby was aghast when informed, for he was desperately worried about an impending invasion by Texans. Chaves was relieved at Fort Fauntleroy and brought to Albuquerque under arrest; Captain Andrew W. Evans took command at the post. Canby then sent Agent John Ward to Cubero, which was to become his headquarters; from there he was to seek out the Navajo and attempt to persuade them to encamp near Cubero so that they could be given the protection of the government. Those who refused this offer were to be treated as enemies on whom war would be made. Of course, the encampment at Cubero was considered temporary; a permanent reservation—and such it would be, although Canby disliked the word—would have to be found. The colonel suggested that the Indians might be colonized in the area of the Little Colorado River west of the Zuñi Pueblo. Late in November he sent word to Colonel Kit Carson, commander of the First Regiment of volunteers, to campaign against raiding Navajo. Carson was not to take male prisoners, but rather to kill any he caught; the women and children were to be sent to their own country.

Little could be done that winter, however, for the Texans indeed were coming to New Mexico. John Robert Baylor invaded the southern part of the territory, capturing Mesilla in July and declaring a Confederate Arizona Territory, which consisted of all of New Mexico and Arizona south of the 34th parallel. Then in December 1861 Henry H. Sibley, a brigadier general in the Confederate army, arrived with orders to capture and govern New Mexico. This led him to Fort Thorn and the Battle of Valverde on February 21; the contest pitted Sibley against Canby—an ironic confrontation in that the two men were former comrades in arms and brothers-in-law. The Confederates won the battle, although they did not capture the fort. Later they would capture Santa Fe and Albuquerque.

As the Confederates approached New Mexico, Canby realized he desperately needed help and wrote to Colorado and California. Volunteers did come south from Colorado to turn back the Texans trying to capture Fort Union; on March 28, 1862, at the Battle of Glorieta Pass, the Rebels were forced to retreat, ending their threat to northern New Mexico. Meanwhile, from California, Brigadier General James Henry Carleton was marching with his California Column. The men swept the Confederates from Tucson and southern New Mexico, Baylor's Confederate Territory of Arizona vanishing. By the end of 1862 New Mexico again was firmly in Union hands, and attention could be given to the marauding Indians who had been relatively free to raid at will.[3] And it was Carleton who faced this task, for in August 1862 Canby had been ordered to Washington.

Carleton was born on December 27, 1814, at Lubec, Maine. Later he lived at Frankfort, the head of navigation on the Penobscot River, his youthful years made lively by the talk of seafaring men. When he was eleven years old, his family was living at the lumbering town of Orono. At that time his father died. The lad grew to manhood hoping for a literary career, but in 1838 came the so-called Lumberjack War between Maine and New Brunswick and he joined the Maine militia in the summer of 1838. Discharged in November 1839, he determined to join the regular army; with letters of recommendation in hand, he journeyed to Washington, passed a test, and was commissioned a second lieutenant of dragoons. His first post was commanded by Captain Edwin V. Sumner, and a fast friendship developed between the two. Duty followed at Fort Gibson, Indian Territory, and Fort Leavenworth, Kansas, as well as at other posts in the vicinity.

In the Mexican War he was part of the column marched by General John E. Wool into Mexico to join Zachary Taylor. He arrived in time to participate in the Battle of Buena Vista; in fact, he finally achieved part of his ambition to write, for in 1848 Harper & Brothers published his *The Battle of Buena Vista*. He emerged from the war to be stationed at Fort Leavenworth again and then be transferred to New Mexico under Colonel Edwin V. Sumner; by 1851 he was a major overseeing escort troops on the Santa Fe Trail. There he fought Mescalero Apache, Jicarilla Apache, and Navajo, and there he became a believer in the scorched-earth policy of securing peace with the natives. He left this territory in 1856, going to Philadelphia to undertake a study of the methods of European cavalry, including those of Russian Cossacks. The year 1858 saw him taking seven hundred recruits to California via the Isthmus of Panama, followed by a tour of duty at Fort Tejon. The outbreak of Civil War found Carleton serving under General Edwin V. Sumner, commander of the Department of California; Carleton was a staunch Union man, and as such was made colonel of the First Regiment of Infantry, a volunteer organization. To him fell command of the California Column and the task of marching it across the Southwest to rid it of Confederates. On April 28, 1862, he was promoted to brigadier general.[4]

The Confederates driven from Arizona and New Mexico, Carleton next turned his attention to the problem of Indian raids, especially those of the Mescalero Apache and the Navajo. From his

years of service at Fort Gibson in 1841-1842, he was a strong believer in the reservation policy, and from his service in New Mexico
in 1851-1856 he remembered the valley of the Pecos River. Therefore he recommended the creation of a reservation forty miles
square at the Bosque Redondo on the Pecos River. On November
4, 1862, he issued Special Orders No. 193 directing a board of officers to "convene at Bosque Redondo, on the Pecos River, New
Mexico, on the 15th of November, 1862, or as soon thereafter as
practicable, and proceed to select the exact site of Fort Sumner,
the new post recently ordered to be established."[5] He chose to
name the post for his old friend, General Sumner (who would die
on March 12, 1863).

The board of officers chosen by Carleton to inspect the site did
not like it, but the general did—and there it would be located. The
nearby Pecos River supplied sufficient water for the needs of soldiers and Indians, and it was more than fifty miles removed from
any town. It was in a large, oblong valley where visibility was almost unrestricted; to the west were mountains where game could
be secured, and to the east was the Staked Plains where buffalo
could be killed. Moreover, a fort at this site would serve as a barrier
to raiding by Plains tribes such as the Comanche and the Kiowa.

Carleton's first Indian campaign was against the Apache (see
Chapter 6 for details). This was concluded swiftly, and on February
1, 1863, he wrote Adjutant General of the Army Lorenzo Thomas
that the Mescalero had been "completely subdued." This freed
him and his soldiers to concentrate almost exclusively on the
Navajo.

Later Carleton would remember his first contact with these
tribesmen after his arrival as commander of the region: "When I
came here this time it not only became my professional business,
but my duty to the residents and to the Government, to devise
some plan which might, with God's blessing, forever bring these
troubles to an end. Soon after my arrival, eighteen Navajo chiefs
came to see me to request a peace treaty. I told them it was not
necessary to go through the *form* of treaty making; that if their
people committed no murders, there would be *peace without a
treaty*. Hereafter, I would judge their sincerity by their acts."[6] Ob-

viously the Navajo intended to come in, sign a treaty, and then be left alone to raid or not to raid—as had been the policy between them and the United States since 1846.

However, they had misjudged Carleton, for he told them in no uncertain terms that "if they were guilty of further depredations, they would be punished, as sure as the sun shone down upon them. It would be a war which they would long remember." Here was talk of a scorched-earth policy. The Navajo responded that never before had they been denied a treaty; apparently Carleton's tough talk did impress them, for they promised to contain their young warriors.[7] "In less than six weeks," Carleton later noted, "robberies and murders were committed" by Navajo. Therefore he began preparing for "a war which they would long remember."

On September 30, 1862, Carleton wrote the adjutant general that he was sending Lieutenant Colonel José Francisco Chavez, second in command of the New Mexican volunteers under Colonel Kit Carson, to take four companies of troops into Navajo country and on the eastern slopes of the Zuñi Mountains to establish a post. On October 7 came Special Orders No. 180, authorizing a board of officers, including engineers, to select the exact site for what would be known as Fort Wingate. The site chosen was at the headwaters of the Ojo del Gallo (Rooster Springs, which is four miles south of the present Grants, New Mexico). The creek provided water, while excellent pasturage was available nearby for horses. Construction began immediately, and by the spring of 1863 it also was ready. The Navajo, watching this post grow and hearing of the campaign against the Mescalero, no doubt were wondering about their own fate. Carleton soon showed his intent, for in April and May he began moving troops from the Apache country of southern New Mexico to the north and west. On April 11 came orders authorizing the hiring of ten Ute warriors and four Mexicans as guides,[8] and then Carleton inspected Fort Wingate himself.

Convinced that yet another fort needed to be built, he issued General Orders No. 15 on June 15. This sent a selection board of officers west to Pueblo Colorado to choose a site for a new post to be known as Fort Canby; however, this site proved unsuitable, and Fort Canby would be erected at Canyon Bonito, which previously

Kit Carson. *Courtesy U.S. Signal Corps, National Archives.*

had been the location of Fort Defiance. That same General Order concerning this post also directed that 315 additional men be sent to Fort Wingate, and it detailed Colonel Kit Carson to "proceed without delay to a point in the Navajo country to . . . prosecute a vigorous war upon the men of this tribe until it is considered at these headquarters that they have been effectually punished for their long continued atrocities." On the shoulders of Kit Carson fell the task of ending centuries of conflict between whites and Navajo—and Carson, an illiterate, was uniquely qualified to achieve results.

Born on Christmas Eve 1809, in the back country of North Carolina, Carson spent his first years in an area actually part of Kentucky. He listened to stories of Indian fighting and trapping beaver and hunting buffalo, tales told by older brothers who had already followed the westward tide of pioneering. His parents planned a legal career for him, and he was the only one of their boys to go to school; he did get three years of primary education after the family's move to Missouri in 1812. Then came the death of his father in September 1818, and eight-year-old Kit, as he was called, stayed home to plow and plant and harvest. In 1825 his mother apprenticed him to a saddle-maker in nearby Franklin, a position he considered distasteful, and a year later he ran away to join a caravan of Santa Fe traders as "cavvy boy"; in this task of herding the caravan's animals, he was employed by Charles Bent, later to be governor of New Mexico. The *Missouri Intelligencer* shortly contained a notice about the runaway apprentice: "NOTICE TO WHOME IT MAY CONCERN: That Christopher Carson, a boy about sixteen years old, small for his age, but thick-set, light hair, ran away from the subscriber, living in Franklin, ... to whome he had been bound to learn the saddler's trade. . . . All persons are notified not to harbor, support, or subsist said boy under penalty of the law. One cent reward will be given to any person who will bring back said boy."[9]

In New Mexico he became known as a trapper and Indian fighter, joining the expeditions of Thomas Fitzpatrick and Ewing Young and Jim Bridger. After years in the mountains, during which time he gained great skill as a frontiersman, he met John

Charles Frémont in the spring of 1842. Frémont, a soldier in the Corps of Topographical Engineers and son-in-law of Senator Thomas Hart Benton of Missouri, employed Carson as a guide on his western expeditions of the early 1840s. Frémont gained fame as "The Great Pathfinder," when in reality he was a "pathfollower" guided over the trails of the Mountain Men by Carson. He served with great distinction in the Mexican War, aiding in the conquest of California before returning to live at Taos, New Mexico, with the Mexican wife he had married in 1843.

He farmed at Taos until 1853 when he was appointed an Indian agent to the Ute. For seven years he held this post and, according to all accounts, rendered honest service to his charges. He was able to write only his name and title; others had to draft the reports he forwarded to Washington. Some of his Ute Indians served as guides to army expeditions against the Apache and Navajo during this time, and Carson frequently went with them; at other times his own Ute raided, and he had to call in soldiers to punish them. In the autumn of 1856 Lieutenant Colonel De Witt C. Peters took down Carson's life story as he dictated it; later this material was rewritten in eloquent style and published as *Kit Carson's Autobiography*; this was published in 1858 and brought great fame to the Indian agent.[10]

At the outbreak of the Civil War, Carson resigned from the Ute Agency and became colonel of the First Regiment of New Mexican Volunteers. He fought bravely against the Confederates at the Battle of Valverde in February 1862 and in the subsequent efforts to drive them from the territory. Next he aided in forcing the Mescalero Apache to accept peace, completing this task in January 1863. Following a leave to be with his family at Taos, he was available in June to begin the campaign against the Navajo.

With Kit Carson preparing to take the field, with Fort Canby prepared, and with additional men at Fort Wingate, Carleton on June 23 sent orders to Colonel Chavez to dispatch word to Delgadito and Barboncito, the two chieftains who had previously asked for peace. Carleton said to inform them that "we have no desire to make war upon them and other good Navajoes; but the troops cannot tell the good from the bad, and we can nor will tolerate their staying as a peace party among those against whom we intend to make war." The peaceful Navajo were given until July 20 to come in to Forts Canby or Wingate, from which point they would be transported to the Bosque Redondo Reservation. The general concluded his message, ". . . after that day every Navajo that is seen will be considered as hostile and treated accordingly; that after that day the door now open will be closed. Tell them to say this to all their people, and that as sure as the sun shines all this will come true."

When the appointed day of July 20 arrived, Carson was ready to take the war to the Navajo as it never had been done before. He had 736 men and officers; they were volunteers, some without horses and many without uniforms. Carson, known among the Navajo as the "Rope Thrower," had brought one hundred Ute scouts with him; Carleton endorsed this policy with the comment to the adjutant general, "The Utes are very brave, and fine shots, fine trailers, and uncommonly energetic in the field."[11] The Ute joined in the hope that captured Navajo women and children would be given to them for sale as slaves. Carson favored such a policy, for the Navajo then would not have to be kept at a government reservation at government expense. However, Carleton vetoed this policy in a most emphatic way, saying that all prisoners "will be sent to Santa Fe, by the first practicable opportunity." He concluded, *There must be no exception to this rule.*"[12]

On July 20 Carson sent out a small party of his Ute scouts. Within a week they reported that they had killed eight Navajo men and had captured eleven women and children. Before the end of July another five Navajo had been killed, but more important was the destruction of all Navajo fields within forty miles of Fort Canby; Carson estimated that 2,000,000 pounds of Navajo grain had been destroyed. Carleton, reading these reports, decided he at last had learned how to fight the Navajo; he sent orders to his officers in the field to pursue the Navajo "not in big bodies, with military noises and smokes, and the gleam of arms by day, and fires, and talk, and comfortable sleep by night; but in small parties moving stealthily to their haunts and lying patiently in wait for them; or by following their tracks day after day with a fixedness

Cave dwellings at Canyon de Chelly. *Courtesy Bureau of Reclamation, National Archives.*

of purpose that never gives up. . . ."[13] In short, the officers were to send their men out in small, mobile—silent—parties; they were to hide themselves near Navajo waterholes and meeting places and attack when given the opportunity. The soldiers were to destroy especially grain fields, orchards, and gardens; moreover, he wanted their animals captured, so he authorized payment of a bounty of twenty dollars for each Navajo horse or mule captured, as well as one dollar for each sheep.[14] And, while the forces were scouting in the Navajo country, Carleton had other troops stationed in the passes of the mountains to halt Navajo raiding parties into New Mexico. Despite these precautions a reported 10,000 sheep were stolen by Navajo in August alone.

Yet the campaign did begin to show results. At the end of September, General Carleton reported to the adjutant general that fifty-one Navajo had been sent to the Bosque Redondo; in October and November another 188 Navajo surrendered.[15] The other Navajo saw that Carleton's new policy would bring starvation, and they responded with their usual tactic: on October 21 a delegation arrived at Fort Wingate to ask for a treaty. To their surprise, the offer was rejected; they were told that no treaty would be made and that their only option was to surrender to be removed to the Bosque Redondo.[16] In November Carson began sending his volunteers out on foot, for the horses were failing; underfed and receiving little grain, they had been in constant use and were no longer fit for service. Carson recommended that they be wintered in the Rio Grande Valley, and on November 15 he personally led a campaign on foot to the west. On this trek he was joined by the Hopi Indians, who were eager to revenge themselves on their ancient enemies.

Meanwhile, General Carleton was trying to effect peace by different means. On November 22 he sent four Navajo from the Bosque Redondo to go among their countrymen and tell them of the food and comfortable quarters awaiting them on the reservation. Delgadito preferred to fight. And he did lead the Diné on raids, attacking and stealing herds belonging to the Mescalero at Fort Sumner.[17]

With a severe winter now descending on the Navajo country, Carson decided to make a determined, decisive move. On January 6, 1864, he left Fort Canby with two detachments. The first, consisting of thirty-three men and commanded by Captain A. W. Pheiffer, an ex-agent to the Ute, was to ride to the east end of Canyon de Chelly, while the second, commanded by Carson and consisting of almost four hundred men, was to ride to the west entrance (near Chinle). He established a supply depot at the west end of the canyon and then swept through it, his men destroying all orchards in the vicinity and capturing a large number of hostiles. On January 23 the colonel again was at Fort Canby, writing to Carleton that he had more than five hundred Navajo ready for transport to Fort Sumner. Well might the soldiers sing a song

which had appeared in the *Rio Abajo* (newspaper) on December
8, 1863:

> Come dress your ranks, my gallant souls, a standing in a row,
> Kit Carson he is waiting to march against the foe;
> At night we march to Moqui [Hopi], o'er lofty hills of snow,
> To meet and crush the savage foe, bold Johnny Navajo.
>   Johnny Navajo! O Johnny Navajo!

Carson made his report in prose, not song, by stating, "I venture to
assert that no troops of the United States have ever before been
called upon to endure as many hardships as did the men of my
command on a scout west of the Oraibi villages."[18]

Carleton was high in his praise of the men and of their campaign. On February 7 he wrote Adjutant General Lorenzo Thomas,
"This is the first time any troops, whether the country belonging
to Mexico or since we acquired it, have been able to pass through
the Cañon de Chelly." Well he might praise the work done by
Carson and his volunteers, for the Navajo had been reduced to extreme circumstances. Some would refuse to surrender, preferring to
retreat farther west and try to live out the winter on piñon nuts,
game animals, and wild potatoes, but most preferred surrender.
During the first week of February 1864 almost 800 of them came
to Forts Canby and Wingate for transfer to Fort Sumner; within
a month this number had grown to 2,500. The Santa Fe *Weekly
Gazette* on March 5 reported that "at the rate they arrive daily [at
Wingate or Canby] we will in less than three weeks have about five
thousand on the reservation."

The day before this article appeared 2,138 Navajo were sent
walking eastward from Fort Canby. They took with them into captivity 473 horses and 3,000 sheep. Government wagons transported
the very young and the very old, along with the sick—and these
were the fortunate ones. At Fort Canby supplies were short, and
dysentery hit among those Navajo waiting for transfer; within one
week's time 126 Navajos died. Later parties marching eastward into
captivity were struck en route by dysentery; some reportedly were
shot by the soldiers when they became unable to march. Carson
grew so distressed by these reports that he pleaded with Carleton for
better care for the surrendered Navajo: "It is here and en route

that we must convince them by our treatment of them of the kind intentions of the Government toward them," the old mountain man wrote, "otherwise I fear that they will lose confidence in our promises, and desert also."[19]

Only Chief Manuelita refused to come in, no matter what the odds. He declared that his God and his parents had lived in the west and that he would not go east. He quoted an old Navajo legend which held that the Diné should never travel west of the Colorado River or east of the Rio Grande, that evil would befall them if they did. Therefore he refused to leave the Chuska Mountains, where he lived with hunger and hardship. Not until November 7, 1866, did he surrender.

All the remainder surrendered, and a living stream trekked the four hundred miles eastward to Fort Sumner. Carleton grew confident at last, writing the adjutant general, "I believe this will be the last Navajo War." Governor Henry Connelly called for a day of prayer and thanksgiving on the first Thursday of April to express the gratitude of New Mexicans for the work done by Carleton, Carson, and the volunteers. And that day a brass band played while the people moved in procession to St. Francis Cathedral for a service of thanks.

Among the captive Navajo, however, there was little sense of thanksgiving. Even Carleton was growing worried, for it now became his task to feed the Indians. At first he had believed the Navajo would number only about 5,000, but the captives dribbled in until they numbered some 8,000. He wrote the commanding officer at Fort Sumner, Major Henry Wallen, to estimate the amount needed to feed these Indians and to keep a fifty-day supply on hand; "There must be no mistake about having enough for them to eat," he wrote, "if we have to kill horses and mules for them."[20] The Santa Fe *New Mexican* on March 5, 1864, urged farmers to raise large crops that year, saying that because of the large number of Indians at Fort Sumner the army would have to make large purchases: "A ready market and paying prices will surely be at hand."

Carleton worriedly wrote lengthy letters to Major Wallen, telling him how to construct dwellings for the Navajo. He told the major to practice economy in every way, even making soup from flour and meat to stretch supplies; and to get the Indians to eat this new dish he suggested, "It must be inculcated as a religion."[21] The Santa Fe *Gazette* on June 9, 1866, noted the method of rationing meat. Every other day twenty to thirty cattle were driven into the butchering pens to be slaughtered four at a time. The Indians brought buckets to catch the blood, which later they mixed with corn meal and ate. The meat was cut into pound-and-a-half pieces, a difficult task because of the thousands of pieces necessary; then at 6:30 A.M. the Indians filed past with their tin buckets to get their ration. Yet there was not enough food, and the ration had to be cut to one pound of food a day; even the soldiers at the post were placed on half-rations.

In desperation the commander of New Mexico sent a long appeal to the adjutant general of the army. His messenger was a former Indian superintendent of New Mexico, Colonel James L. Collins, who was also to act as lobbyist for Carleton's request. To General Thomas, Carleton wrote, "The War Department has performed its whole duty in bringing these Indians into subjection and now, in my opinion, stands ready to transfer them to the Department of the Interior. Other tribes are on the war path and we should not be embarrassed with the care of Indians no longer hostile. Laws should be passed to care for them." As to immediate needs he asked for 2,000,000 pounds of food, 13,000 yards of cloth for clothing, 7,000 blankets, 20 spinning wheels, 50 mills for grinding corn, along with farming machinery, seed, and—astonishingly—600 cotton handkerchiefs. He stated his belief that a congressional appropriation of $150,000 would cover all that he asked. In his letter, Carleton gave reasons to satisfy any questioning politicians that the price was low: "When it is considered what a magnificent pastoral and mineral country they have surrendered to us, the mere pittance which must be given to support them sinks into insignificance as a price for their natural heritage."[22]

Colonel Collins apparently proved a persuasive lobbyist, for Congress did appropriate $100,000 for the care of the Navajo (one senator, when told he was voting on a measure dealing with the captured Navajo, responded, "Was there an Indian War?"). Carleton was given 500,000 pounds of flour from Colorado and 2,000 head of cattle, with the promise that additional food would be sent.

Two and one-half years passed before the army was able to rid itself of care of these Indians, however. During this time the Bosque Redondo became a large agricultural enclave. On June 30, 1864, Congress enlarged it, and on this vast tract of land bordering the Great Plains the soldiers tried to teach the Indians how to farm. Thirty miles of irrigation ditches were built to bring water from the Pecos River, where a dam had been built (at the next major rain the dam held, but it diverted the flood onto the Indians' farm land and washed them out). Corn, wheat, sorghum, and rice were planted, along with 12,000 trees intended to supply fuel in the future. Kit Carson came on July 11, 1864, to assume the task of overseeing the reservation, but this proved frustrating. The Apache and Navajo hated each other bitterly, and quarrels were frequent. Cutworms attacked the crops that autumn, while the natives proved unable to wait for the sorghum to mature; at night they cut the canes and ate them like candy. The rice simply withered away to nothing.[23]

To Carson also fell the task of trying to build villages for the Indians. The Navajo traditionally had lived in scattered villages, each under its own chief. Carleton wanted them to live in tents, but the condemned army tents which he sent for this purpose were cut up and sewn into sacks in which to store and transport grain. The general then proposed the construction of Navajo "Pueblos," each building to be "one story high" and facing a central plaza; he believed the Navajo could construct these in their spare time.[24] Carson was unable to put this plan into effect, however, for the Navajo refused to live in a dwelling where death had occurred. At last the two compromised; the Navajo would live in rows of adobe hogans, and when there was a death the family could move out and build a new home at the end of the row.[25]

By the autumn of 1864 conditions at Fort Sumner and the Bosque Redondo, "Fair Carletonia" the soldiers called them with contempt, were desperate. All the general could offer the Navajo was sympathy, however; he told his officers to exhort them to be "too proud to murmur at what cannot be helped. We could not foresee that frost, rain and hail would come and destroy the crops." He continued, "Tell them not to be discouraged but to work hard, every man and woman, to put in large crops next year, when if God smiles upon our efforts, they will, at one bound, be forever placed beyond want and be independent."

Simultaneously there came a quarrel with Michael Steck, Superintendent of Indian Affairs for the Territory. Steck argued that the Navajo should not have been removed from their own country, especially not to the same area as their traditional enemies, the Apache. Speck soon was writing to his superiors to urge that the Navajo have their own reservation and in their own country. Because of Steck's protests, the Commissioner of Indian Affairs, William P. Dole, recommended to his superior, the Secretary of the Interior, that his bureau should not assume responsibility for the Indians; rather he urged that the army be left to administer to them. This quarrel between the army and the Bureau of Indian Affairs came to a head in May 1865 when Steck was fired, to be replaced in New Mexico by Felipe Delgado.

During 1865 Carleton continued his fight to make a success of the reservation at the Bosque Redondo. However, fate seemed against him, for crops failed that year as they had the year before, and Congress proved reluctant to vote funds to feed Indians who had fed themselves for centuries. To the army's vast relief General Ulysses S. Grant on December 31, 1866, issued Special Order 561, which stated, "Turn over Navajo Indians now held at Bosque Redondo to the Indian Agent; the settlement of supplies should be agreed upon by the two Departments; the commanding officer will afford the necessary and usual aid to the Indian Agent to control the Indians but without going beyond strict duties and administration."[26]

At last, eighteen years and more after the meeting between Colonel Alexander W. Doniphan and the Navajo at Bear Spring, the Indians had ceased to be a vexing problem for the soldiers stationed in New Mexico. And very shortly after they were transferred to the Bureau of Indian Affairs, they ceased to be a problem at the Bosque Redondo—for they were given their own reservation. In the summer of 1866 General John Pope came to New Mexico on a tour of inspection; his recommendation was that the Navajo be sent further east to the Indian Territory. Then in the spring of 1868 General William T. Sherman visited Fort Sumner; his telegram to Senator J. B. Henderson told what happened: "I have had four long interviews with the Navajos. Without absolute force, they will not remain here or move farther east. Colonel S. F. Tappan and I have concluded to let them return to a reservation in northwest New Mexico and on the faith of the $150,000 proposed, I will put them in motion at once."[27]

A treaty to this effect was drawn, one wherein the government promised each head of family 160 acres plus $150 over three years for the purchase of seeds and implements; in addition, the government promised 15,000 sheep and 500 cattle for each tribe, a teacher and school for each 30 children, and $150,000 to finance the move westward. In return the Navajo promised not to attack or rob Americans. They departed the hated Bosque Redondo on June 18, 1868, to return to their homeland, now their reservation, with the agency headquarters to be at Fort Wingate. The march westward became a trail of tears for them, tears for those who died returning home and tears of joy at returning to their country of red desert and sandstone mountains. By the end of July the "Long Walk," as it became known, was ended. The Navajo no longer were the lords of New Mexico. They were weavers of blankets, makers of jewelry, herders of sheep, and objects of interest to tourists—as well as a source of profit for cheating agents. Moreover, they would be the unwilling recipients of the attentions of generations of do-gooders, and the subject of countless interviews by anthropologists. Decades would pass before the Navajo would try to assume control of their own destiny again—and that goal has not yet been reached.

4
THE COMANCHE BARRIER

On August 10, 1780, Domingo Cabello y Robles, governor of Texas, wrote Commandant-General Teodoro de Croix that the soldiers of his province, although valiant, without exception openly expressed their fright at the mere mention of the word "Comanche." Croix realized the seriousness of this problem; he in turn informed the viceroy in Mexico City that if the Comanche continued to raid Texas so fiercely, "the desolation of the province will be consequent, irremediable, and immediate. . . ." And to Governor Cabello he sent only advice: he suggested trying to pacify the Comanche by persuasion, emissaries, and presents; to show them the benefits of peace; and to overlook their raids.[1]

Perhaps this was good advice, for in the years that followed a patchwork peace was effected. Treaties were solemnly made and even observed for a period of time. Then a raid would occur, and the chiefs, when questioned, would blame the "crazy boys"—irrepressible young warriors who could not be restrained. When this excuse wore thin, the Indian leaders would solemnly explain that they had heard rumors that the Spaniards were planning to attack and had struck first. Finally the raids would become too numerous and the stealing too flagrant, whereupon the Spaniards would stop their annual distribution of presents; then the chiefs would send delegations to ask peace and forgiveness. Invariably the hard-pressed governors were in no position to refuse, and then the cycle of raids and explanations would begin again. In truth, the Comanche were the real masters of Texas, at least from the timber line westward.

In the summer of 1812 the Indians demonstrated their contempt for the Spaniards, as well as their sense of humor—and the desire of one chief to count coup. On July 12 that year he and his warriors struck the Spanish outpost at San Marcos (fifty miles northeast of San Antonio), driving off 205 horses. The chief knew there would be no pursuit, for the soldiers there had no mounts on which to give chase, and he knew that it would be several days before news of the raid reached the governor at San Antonio. Therefore he and 200 of his followers sauntered into the capital city as if on a trading expedition. The next day one of his warriors rode breathlessly into the city to tell of the attack at San Marcos and to call the Comanche away. Through this deception the governor of the province was convinced that another tribe, not Comanche, were guilty of the attack at San Marcos.[2]

In 1821, just at the time of Mexican independence, American colonists began arriving in Texas under the direction of Stephen F. Austin. The following spring Austin and two companions were surrounded by fifty Comanche near the Nueces River; in this, one of the first meetings between this tribe and Americans, the three had all their possessions taken away. When the Indians learned the nationality of the three, however, they returned the property and released them. Apparently they considered the newcomers to be friends—or else unworthy of their attention. In the years immediately following this incident, the Americans were too busy colonizing the province and then fighting for their own independence to take note of the bold raiders of the plains country to the west.

In 1836, after Texas became a republic, the first president was Sam Houston, who at one time had resigned as governor of Tennessee to live among the Cherokee. Houston was friendly to all Indians, and his policy toward the Comanche was one of peace. In 1838, however, the Comanche became concerned about the westward advance of the American frontiersmen, who were venturing out onto the plains not only to hunt but also to settle. Early in

Mirabeau B. Lamar (from a painting), the president of the Republic of Texas who was determined to drive out the Indians. *Courtesy Western History Collections, University of Oklahoma Library.*

1838 they requested a treaty with the Texans; Sam Houston refused to make such an agreement, for the Comanche had requested a definite boundary between the two peoples. As a result the Indians began waging a devastating series of raids along the frontier.

In the election that fall, Mirabeau Buonaparte Lamar was elected the chief executive of the infant republic, and his attitude toward Indians was far different from that of Houston. Born in Georgia in 1798, Lamar was well educated before failing at mercantile activity. He had been private secretary to Governor George M. Troup of Georgia and had actively participated in the expulsion of the Creek and Cherokee Indians from that state. After his wife died in 1833, Lamar ran unsuccessfully for Congress, then moved to Texas in time to participate in the wars for Texan independence. Although he was a poet, a dreamer, an idealist, and a man keenly interested in history, he bitterly hated Indians. One of his first moves was to order a series of frontier forts and to prepare punitive expeditions against the raiders. Texans were happy to join such projected forays—the Comanche had been kidnapping their women and children. A few such captives had been taken by the Comanche to New Mexico on their trading expeditions, and they had been ransomed by New Mexicans—for sale to their families in Texas. The Lamar administration knew that various Comanche bands were holding several additional white captives, but he was unable to recover them.

In January 1840, to Lamar's surprise, three Comanche chiefs rode into San Antonio. They stated that they represented a general council of their fellow chiefs, and that they wanted to convene a council with the Texans in order that a treaty might be drafted between the two people. Henry Karnes, who negotiated with the three, suggested that the conference take place in mid-March at the Council House in San Antonio and that the Comanche bring in all their white captives for sale to the Texas peace commissioners. The Indians agreed, fully intending not to honor their pledge; they preferred to hold such captives for ransom one at a time. Karnes was equally guilty of deception, for he intended that the Texans capture whatever chiefs came in for the council and to exchange them for the white captives.

The meeting took place on March 19 as scheduled. That morning two runners came into town to announce that sixty-five chiefs, warriors, women, and children were arriving, but only one white prisoner was with them. This proved to be Matilda Lockhart; she was both starved and tortured, the flesh burned away at her nostrils by live coals and her body covered with bruises. To the Texans with whom she was allowed to converse, she said that "she had seen several of the other prisoners at the principal camp a few days before she left; and that they brought her in to see if they could get a high price for her, and if so, would bring in the rest one at a time."

Colonel William G. Cooke, the acting secretary of war, gave the order for Texas Rangers to begin placing themselves around the Council House. "Where are the prisoners you promised to bring to this talk?" asked one of the Texans, to which Chief Muke-war-rab replied, "We have brought in the only one we had; the others are with other tribes." Texan negotiators stalled for time, waiting for the Rangers to get into place, by explaining the provisions of the treaty which the Lamar administration would make with the Comanche after the captives were brought in. At last the Rangers were in place, whereupon the Comanche were told that they were prisoners and would be held hostage for the return of whites held by the Indians. The chiefs drew their knives and warriors readied their bows, and all rushed for the doors. "Fire," yelled the Ranger captain. When the bloody fighting ended, according to Colonel Hugh McLeod (who, along with Colonel Cooke, constituted the Texas commission), "The loss of the enemy was total . . . . 35 killed, including three women and two children—and 27 women and children and two old men captured." A total of seven Texans died, while another eight were wounded.

Colonel McLeod moved immediately to take advantage of the hostages. According to his report the following day to President Lamar, ". . . A squaw has been liberated, and well mounted, to go to the main tribe and tell them we are willing to exchange prisoners. She promises to return in four days with our captive friends. . . ."[3]

She did not return in four days—or ever. Instead the Comanche who had camped near San Antonio, members of the Penateka branch of the tribe, withdrew to the plains country to cry for their dead and to consider what they thought to be an act of great treachery on the part of the Texans. Reportedly they tortured a dozen of their prisoners to death, and they plotted revenge. White residents of the Republic of Texas, meanwhile, brooded about what they considered to be the Comanche treachery in failing to bring all their prisoners to the Council House. They congratulated themselves that they had inflicted so severe a defeat on the Indians that henceforth the settlements would be left in peace. Spring gave way to summer, and still the Comanche had not attacked.

Then on August 5, Dr. Joel Ponton and Tucker Foley were on their way from Columbus to Gonzales. Suddenly they were confronted by twenty-seven Comanche warriors, who chased them for three miles, killing Foley and wounding Ponton; the doctor did manage to reach his home and to spread the alarm. Thirty-six Texans immediately took the trail only to meet other groups of armed Texans who reported raids at different settlements; soon 125 volunteers were riding under the command of Captain John J. Tumlinson—little realizing that as many as 1,000 Comanche were in the vicinity bent on killing as many Texans as possible. At the town of Victorio they struck without warning and killed 13 people; the next day, August 7, they rode toward the coast, driving from 1,500 to 2,000 horses with them, as well as taking several women and children captive.

On August 8 came the great Comanche raid at Linnville, a small port village on the Gulf Coast. At eight o'clock in the morning they thundered into town, riding in a half-moon formation that surrounded the village. Most of the frightened whites boarded small boats and fled into the bay; there they sat through the day, watching the Comanche burning houses one at a time, butchering cattle indiscriminately, and parading up and down the beach dressed in stolen bits of finery. The Texans had no guns with which to fight and thus witnessed in helpless fury this destruction of their town—as well as the death of five men, including H. O. Watts, collector of customs, and the capture of two women and a child.[4] At dark, loaded with booty, the Comanche withdrew from the town, riding leisurely back to their plains haunts.

The following day the raiders were confronted by the Tumlinson party of 125 angry Texans, but Tumlinson proved indecisive. Despite the counsel of the impatient Ben McCulloch, who later would gain great fame as a Texas Ranger, Tumlinson refused to charge the Indians; thereupon the Comanche slipped away. However, word of the Linnville and Victorio raids had spread, and volunteers hastened to form companies; they gathered at Plum Creek at a point where the Comanche would return. There, under the command of General Felix Huston, General Edward Burleson, and Ben McCulloch, who had ridden a horse virtually to death to arrive in time for the fight, some two hundred men waited. On August 12 they fought what was called the Battle of Plum Creek, one of the few pitched battles between Comanche and whites; some seventy to eighty Indians were killed that day, several hundred of the horses recovered, and three of the white captives were recovered.[5] Most of the Indians eluded the Texans, however, slipping around them with their captive horses and fleeing to the plains. Yet because of the Battle of Plum Creek, thereafter they never came in large numbers to attack Texas towns; instead they resorted to guerrilla warfare, attacking in small parties to steal horses, kill men, and capture women and children.

John H. Moore, sometimes called the most experienced Indian fighter in Texas during the days of the republic, wanted revenge on the Comanche for the Linnville raid, more than had been exacted at Plum Creek. Gathering 275 men, he left the city of Austin on October 5, marching up the Colorado River of Texas. On October 23 on the Red Fork of this river (in present Mitchell County) his spies found a Comanche village of 60 lodges and 125 warriors; at dawn the next day the volunteers, usually called Rangers, poured into the encampment with total surprise on their side. The Indians fled toward the river; some were shot before they could reach it, others drowned in it, and the ones who crossed were pursued for four miles. Moore, in his report of the battle, said, "The river and its banks now presented every evidence of a total defeat of our savage foe. The bodies of men, women and children were to be seen on every hand wounded, dying, and dead. . . ." One hundred and thirty Comanche died in this engagement, and plunder and livestock from the Linnville Raid was recovered, while the village itself and its contents were burned.[6]

During the remaining years of the Republic of Texas, battles with the Comanche were sporadic and raids isolated. A settler was killed here, a child stolen there, a house was burned, a field destroyed. Comanche hatred of the Texans likewise increased as former hunting lands were plowed under, individual Indians were killed by whites, and property was destroyed. Leading the Texans in their fight against the various Comanche war chiefs and their followers were the Rangers, a force which had its origins in the days when Stephen F. Austin was colonizing the Mexican state of Texas. Citizens in the infant colony had banded together into "ranging forces" to protect themselves against the Indians; to do so they learned to ride hard and travel light, much in the fashion of the Indians themselves, just as they also developed a pathological hatred for the natives of Texas.

In 1837, shortly after Texas achieved its independence from Mexico, the Congress of the republic realized a need for some force to protect the western frontier, and in May 1837 it created the Rangers by appropriating $100,000 and by giving President Sam Houston a thirty-day leave of absence from his official duties in order to organize the body. Houston soon had established six companies of Rangers, who were ordered to construct blockhouse forts along the frontier to keep the Indians on the western side of this line. The Rangers quickly developed an *esprit de corps* that attracted spirited young men in search of adventure—which they found in measure aplenty. From then until the end of the Republic, it was the official duty of the Rangers to pursue raiding Indians; when such attacks came in large numbers, the Rangers were reinforced by civilian volunteers, as during the Linnville Raid, but usually the Rangers were able to cope with the small bands of Comanche raiders by themselves.[7]

In the election of 1841, Sam Houston returned to the presidency of Texas, and he moved to restore peace with all the tribes alienated by President Lamar. By 1843 he and his agents had succeeded with most tribes, but not with the Comanche. That summer J. C. Eldredge, who was general superintendent of Indian affairs, visited the Comanche country and reported that the Indians yet remembered with bitterness and anger the Council House Fight and that they were reluctant to agree to any meeting with Texans. Nor

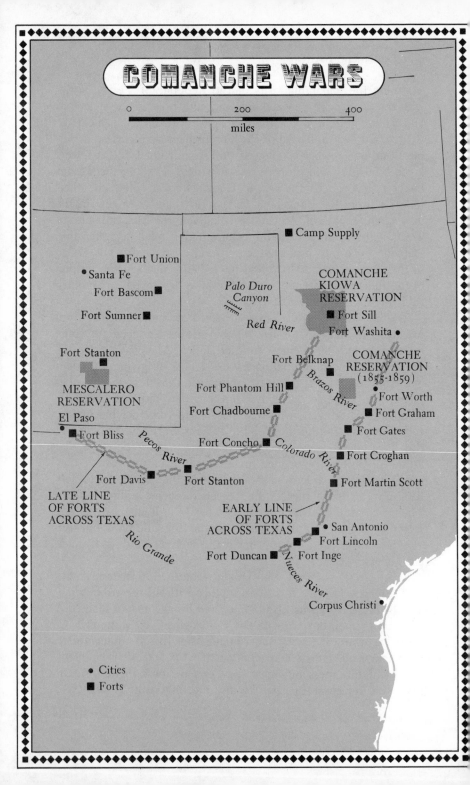

would they agree to release any of the white prisoners they held. The following year Chief Buffalo Hump of the Peneteka did meet with President Houston to discuss a treaty; however, Buffalo Hump insisted that a boundary between the two people should run southward along the Cross Timbers, by Comanche Peak in central Texas, just west of San Antonio, and end at the Rio Grande near the town of Eagle Pass. To this Houston angrily refused, and negotiations ended. In fact, within a year frontiersmen would be pushing west of this line—with Indian raids, Ranger counterattacks, and hatred the result.

On December 29, 1845, Texas was annexed to the United States, whereupon federal soldiers became obligated to assume the frontier defense as they were in all states. However, the United States Army was too busy fighting Mexico to spare men for western Texas until 1848, and the Rangers had to continue protecting the frontier until soldiers at last could move to the region (Texas billed the United States for this service). In December 1848 federal soldiers at last arrived. Their commanders assessed the local situation and decided that the Texans had been right in constructing a line of forts as a means of containing the Comanche; therefore between December 1848 and July 1849 the government built, from south to north, Forts Duncan, on the Rio Grande at Eagle Pass; Inge, near the town of Uvalde; Lincoln, on the Seco River fifty-five miles west of San Antonio; Martin Scott, on the Pedernales River at Fredericksburg; Croghan, on Hamilton Creek near the present Burnet; Gates, on the Leon River; Worth, at the present Fort Worth; and Graham, on the Brazos River.

The soldiers sent to garrison the posts were infantrymen, not the cavalrymen so desperately needed. As one Texas newspaper editor bitterly declared in 1849, "The idea of repelling mounted Indians, the most expert horsemen in the world, with a force of foot soldiers, is ridiculous." Moreover, most of the companies sent to Texas were understrength, while the Indians had a superior knowledge of local geography. Thus the Comanche had little difficulty in slipping past the new line of forts, and their raids grew in intensity. As a result the Texas settlers petitioned their state government for contingents of Texas Rangers to give them protection. In response to protests from the Lower Rio Grande Valley, the state did send a force of Rangers under command of Captain John S. "Rip" Ford to that area. Early in 1850 Ford established his headquarters north of Rio Grande City, and from there his men scouted for Comanche. Because of his efforts the number of raids in that area did diminish considerably.

Meanwhile, the United States government was eager to come to terms with the Comanche in order to halt their raids into Mexico; by the terms of the Treaty of Guadalupe Hidalgo, the United States was supposed to contain the Indians within its area of jurisdiction. Therefore on December 10, 1850, John H. Rollins, the superintendent of Indian affairs for Texas, met with thirty-four chiefs of the Comanche and other tribes on the San Saba River (to the northwest of San Antonio). The chiefs signed a treaty with Rollins; they did so, they said, because they feared the military might of the United States. The agreement stipulated that the Comanche would not raid south of the Rio Grande, nor were they to penetrate east or south of the line of posts established the year before. Finally, this treaty stipulated that the Comanche would free their white captives.

The immediate result of the treaty, which was never submitted to the United States Senate for ratification, was that white settlers began moving westward onto lands formerly dominated by the Comanche; and it led to further quarrels between the Comanche and the United States government, for it had made no mention of Mexican prisoners. When American officials implied that the Comanche had to give up these people, the Indians asked for yet another conference. This occurred on October 28, 1851, when Agent John A. Rogers met the Penateka on the San Saba and secured a new agreement. The northern Comanche were angered by this new agreement, for they held many Mexican prisoners, and they began raiding both the Texans and their southern kinsmen. Thereupon the government decided to move its line of forts even farther west to more strategic locations. Between June 24, 1851, and November 18, 1852, seven new forts were established, most of them at least a hundred miles west of the line of 1849. These were Forts Clark, near the present town of Bracketville; Mason, at the present town of the same name; Terrett, on the North Llano River; Mc-Kavett, on the upper San Saba; Chadbourne, on Oak Creek; Phantom Hill, fourteen miles north of the present Abilene; and Belknap, on the Brazos River.

As soon as the posts were erected, there was a rush to the land intervening between them and the old line. With the new posts undermanned and the Comanche raiding the new settlements, civilian demands for protection mounted. In response to these pleas, Governor Peter H. Bell ordered more Rangers to the frontier, and Indian raids slowed. Then, in 1853 when the Franklin Pierce administration came to power in Washington, Secretary of War Jefferson Davis proved sympathetic to the Texans. He suggested to Governor Bell that Texas might wish to set aside land for reservations for the southern Comanche, who by this time were willing to settle on them. They had been pushed westward by the new line of forts and by the Rangers, and were subsisting largely by raiding into Mexico. However, their great war trail into Mexico was no longer safe because of the new line of forts. When Agent Robert S. Neighbors asked some of the Penateka if they were ready to settle on a reservation, one chief replied: "Over this vast country where for centuries our ancestors roamed in undisputed possession, free and happy, what have we left? The game, our main dependence, is killed and driven off, and we are forced into the most sterile and barren portions of it to starve." Looking at the future the chief concluded, "We see nothing but extermination left for us, and we await the result with stolid indifference. Give us a country we can call our own where we may bury our people in quiet."

Early in 1854 the Texas legislature, eager to give the Comanche a "country we can call our own," authorized the Indian Bureau to select as many as three reservations. These were to total no more than twelve square leagues of land (or approximately 50,000 acres) to be taken from the public domain of the state. Captain Randolph B. Marcy of the Corps of Topographical Engineers and Indian Agent Neighbors were chosen to make the locations. They chose one site of eight square leagues on the Brazos River (near the present town of Graham); this was for the sedentary tribes of central and eastern Texas who had been driven west and who were homeless. The other site chosen consisted of four square leagues of land (about 17,500 acres) on the Clear Fork of the Brazos; this was to be the new home of the Penateka Comanche. By November 1855 Agent Neighbors was ready to open these two agencies.

At first it seemed that the Comanche reservation would be successful. Neighbors found 1,200 Penateka waiting for him at the reservation, but word soon spread among the tribesmen that the army planned to kill all of them, and Chiefs Buffalo Hump and Sanaco fled north with 800 of their people. Thereafter the number of Comanche at the reservation varied from 250 to 550, with an average of perhaps 350 there most of the time. Yet that year of 1855, the war department sent Colonel Albert Sidney Johnston to the Texas frontier with the newly organized Second Cavalry, and because of his vigilance the frontier grew very quiet. Johnston sent Colonel Robert E. Lee with four companies of the Second Cavalry to establish Camp Cooper near the Comanche reservation, and this also contributed to peace.

Beginning in 1857, however, the northern Comanche renewed their war in Texas with great ferocity. In August that year, Colonel Johnston and most of his Second Cavalry departed for Utah to participate in the so-called Mormon War, and the Nokoni Comanche swept down from the north that fall in one great raid, stealing an estimated 500 horses and killing several whites. Governor Elisha M. Pease responded by sending a company of Rangers and authorizing several companies of volunteers to take the field. Agent Neighbors likewise was alarmed, for he feared the Texans would kill reservation Comanche along with the raiders; he wrote General David E. Twiggs, commander of the Fifth Military District (Texas), to urge that the army also take the field. Twiggs, portly and profane, agreed and secured permission from the war department to abandon the passive defensive posture in the state in favor of an aggressive campaign. Before he could take the field, however, impetuous Texans had swept into the area.

In January 1858 the Texas legislature authorized $70,000 of state funds be spent to punish the Comanche raiders. Governor Hardin R. Runnels likewise was empowered to call out as many Rangers as were needed. He responded by sending Captain Rip Ford to conduct a campaign. In the spring of 1858 Ford crossed the Red River with 215 Rangers and friendly Indian scouts from the Brazos Agency, and on May 12 he fought a decisive battle against the Kotsoteka Comanche in the valley of the Canadian River. In this engagement seventy-six Indians, including Chief Iron Jacket, were killed, and eighteen were taken prisoner, while only one Texan and one Indian scout were killed. Convinced that this victory would halt the raids, as well as being desperately short of supplies, Ford then marched his command home.

That fall the army at last was marching. In mid-September 5 companies of soldiers and 125 Indian allies departed from Fort Belknap under command of Major Earl Van Dorn. A West Pointer, class of 1842, Van Dorn had been serving at Camp Cooper under Lieutenant Colonel Robert E. Lee and had campaigned against the Comanche renegades in the summer of 1856. His Wichita Expedition, as it came to be called, made one forced march of thirty-six hours in the saddle in order, on October 1, to surprise Buffalo Hump and his band of Penateka Comanche near the present Rush Springs, Oklahoma. When this battle ended, 70 Indians (including women) were dead, while only 5 of Van Dorn's command had been killed. Among the wounded, however, were Van Dorn, who had one arrow through his navel and another through his wrist, and Lawrence Sullivan Ross, later to be a Ranger captain, Confederate general, and governor of Texas.

Van Dorn was not expected to survive his wounds, but he recovered and in May 1859 again was on the trail of the raiding Comanche. That month he and his soldiers surprised Chief Buffalo Hump a second time; this time Van Dorn either killed or captured almost the entire band. This American invasion of land considered safe for hunting and camping caused the northern Comanche to strike back in force. In September 1858 they had hit settlements in north-central Texas with great fury, and in the months that followed they made their presence felt—and feared—as far south as Fredericksburg, just fifty miles from San Antonio.

Texans grew increasingly frustrated at these raids, their hatred finally turning on the Comanche reservation. Their pent-up wrath finally exploded on December 28, 1858, when one group of Tex-

John Robert Baylor in 1858. *Courtesy Western History Collections, University of Oklahoma Library.*

ans happened upon a small party of Indians from the reservation; the natives had a pass from their agent to hunt grazing land for their horses, but the Texans refused to listen. They killed four men and three women, and wounded most of the rest. Some Texas officials were appalled at this deed. A district judge, backed by Governor Runnels, ordered the culprits arrested, but both sheriffs and Texas Ranger leaders, including Rip Ford, ignored the order; moreover, a grand jury convened to look into the matter not only refused to return indictments, but also recommended that the perpetrators be commended for performing a public service.

Federal officials, after this event, finally conceded that a reservation for the Comanche in Texas was unworkable. The Indian Bureau in Washington decided on March 30, 1859, to move the southern Comanche to the Indian Territory (Oklahoma) as soon as space could be arranged for them there. However, even this decision failed to appease the Texans. On May 23 a group of 250 angry frontiersmen appeared at the Comanche reservation determined to exterminate the Indians or else to drive them from the state. Leader of this band of fanatical frontiersmen was John Robert Baylor.

Born in Kentucky in 1822, Baylor in many ways typified his Texas neighbors. The son of a doctor, he attended a university in Cincinnati for a time and was well educated by the standards of that day. Arriving in Texas in 1840, he fought the Indians on several occasions, including the expedition led by John H. Moore in 1840. After farming at Rose Prairie in Fayette County, he was elected to the state legislature in 1853. His service terminated when he was appointed one of the agents at the Comanche reservation. His time there proved short, for he violently disagreed with Indian Superintendent Robert S. Neighbors and was fired. He then moved to a site about thirty miles west of Fort Worth and began ranching—and watching developments on the reservation, totally convinced that the Indians there were using the reservation for protection and were slipping from it when convenient to raid, loot, and kill.

That spring of 1859 he helped organize the 250 frontiersmen bound for the reservation and was elected their leader. Arriving at the reservation on May 23, he demanded that the Indians guilty of crimes be turned over to the party. They then fought a hot skirmish with the Comanche—while United States Army troops stood by and watched, their commander stating that he had no jurisdiction over Indians when they were off the reservation. Baylor and his men were forced to withdraw, but they kept close watch from a nearby vantage point; obviously they intended another attack when circumstances favored them. Governor Runnels was so angered by this attack that he called out a company of militia to disperse the attackers, only to disband the militia in alarm when he learned that they intended to join Baylor in slaughtering Comanche.

Indian Superintendent Neighbors used this attack to convince his superiors that the reservation in Texas must be abandoned. Approval for this was finally granted on June 11; a month and a half later, protected by three companies of soldiers, Neighbors departed with 384 Comanches and 1,112 natives from the Brazos agency for Oklahoma. In the rush to leave Texas, the Penateka Comanche were able to gather only a small portion of their livestock, which were valued at $9,550; they left behind other animals valued at $14,922.50. On August 8 the cavalcade crossed the Red River, a curious spectacle of Indians, soldiers, livestock—and militia sent along to see that no Comanche straggled away to attack settlements. Eight days later the party arrived at a new reservation selected for them, a site on the Washita River (four miles northeast of the present Fort Cobb, Oklahoma). The removal of the Comanche from Texas and the closing of the two reservations did not end the hatred they had caused, however; when Superintendent Neighbors returned to Texas, bound for San Antonio, he was murdered on the streets of Belknap by an irate citizen who thought he had been giving renegade Indians sanctuary on the reservation.

That year in the gubernatorial race in Texas, Sam Houston campaigned against the incumbent Runnels, stating that his opponent had failed to protect the frontier. Houston's election reflected that the public believed this charge. Houston therefore took office pledged to halt these depredations; this he undertook despite his earlier sympathy for the natives. The raids were growing more intense as the northern Comanche and their Kiowa allies, joined by the southern Comanche driven into Oklahoma, congregated between the Arkansas and Canadian rivers and sent war parties south into Texas. Houston responded in February and March 1860 by sending seven companies of Rangers to the exposed area and by authorizing each county there to raise a company of no more than twenty volunteers. The mounted troops brought a temporary peace by their numbers, but their success was not great.

The most notable victory at this time was gained by one of the Ranger captains appointed by Governor Houston. In late 1859 when he sent the seven companies north, one of them was under Lawrence Sullivan Ross, who had recovered from the wounds he had received on the Wichita Expedition led by Major Van Dorn. Born in Iowa in 1838, Ross had come to Texas the following year; there his father, Shapley Prince Ross, had been an agent on the Brazos reservation, and the young lad had learned much about the Comanche during this time. For a time he was a student at Baylor University in Texas, and in 1859 he had graduated from Wesleyan University in Alabama; in fact, he had joined the Wichita Expedition while home during recess from his studies.

In December 1859 the twenty-one-year-old Ranger captain, leading twenty soldiers from Camp Cooper and seventy inflamed and aroused volunteers, pursued a Comanche raiding party into northwestern Texas. There, in crossing the rough buttes and canyons along the Pease River, the party surprised a large Nokoni Comanche camp. In the battle that followed, a number of hand-to-hand encounters occurred; in one of these Ross killed an Indian believed to be Chief Peta Nocona (although later the Comanche denied this). And to the amazement of the Texans, they found Cynthia Ann Parker in this camp and brought her back with them.

Cynthia Ann Parker, born about 1827, was approximately nine years old when on May 19, 1836, her father's trading post in Texas, known as Fort Parker, was attacked by several hundred Comanche. In the battle that followed, her father was killed, while she, a younger brother, two women, and another boy were taken into captivity. Five years later a trader saw her with Comanche on the

Canadian River and tried to ransom her from the Indian family that had adopted her, but he was unsuccessful. Two years later another trader saw Cynthia at the same location, only to learn that the sixteen year old had married Peta Nocona, a Comanche chief. She later gave birth to two sons, Pecos and Quanah Parker, and a daughter, Prairie Flower. In the battle in December 1860 she and her daughter were captured. In almost every way she resembled the Indian taken with her, but she had blue eyes and light skin, and Captain Ross guessed her real identity.

Ross brought Cynthia Parker to Camp Cooper where her uncle, Isaac Parker, came to claim her. She did recognize her American name, but she definitely preferred the company of the Comanche. The state legislature in 1861 voted her a pension and a league of land, but she kept trying to run away to rejoin her adopted people. Just after the death of her daughter in 1864, she also died—the more romantic say of a broken heart at separation from the Comanche.[8]

As the year 1861 arrived, the Comanche were still actively raiding the northern Texas frontier, but Texans were no longer as concerned about it. Instead they chose to involve themselves in the question of states' rights and of secession and of the "War for Southern Independence." In the years that followed, they would secede, oust Governor Houston, join the Confederacy, spend millions of dollars, and see the cream of their young manhood die in their vain hope of becoming part of a separate Southern nation. Only at the end of that conflict would they again turn their attention to the Comanche menace on their northern border. The Comanche had been confronted, but not conquered.[9]

While the Texans were fighting the southern Comanche, the northern and western members of this tribe were living in peaceful —even profitable—harmony with other Americans, principally those in New Mexico. This relationship had started while the flag of Spain still flew at Santa Fe; Governor Juan Bautista de Anza in 1786 had negotiated a treaty with the northern Comanche providing for trade. The Comanche respected this traffic and did not raid in New Mexico, for they profited from it; there they exchanged the horses, booty, and even captive women and children taken in

raids in Texas and northern Mexico for the manufactured goods
and alcoholic beverages they desired. This practice not only supplied the Comanche with the means of war, for arms and ammunition were among the items they purchased, but also gave them
an incentive to raid. Soon annual caravans of traders, called *Comancheros*, left New Mexico each spring to journey onto the
plains to trade. Some of the Comancheros were lower-class New
Mexicans, while others were Pueblo Indians. During the Mexican
years, 1821 to 1846, this traffic grew so rapidly that the cart trails
from New Mexico into western Texas grew broad and deep.

In 1849, after the American conquest of New Mexico, Superintendent of Indian Affairs James S. Calhoun was astonished by
the Comanchero trade. To his superiors he wrote that the trade
should be "gently and quietly stopped," but he allowed it to continue, even licensing both Pueblo Indians and New Mexicans as
traders; however, he did try to prevent the traders from trafficking
in arms and ammunition with the plains raiders.[10] Early American
travelers in the region were not impressed with the Comancheros.
Captain Lemuel Ford of the First Dragoons met a party of them
in eastern Colorado, and in his diary noted his impressions: "These
Spaniards are the meanest looking race of People I ever saw, don't
appear more civilized than our Indians generally. Dirty filthy looking creatures." Another American in southeastern Colorado, Jacob
Fowler, noted with distaste that he saw the Comancheros catch
their lice and eat them.[11]

Every August and September the traders would depart New
Mexico in their huge carts. These *carretas* with their wooden
wheels were little changed from the vehicles of Biblical days, but
on these screeching wheels they carried as much as a ton of goods
to be traded: tobacco, saddles, dried pumpkins, onions, barley
meal, and dry goods—and bread made from corn meal and flour;
the Comanche came to treasure these loaves so much that they
would trade a horse for one sack of them. In return the Comancheros received horses, mules, buffalo hides, and meat. The major
menace to the traders was not the Comanche, who valued their
friendship and the goods thus received, but the Kiowa; these tribesmen were regarded by New Mexicans as treacherous, for they

Ox carts such as were used by the Comancheros. From *Harper's New Monthly Magazine* (1859).

often killed the Comancheros and took their goods rather than trade for them. On occasion the Comanche punished their Kiowa allies for such misdeeds.

The Comancheros performed one other valuable function—the ransoming of captives from the lords of the plains. During the Spanish period the New Mexicans had purchased principally Indian slaves from the Comanche; they were used as servants and miners in New Mexico, and the Comanche regularly took captives for this purpose on their raids. Later, however, the New Mexican traders began ransoming people captured by the Comanche on their forays into Texas, Coahuila, and Chihuahua. The New Mexicans then would try to secure a higher price from the captive's kin, else they held him in virtual slavery. Indian Superintendent

Calhoun was horrified when he first learned of this practice, but he and his successors soon were using the Comancheros to ransom white captives from the Comanche.

At first American officials in New Mexico did nothing to disrupt the traffic between local citizens and the plains raiders. Indian Superintendent and later Governor Calhoun licensed the trade, while Colonel John Munroe, commander of the Department of New Mexico, allowed it to continue, writing to his superiors that New Mexicans in the Pecos Valley and Comanche visitors coexisted happily, "no one having any fear of the Comanches." New Mexicans even were moving eastward in the Pecos Valley, running their sheep and cultivating a few acres of beans and chiles without Comanche interference. Calhoun in 1851 even invited a Comanche chief to dine with him in Santa Fe; Chief Eagle Feather and several warriors came, ate his food, and sold him a Mexican captive.

However, in the mid-1850s American ranchers began settling in eastern New Mexico just when Texas Rangers and federal soldiers were forcing the Comanche westward from the Lone Star State. In 1855 Colonel John Garland, then commanding the Department of New Mexico, complained of Comanche warriors coming into his region from Texas. That spring Chiefs Sanaco and Pahanca arrived with their followers in the Pecos Valley and proceeded to barbeque cattle from the ranch of James M. Giddings and Preston Beck, who had settled south of Antón Chico. Then in July a band of Kotsoteka Comanche struck the ranch of Lucien Maxwell in the Canadian Valley and killed two hundred sheep, promising to return in the fall when the corn ripened. The American ranchers angrily demanded military protection.

Colonel Garland, in response, sent 150 soldiers to the eastern part of the territory with orders to warn the Comanche to stay away and to attack the Indians if they continued their demands and raids. However, this action did not deter the plains natives, for the following year they returned as insolent as ever. In September 1856 Chief Esaquipa encamped on the Gallinas River and ate the corn from Alexander Hatch's fields; Hatch, like Giddings and Beck, was farming and ranching in the Pecos Valley near the village of Antón Chico. In addition, bands of Kiowa on their way to raid the Navajo stopped at Hatch's place to eat their fill, and he, like the others, angrily petitioned Colonel Garland for protection.

That fall Garland finally acted. He sent Captain W. L. Elliott to locate a site for an army post in the Pecos Valley. After a survey of the region, Elliott recommended Hatch's ranch as the best site; located thirteen miles north of Antón Chico and thirty-three miles southeast of Las Vegas, Hatch's place had buildings suitable for troops, and water, firewood, and corn could be had in ample supply. The location approved, Elliott in November established a post that would be called Hatch's Ranch until it was abandoned at the outbreak of the Civil War. This post did lessen Indian visits to the region, and, moreover, it proved an economic boon to Hatch and other settlers in the area; as always, Indian wars proved good business for local merchants. The soldiers stationed at the post required food, as did their horses, and after payday the troops wanted entertainment. Lieutenant J. H. Beale, an army engineer at the post in 1858, commented, "Hatch settled a year or two since . . . and by the fruitful product of the country has made himself independent. When we arrived he had already collected some ten thousand bushels of corn which he was selling at over one dollar a bushel *to the government* and others." In addition, Hatch served as post sutler. Other Americans came to the area because of the military protection, and this caused land values to rise. Finally, Mexicans settled at a nearby town called Chaparito to establish *cantinas* at which the soldiers could purchase a wretched grade of alcoholic drinks and cater to their other appetites. This town, three miles from Hatch's Ranch on the Gallinas River, ironically became a stronghold for the Comanchero traders.

Because of the moves by the military commander of the Department of New Mexico, the Comanche were peaceful in 1857. J. L. Collins, newly appointed superintendent of Indian Affairs there, did note some Kiowa and Comanche threats that year, but added that when warned by army officers the Indians were cooperative. Yet the year 1857 proved a turning point in the territory, for the Comanche were increasingly angry at the intrusion of American ranchers onto land where previously the Indians had hunted. In March 1858 the Comanche decided to make an example of a ranch established by Samuel Watrous on the Canadian River 130 miles south of Fort Union. Three Mexicans who had lived for years among the Comanche came to the ranch and secured employment. Then, a few days later, four Comanche arrived on a pretext that they wished to trade; satisfied that no troops were there, the Indians then killed the foreman, burned the ranch buildings, and drove off the cattle. The Mexican hands employed at the ranch were allowed to depart unharmed, but were given instructions to tell other Americans that the Comanche would kill any ranchers who ventured into that region. In fact, to show that this raid was no accident, the Comanche also sent word to army officers that the attack had been planned in a council beforehand and that they intended to halt all settlement east of Hatch's ranch.

And the following year, 1859, when surveyors came into the Canadian Valley, the Comanche rode in and captured the entire group. The Comanche obviously understood that settlers quickly followed in the wake of surveyors. The contractor conducting this survey, R. E. Clements, pleaded for four hours for his life, promising never to return. Apparently the Comanche believed him, for he was released with a stern warning. Indian Superintendent Collins, after hearing of this incident, commented that no settlers could venture into the Canadian Valley without a fort nearby to give them protection. Collins doubtless was irked with the surveyors, for in 1859 he had been given the task of negotiating safe passage through Comanche country for a mail and stage line that was to run from Neosho, Missouri, to Santa Fe and on to California. Collins used the incident of the surveyors to demand military protection from Colonel B. L. E. Bonneville, the new commander of the Department of New Mexico. Bonneville agreed, and on July 18 took 130 soldiers with him when he accompanied Collins to meet the Indians. However, the conference never took place because the Comanche became alarmed at the large party of soldiers and fled eastward, fearing the conference was a trap at which they would be massacred.

That fall the Comanche increased the frequency and intensity of their raids in eastern New Mexico, obviously intending to drive all ranchers from the area. And on these forays, during which cattle were killed and horses stolen, they attacked Mexican ranchers as well as American; however, they did not kill the New Mexican herders, with whom they traditionally had been friendly. When troops took the field to pursue the raiders, the Comancheros gave them false information about the Comanche so that' frequently they made long but fruitless marches. The officers quickly determined that the traders were, as one officer said of them, a "set of villainous vagabonds" in league with the Comanche—which indeed was true. In New Mexico at this time the Comancheros, generally the lower-class citizens, considered themselves the allies of the plains Indians and the enemies of the Americans living in the territory, both military and civilian.

Because of the increasing number of raids, officials in Washington determined to punish the Comanche and Kiowa in the late spring of 1860. A three-pronged offensive was planned, one column to come southwest from Fort Riley, Kansas; the second northwest from Fort Arbuckle, Oklahoma; and the third down the Canadian River from Hatch's ranch. Each column was to consist of six companies, making a total of approximately 850 troops involved. The commanders of the columns were told not to negotiate but to attack Comanche wherever encountered. The campaign, however, failed, in part because of dry weather, which caused men and animals to suffer, and mainly because the Comancheros both warned the Indians and also gave the troops false information. Major C. F. Ruff, who led the column from Hatch's Ranch and who marched far afield on the basis of Comanchero information, later called the traders "lying Mexicans who never tell the truth, if a falsehood can possibly be made to answer the purpose."[12] The columns stayed doggedly in the field during the summer months, but few engagements resulted. As autumn approached, the troops were called in.

That fall, after a band of Comanche trading at Chaparito were attacked by soldiers from nearby Hatch's ranch,[13] the plains Indians raided relentlessly at ranches in eastern New Mexico. Hundreds of head of livestock were driven off, but Mexican herders were left unharmed, causing Americans to believe that the lower-class New Mexicans were in league with the natives. Lieutenant Colonel George B. Crittenden at Fort Union determined to chastise the raiders. He organized an expedition in total secrecy, telling only a few select officers of his plans; slipping out of the post with sixty men, he rode through late December snow and on January 4, 1861, attacked a Comanche village of 150 lodges, killing 10 Indians, capturing 40 horses, and destroying the camp.

Perhaps this raid caused the Comanche to consider their need of New Mexico as a place for trade. Early in 1861 they sent emissaries to the territory to ask for peace. Officers at the frontier posts wanted to ignore them, but Colonel T. T. Fauntleroy, commander of the Department, chose to listen because he wanted to concentrate on punishing the Mescalero Apache who were raiding in southern New Mexico. Therefore a peace conference took place on May 10-11 at Alamo Gordo Creek, a tributary of the Pecos; Captain R. A. Wainwright and Indian Superintendent Collins negotiated with Chiefs Eagle Feather, Esaquipa, and Paracasqua. The result was an agreement calling for an American armistice in return for which the Comanche promised not to raid the ranchers or wagon trains and to trade only at places designated by New Mexican authorities. This truce collapsed almost immediately, however, for about a week later Chief Esaquipa, with a small band, came in to trade at Chaparito, whereupon Captain Thomas Duncan attacked with troops from Hatch's ranch.[14]

Settlers in eastern New Mexico, fearing renewed Comanche raids, charged that the soldiers were guilty of unprovoked attacks and thus were responsible for any future trouble. The soldiers responded that the culprits were the New Mexicans who traded with the plains raiders—the Comanche came in to the settlements where they invariably caused trouble.

Just at this critical juncture came the outbreak of Civil War, and most soldiers were withdrawn from eastern New Mexico, either to the Rio Grande Valley to fight an anticipated Confederate invasion or to the eastern part of the United States. Surprisingly, however, the result was peace, for the Comanche immediately resumed their old peaceful—and mutually profitable—relationship with the

New Mexicans. Again the Comanchero carts rolled eastward onto the plains to exchange tobacco and bread and other items, including guns and whiskey, for whatever the Comanche stole in Texas and Mexico. In the fifteen years that the United States Army and officials from the Indian Bureau had been in New Mexico, the trade had not been halted and, if anything, had been strengthened; moreover, the trade had taken a new turn, for the Comancheros by 1861 were more openly allied with the Indians against Americans, more willing to furnish them with arms and ammunition, more willing to give the Indians information, and more willing to take stolen property in exchange.[15]

5

WAR FOR THE SOUTH PLAINS

The outbreak of the Civil War caused a dramatic change of attitude on the part of Union officers in New Mexico. Suddenly the Comancheros were valuable, not a "miserable" or "degraded" people; rather they were "allies" to be treated with kindness. They were openly given food and ammunition from army stores, and they were encouraged to trade freely with the plains raiders. In fact, some of them even went on the army's payroll; at a time when common soldiers received twelve dollars a month, some Comancheros were paid $1.75 to $3.00 a day. The New Mexican traders were considered scouts and spies for the Union Army in New Mexico, their task to listen and watch for any Texan invasion.[1]

Nor in the months immediately following the outbreak of war were the Comanche and Kiowa hampered from trading in the territory, for from them might be gained word of Confederate activity on the plains. Orders went out to local commanders to restrain their troops and to treat the Comanche with friendship and kindness.

With the arrival of General James H. Carleton and the California Column, however, the Union posture in New Mexico dramatically improved—to the extent that Carleton no longer needed the Comancheros. Therefore the traders were dropped from army payrolls, and Indian Superintendent Collins even began refusing to license the Comancheros to make their trek to the plains. Yet Carleton and Collins were thwarted in their effort to halt the trade, for many of the men garrisoning New Mexican posts during the Civil War were New Mexican natives who were sympathetic to the traders and to the Comanche. Carleton thereupon ordered Captain William H. Backus to establish a post in eastern New Mexico; to accomplish this order of October 31, 1862, Backus had only one company of Colorado volunteers, but he was successful. The outpost, known as Camp Easton, was erected on the Canadian River fifteen miles above the mouth of Utah Creek.

So small a detachment could easily be overrun by Comanche, Carleton realized, and therefore he wanted friendship with these plains raiders. He asked Indian Superintendent Collins to send an agent to the Comanche at the outpost; Collins responded by sending William B. Stapp, formerly an agent to the Mescalero Apache, but Commissioner of Indian Affairs William Dole, from the safety of Washington, overruled Collins and ordered Stapp withdrawn. Despite this setback, Captain Backus and his successors did maintain friendship with the Comanche through 1863.

At the same time General Carleton was promoting the settlement of the Canadian Valley by civilians. He used army personnel to survey the region around Camp Easton, which was renamed Fort Bascom in August 1863, and he announced through the newspapers that the soldiers there would guard any settlers in the area.[2] This move, of course, angered the Comanche, who for years had fought the settlement of this region, but the end to cordial relations with the Indians came because of a feud between the army and the Indian Bureau. At Fort Bascom the Comanche were repeatedly given food and gifts, and Carleton sent the bills along to the superintendent of Indian affairs for payment. By this time, early in 1864, Collins had been succeeded by Michael Steck, a physician from Pennsylvania who previously had served as agent to the Mescalero Apache. This dour individual in turn sent the bills to Indian Commissioner Dole in Washington, who promptly refused to pay them. Carleton, informed of Dole's refusal to pay for food and gifts to the Comanche at Fort Bascom, or to provide an agent for them there, ordered no more rations be given the Co-

Plains Indians attacking an Overland stage. *Courtesy Library of Congress.*

manche. In February 1864 Chief Esaquipa came to Bascom with a fanciful report of Confederate invaders only to be told he would get no presents. He left in a huff, highly offended.

This event alone did not cause the war that followed. Several other factors contributed strongly. The Comanche were always attracted to warfare, and the diversion of soldiers elsewhere during the Civil War caused them to be severely tempted. Moreover, the Comancheros apparently were inciting them to kill *gringos* (a derisive word for the Anglo-Americans); according to Robert North, who went among the Comanche late in October 1863 to attempt the ransom of a white captive, the Comancheros had been among the plains Indians recently to urge them to fight and promising that "a great many Mexicans would come up from New Mexico" in the spring to aid in the killing.[3] Finally, the Comanche were stirred in 1864 by the Cheyenne, who in Colorado that spring were taking to the warpath and inviting the Comanche and Kiowa to participate. Many of these warriors did ride to Colorado, and that summer they disrupted mail and stage service, plundered small communities, and killed more than fifty Coloradoans.

At first this war in Colorado seemed of little concern to New Mexicans, but in August that changed. That month seventy Comanche came into a camp of teamsters on the Santa Fe Trail at Lower Cimarron Springs; the Indians pretended they wanted to trade and then killed and scalped five Americans. The Indians spared three New Mexican teamsters in the camp. Carleton interpreted this act as proof that the Comanche and the New Mexicans were united in a war against Anglo-Americans, and he sent orders to all post commanders in the eastern part of his department to prepare for war. Comancheros warned the plains Indians of these preparations, and ten Comanche and Kiowa chiefs came to Fort Bascom, led by Chief Ten Bears, under a flag of truce to ask for peace. Carleton, informed of the request, spurned it, saying that the Comanche and their allies had committed many atrocities and that there would be no negotiations until all stolen stock was returned and those Indians guilty of the killing at Cimarron Springs were turned over to the army. The Indians departed from Fort Bascom aware that war was in the offing.

Carleton could ill spare men for a punitive expedition to the plains country, but he patiently gathered as many as possible. Indian Superintendent Steck tried every way possible to halt these preparations, and openly spoke against the plan. And Governor Henry Connelly, when asked by Carleton to send along elements of the territorial militia, bluntly refused, saying the Comanche were at peace with the people of New Mexico and that it was wrong to attack them.[4] Finally Carleton did ready 335 cavalry, mainly New Mexican volunteers, and 75 Indian allies, principally Ute. At their head he placed Colonel Kit Carson, who the previous winter had conquered the Navajo and who had spent that summer as a very frustrated agent at the Bosque Redondo reservation.

As autumn approached in 1864, Carleton on October 22 requested that Steck and Governor Connelly give no more licenses to Comancheros. Both refused to honor the request, and parties of traders did leave for the Texas Panhandle; not only did they inform the Comanche of the impending attack, but they also supplied the Indians with guns and ammunition. However, a party of Comancheros informed Carleton of the Comanche location, and on November 12 Carson departed Fort Bascom with his command, taking with him two mounted howitzers. He urged his men forward through two snowstorms, and found his quarry on November 25 at Adobe Walls. This was the ruins of a trading post established in 1843 on the South Canadian River by William Bent; however, it had been abandoned owing to Indian hostility and had gone to ruin—to remain a well-known landmark on the High Plains.

At this site, 200 miles northeast of Fort Bascom, were encamped an estimated 3,000 Comanche, while a few miles upstream were 600 to 800 Kiowa, the followers of Chief Little Mountain. In this Kiowa village was Satanta, himself later to be a prominent chief. Carson began his attack at dawn on November 25, striking Little Mountain's 150 lodges. The women and children fled the village, while warriors dashed downstream to fetch Comanche allies. Soon a force of more than 1,000 warriors encircled Carson and his 400 troops at Adobe Walls. Hours of fighting followed in which only the two howitzers, firing exploding shells, prevented a massacre of epic proportions. Carson finally ordered a retreat to the Kiowa village, which had been reoccupied by Kiowa; the two howitzers blasted them out once again, whereupon some of the soldiers explored the 150 lodges while the rest fended off repeated attacks. In the village Carson's men found conclusive evidence of Kiowa attacks on whites: the uniform of a soldier, clothes belonging to white women and children, and scalps. Everything, save what the soldiers took for themselves, was set afire: 150 lodges, the Kiowa winter supply of food, ammunition, clothing, all went up in flames. Carson later learned that the Kiowa had five white women and two white children captive in the camp at the time of his attack and had spirited them away.

Retreating to Fort Bascom, Carson reported that he had killed or wounded an estimated sixty Indians while suffering only three dead. He concluded that he had "taught these Indians a severe lesson."[5] Indeed he had, more than even he realized, for his sudden and unexpected attack, along with the destruction of a major village and of winter supplies, so demoralized the plains raiders that they asked Confederate agents for peace in February 1865; they wanted to avoid a two-front war (this effort came to naught when the Confederacy collapsed that spring).

Carson, upon his return, learned that Indian Superintendent

Steck on October 27 had issued passes to Comancheros to go among the plains Indians. This was five days after Carleton had requested that no additional licenses be given. Carson included in his report a comment about the Indian commissioner: "I blame the Mexicans not half as much as I do Mr. Steck . . . who [knew] that the Mexicans would take what they could sell best, which was powder, lead, and caps." Carleton likewise seized on this incident; he sent a full report to Washington, and on May 1, 1865, Steck was asked to resign. He was replaced by Felipe Delgado, a hack politician from New Mexico—who proved far more sympathetic to the Comancheros than had Steck.

The Adobe Walls campaign had other results. In the spring of 1865 it was an issue in the hot race for New Mexico's territorial delegate to Congress. Carleton was backing Francisco Perea, who claimed that the campaign had produced results, for that spring Chief Skeer-dee-na-kwaugh, a Comanche leader, had come to Fort Bascom to ask for peace. Those opposed to Carleton stated in the Santa Fe *Weekly New Mexican* that the whole campaign was a bad mistake that had served only to anger the Indians. Carleton, hoping his man would win the election, relaxed his restrictions on the Comanchero trade, and that spring it flourished to an extent rarely seen before. This, coupled with the collapse of the Confederacy and the resulting chaos in Texas, brought profits to both Indians and Comancheros. Cattle were what made these profits, longhorn cattle which ran on hundreds of Texas ranches and which were driven west by Comanche to be exchanged for the bread, tobacco, guns, and other items they desired. The New Mexicans, in turn, sold the cattle to the army and to the reservations where the Indians had been promised food rations. For a decade this traffic would flourish, tens of thousands of longhorns journeying west to enrich New Mexicans who asked few questions about brands or for papers of ownership from the Comanche raiders. Only the total confinement of the Comanche and Kiowa on reservations in Oklahoma would halt the annual caravans of *carretas* creeking their way eastward from New Mexico and the traffic in cattle westward.[6]

In Texas, few citizens were in a position to complain about this traffic, especially during the Civil War. When that conflict began, the federal soldiers manning the line of posts had been withdrawn or else captured, and the frontier was left without protection. The legislature thereupon authorized each of the thirty-seven frontier counties to raise a militia company for self-defense, while Albert Pike, the Confederate Indian agent, negotiated a treaty with the Comanche and Kiowa promising the two tribes a reservation in Oklahoma, in return for which they could hunt on the High Plains of the Texas Panhandle. Both the militia companies and the reservation failed, however, and the legislature late in 1861 replaced this system with the Frontier Regiment, which was to consist of ten mounted companies. In January 1862 James M. Norris was commissioned colonel of the regiment, and he managed to organize nine companies. These totaled 1,089 men, who generally were called Rangers.

Norris made a tour of inspection of the frontier and then created eighteen Ranger posts stretching from the Rio Grande northward to the Trinity River. Each company had to man two camps, which meant approximately fifty Rangers had to patrol the country in between it and the next camp. Naturally the Comanche, who began raiding in great force in October 1862, were able to slip around these patrols to commit their depredations. In 1863 Norris was succeeded by J. E. McCord, who dropped the patrols in favor of irregular scouting expeditions. This tactic had a little more success, but the difficulty was in keeping men. Young Texans who might have considered such duty in peacetime wanted to participate in the great war then occurring in the east; moreover, those who did sign up for this duty frequently were transferred to Confederate service elsewhere, as happened to the entire Frontier Regiment early in 1864.

When this happened, the legislature again authorized local militia units, but was unable to supply and equip them. And by this time few young men were left to be recruited; often those who joined did so only to escape conscription into the Confederate Army and proved virtually worthless. Finally, in December 1864, the state named James W. Throckmorton brigadier general and gave him authority to reorganize the defense of the Indian frontier. He recruited 1,400 men and put them in twenty-six companies; the following February he sent 500 of these men into Oklahoma to attack the raiders. However, the Comanche, smarting from the winter raid of Kit Carson and federal troops from New Mexico, asked to make peace; Throckmorton negotiated a treaty with them which might have brought a slackening in the raids, but then the Confederacy collapsed—as did the treaty. The net result of the Civil War, so far as the Comanche wars in Texas were concerned, was an eastward retreat of the line of settlement by 150 to 200 miles.[7]

The frontiersmen of northern and western Texas at first thought that the end of the war in the spring of 1865 would mean an early return of federal soldiers to the old line of forts, thereby giving them protection. In this they were mistaken, however, for the process required several years. In the interim the Comanche and Kiowa raids came on a scale never before seen. During this period Little Mountain, the head chief of the Kiowa, died, and was replaced by Lone Wolf. Lone Wolf proved an ineffective leader, and war chiefs such as Satank and Satanta raided at will, commanding huge followings.[8] Governor J. W. Throckmorton reported that from May 1865 to July 1867, Indian raiders had killed 162 people, wounded 24, and captured 43, and he telegraphed President Andrew Johnson that unless the federal government took radical steps the state soon would be depopulated.[9] In fact, the legislature, desperate to take action, voted to raise a state force to be commanded by federal officers, but General Phillip H. Sheridan, commander of the Department, vetoed the project; he wanted no armed body of ex-Confederates riding about, even if commanded by Union officers.

At first officials in Washington believed the protests about Indian raids made by Texans were incorrect, or, if true, that the Texans were ex-rebels who should be made to suffer. Thus no action was taken except to veto all suggested means of remedying the situation. And the Indians grew bolder. The Kiowa war chief Satanta in August 1866 raided in northern Texas to kill and capture, and then in September he rode boldly into Fort Larned, Kansas, to tell the post commander that he had white captives for ransom. He was paid $2,000 for them.[10] One reliable government official reported at this same time that he had seen Kwahadi Comanche in northwest Texas with a herd of 15,000 horses, several hundred mules, and so many cattle that he could not count them. Still high military officials chose to disregard the evidence. General William T. Sherman, commander of the Division of the Missouri (which included both Texas and Kansas), stated in his annual report in the summer of 1867: "During the past year we have been infinitely embarrassed by many causes which I trust will not occur again. In the early part of the year there seemed to be a concerted and mischievous design to precipitate hostilities, by a series of false reports almost without parallel."[11]

At this time the western part of Kansas was virtually in a state of siege from Comanche and Kiowa attacks, as well as incursions by Cheyenne. The citizens of this region also were protesting to Washington; these were not former Confederates, moreover, and their protests could not be ignored. Moreover, a congressional committee created in 1865, the Joint Special Committee on the Condition of the Indian Tribes, made its report that year of 1867; it showed conditions in the West to be chaotic, noted graft and thievery in the Indian Bureau, and concluded with a slap at the army: "While it is true many agents, teachers, and employees of the government are inefficient, faithless, and even guilty of peculations and fraudulent practices . . . , it is equally true that military posts among the Indians have frequently become centers of demoralization and destruction to the Indian tribes, while the blunders and want of discretion of inexperienced officers in command have brought on long and expensive wars. . . ."[12] On July 20, 1867, Congress passed an act creating a peace commission to negotiate with "certain hostile Indian tribes." This included the Comanche and Kiowa. Invitations accordingly were sent to the chiefs to gather, and they met on October 19 at Medicine Lodge Creek, Kansas.

The American commission consisted of the commissioner of Indian Affairs, three politicians, and three generals, and was accompanied by five hundred cavalrymen. Five thousand Indians greeted them, to be given gifts of clothing, tobacco, and cutlery and served generous portions of food and coffee. The natives responded by giving a great feast for the commissioners at which they served a Comanche delicacy—cold, fat dog. Then the speeches began; the Indians were masters of oratory. One after another they told of

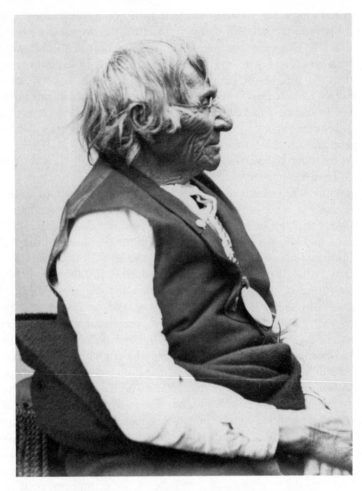

Ten Bears at an advanced age. *Courtesy Bureau of Indian Affairs, National Archives.*

great wrongs committed on their people by whites, of infinite Indian patience at last strained to breaking, and of a strong desire to live in peace with Americans. Ten Bears, a Comanche chief, delivered a typical speech:

> My heart is filled with joy when I see you here, as the brooks
> fill with water when the snows melt in the spring; and I feel glad
> as the ponies do when the fresh grass starts in the beginning of
> the year. . . . I knew that you had come to do good to me and
> to my people. I looked for benefits which would last forever, and
> so my face shines with joy as I look upon you. My people have
> never first drawn a bow or fired a gun against the whites. There
> has been trouble on the line between us, and my young men have
> danced the war dance. But it was not begun by us. It was you
> who sent out the first soldier and we who sent out the second. . . .
> You said you wanted to put us upon a reservation, to build us
> houses and make us medicine lodges. I do not want them. I was
> born upon the prairie, where the wind blew free and there was
> nothing to break the light of the sun. I was born where there
> were no enclosures and everything drew a free breath. I want to
> die there and not within walls. . . .
> When I was in Washington the Great Father told me that all
> the Comanche land was ours, and that no one should hinder us in
> living upon it. So, why do you ask us to leave the rivers, and the
> sun, and the wind, and live in houses? Do not speak of it
> more. . . .
> The Texans have taken away the places where the grass grew
> the thickest and the timber was the best. Had we kept that, we
> might have done the things you ask. But it is too late. The whites
> have the country which we loved, and we only wish to wander on
> the prairie until we die. Any good thing you say to me shall not be
> forgotten. I shall carry it as near to my heart as my children, and
> it shall be as often on my tongue as the name of the Great Spirit.
> I want no blood upon the land to stain the grass. I want it all
> clear and pure, and I wish it so that all who go through among my
> people may find peace when they come in and leave it when they
> go out.[13]

The commissioners listened sympathetically, and then on October 21 signed a treaty with the Comanche and Kiowa. This promised the tribes a reservation in Oklahoma of 2,968,893 acres between the Red and Washita rivers and between the 98th and 100th meridians; in return for surrendering all claim to their former lands, they would be given food, clothing, and an annuity. Further, the government promised to provide schools, teachers, doctors, carpenters, and blacksmiths, as well as give instruction in farming; in turn, the Indians promised to remain peaceful, to avoid roads used by Americans, and to allow the railroads to be constructed through their country.[14]

About this same time—late 1867 and early 1868—the federal government at last ordered the re-establishment of the old line of frontier forts in Texas. These included Forts Davis, Stockton, Clark, Concho, Griffin, Richardson, and McKavett. However, these proved largely ineffective, for the forts averaged eighty-five miles apart, and the pitifully few soldiers in them could not patrol such distances properly; moreover, the troops sent to garrison these posts were inexperienced, green recruits with little knowledge of Indian warfare—and, said Texans, little stomach for it.

Complicating matters still more was the tardiness of the federal government in establishing the promised agency for the Comanche and Kiowa in Oklahoma. Nor did it send the supplies stipulated by the Treaty of Medicine Lodge Creek. Finally, there was the intransigence of the Indians themselves; when at last on July 1, 1869, the Indian agent arrived at the Oklahoma reservation, an estimated 1,500 of the 2,416 Kwahadi and Kotsoteka Comanche refused to live at the designated site. They preferred the excitement of the chase and the glories of the warpath to the monotonous and idle life they found in the vicinity of Fort Sill, a post established near the new reservation. Those Indians who did report to the agent slipped away at will to join the raiders and to hunt, and when pressed hard by soldiers they returned to it for sanctuary; the troops could not trespass on the reservation without permission of the agent, and this he refused to give.

The agent was Lawrie Tatum, a sincere, devout Quaker, part of President Ulysses S. Grant's vaunted "peace policy." In the spring of 1869, just after coming to office, the President accepted the recommendation of eastern "experts" who believed that the Indians would best respond to kindness, religious instruction, and training in agrarian methods. Army officers were forbidden to act as agents, which sometimes had occurred previously; instead, the agents would be selected from the nominees of the various religious denominations. The most active denomination in naming such agents was the Society of Friends, better known as the Quakers, and thus in the public mind Grant's new policy was labeled the "Quaker Peace Policy." Lawrie Tatum came to his post with great enthusiasm and equally great ignorance; he did possess courage, honesty, and intelligence, however, and he gained the respect of many of his Comanche, Kiowa, and Kiowa-Apache charges—but he largely was unsuccessful in getting these lordly warriors to harness their mounts, break ground, and plow the earth. Instead, he found that the chiefs and warriors respected only force and that as long as possible they would remain on their plains homeland.

Tatum's ignorance, combined with the Indians' restlessness, the inexperience of the troops manning the posts in Texas, and the relative helplessness of ex-Confederates in the Lone Star State, brought on large-scale raiding in 1869 and 1870. These were the bloodiest years in Texas history, with war parties haunting the outskirts of frontier villages and a steady stream of Texas cattle being driven to the High Plains to be traded to the Comancheros. Major General J. J. Reynolds, commander of the Department of Texas, complained to Agent Tatum that his charges were guilty. Tatum, in turn, warned Comanche and Kiowa chiefs that the raids must stop, whereupon one chief told the astonished Quaker that if Washington wanted his warriors to stop their forays it must move Texas far away where the young men could not find it. Moreover, they said, if they increased their raids, then government officials would come and again make peace with them, in the process showering them with presents. By 1870 not only were the Kiowa stealing in Texas, but also on June 12 that year they stole the army mules at Fort Sill. Yet regularly they returned to the Fort Sill agency to protest their friendship, draw their rations, and ride out again. It seemed that the Kiowa and Comanche were determined to drive back the white line of settlement by dozens—if not hundreds—of miles.

The state of Texas was helpless to meet these incursions, for it was in the iron grip of reconstruction by Radical Republicans more interested in personal enrichment than in protecting citizens—and more fearful of armed militia than of Indian depredations on the frontier. E. J. Davis, the carpetbag governor, wanted no Texas Rangers, and there were none for nine years following the Civil War. On June 13, 1870, the legislature did pass an act providing for twenty frontier companies of militia, each to have sixty-two men; a few such companies were organized, but the state legislature had appropriated so little money that even these had to disband. And the legislature tried again the following year; on November 25, 1871, came an act allowing each of the twenty-four frontier counties to raise a company of twenty volunteers. This effort was little more successful than that of the previous year and for the same reason. Therefore protection from the ravages of Comanche and Kiowa attacks on the Texas frontier had to come from the army.

By the spring of 1871 the army at last had come to believe that the raids were genuine. To meet the onslaught expected that year the Sixth Cavalry had been moved to Kansas in March, and Colonel Ranald S. Mackenzie and the 4th Cavalry had been sent to Texas. This change placed 179 men at Fort Davis, 259 at Fort Stockton, 560 at Fort McKavett, 499 at Fort Richardson, 444 at Fort Griffin, and 369 at Fort Concho; Mackenzie made his headquarters at Fort Concho, and from it he would mount effective expeditions against the plains raiders in the years that followed, for he was an exceptional officer.

Born on July 27, 1840, in New York City, Ranald S. Mackenzie grew to manhood in a stern and military environment (his father, Alexander, a naval commander, gained national prominence in 1842 when he hanged, without benefit of trial, Midshipman Philip Spencer, son of the secretary of war, and two others for plotting mutiny). Graduating from West Point in 1862 first in his class, Ranald served at first as an engineer but longed to command fighting troops; that opportunity came in 1864 when he became colonel of the 2nd Connecticut Volunteers. At the Battle of Petersburg he had two fingers shot off his right hand (which later caused the Indians to refer to him as "Bad Hand"). He emerged from the war a brevet major general of volunteers and brevet brigadier general in the regular army. However, at the end of the conflict he resumed

Ranald S. Mackenzie as a brigadier general. *Courtesy U.S. Signal Corps, Brady Collection, National Archives.*

his permanent rank of captain of engineers. Those who knew him well at the time stated that he bore a remarkable resemblance to Ralph Waldo Emerson, a man of "ascetic, hawk-like face and the air of a crusading Norman bishop," according to one.

In order to return to a fighting unit, he accepted command of the 41st Infantry Regiment, a Black unit, and as its colonel went with it to the Rio Grande Valley where he served until 1870, after which his unit was the 4th Cavalry. Such was the background of the man Ulysses S. Grant had been moved to call "the most promising young officer in the Army."[15] He was one of those rare officers who inspired devotion from his troops and who led them by personal example rather than through rigid and authoritarian discipline.

While Mackenzie was readying the men of his command for the field, an event occurred that changed the opinion of officials in Washington about the Comanche and Kiowa. The Texans had been complaining for years, but late in 1870 came a resolution from the legislature of the state to Congress stating that in the preceding five years the raiders had murdered "several hundreds of citizens of Texas, have stolen and destroyed property to the amount of millions of dollars in value, have not only retarded the settlement of the frontier counties of the State, but have almost depopulated several counties thereof."[16] At last General William T. Sherman, now commanding general of the army, set out to see the truth for himself. He journeyed to San Antonio, there to be joined by Inspector General Randolph B. Marcy, an officer who had long served on the frontier; the two left San Antonio early in May, accompanied by seventeen troops of the Tenth Cavalry.

The party traveled through fair weather to Forts McKavett, Concho, and Griffin, seeing no Indians but hearing of depredations. Even General Marcy was astonished, however, for as he observed in his journal, "This rich and beautiful country does not contain today so many white people as it did when I visited it eighteen years ago, and if the Indian marauders are not punished, the whole country seems to be in a fair way of becoming totally depopulated." Reaching Fort Richardson on May 17, he conferred with Colonel Mackenzie, who happened to be there, and he listened to residents of the area complain of Indian depredations. These he scarcely believed, however, for the country had seemed too peaceful.

Late that night, however, a wounded teamster came to the post. In a state of exhaustion he told of how 150 Kiowa had attacked a government wagon train on which he was employed. He and the

General William T. Sherman in 1865. *Courtesy U.S. Signal Corps, Brady Collection, National Archives.*

other teamsters had fought, but when five of their number were killed the rest had fled. The wounded teamster, Tom Brazeale, told where the train had been when attacked, and to General Sherman's astonishment it was on the same road over which he had passed and just a few hours after his own journey. Two additional bodies were recovered, one of which had been tied to a wagon pole and burned.

Sherman ordered Mackenzie on the trail of the raiders, while he proceeded to Fort Sill. Arriving there on May 23, he found the names of the guilty four days later: Satanta, Satank, and Big Tree were openly bragging about their murder of the seven teamsters in Texas. Sherman ordered their arrest and sent them in chains to stand trial in Texas. On the way Satank tried to escape and was killed, but the other two were taken to Jacksboro, tried in civil court for murder, found guilty, and sentenced to hang. However, Governor Davis commuted their sentences to life imprisonment, and they were sent to Huntsville State Prison.

General Sherman at last was convinced of Comanche and Kiowa raiding, and he ordered Mackenzie to take the trail. In addition, he replaced General J. J. Reynolds as commander of the Department of Texas with General C. C. Augur, an experienced plains campaigner and a tough soldier. Mackenzie with his 4th Cavalry stayed in the saddle much of 1871 and 1872, leading 600 men to the High Plains the first year, and the second attacking a Comanche village on the North Fork of the Red River in September, killing 23 warriors and capturing 124 women and children as well as hundreds of horses. These raids produced peace in 1873—during which year, as one of his last official acts before being forced from office Governor E. J. Davis pardoned the Kiowa chiefs Satanta and Big Tree. General Sherman indignantly telegraphed a protest and predicted that the two would return to the warpath; he concluded, "If they are to take scalps I hope yours is the first. . . ."

With Mackenzie occupied in South Texas, chasing Kickapoo Indians living in Mexico, and the frontier forts again short-handed, and with Satanta and Big Tree once again free, the Kiowa and Comanche resumed their raiding ways in 1874. They were especially angry at the hordes of buffalo hunters swarming across the plains

Chief Big Tree. *Courtesy U.S. Signal Corps, National Archives.*

that spring, for the Indians well knew that the death of the buffalo would end their old free, roaming ways forever. While the Comanche concentrated on this problem, Satanta and Big Tree gathered bands of followers and raided directly to the south, leaving a trail of death and destruction in their wake. Returning to the reservation, they were detected and arrested. General Sherman thereupon recommended to President Grant that the two be returned to prison in Texas. Despite pleas for clemency for the two from various functionaries in the Indian Bureau, Grant approved Sherman's recommendation, and the two were returned to Huntsville Prison. There Satanta committed suicide on November 11, 1878, by throwing himself out a window.[17]

Lawrie Tatum, meanwhile, had grown weary of his labors, as well as disillusioned about his Comanche and Kiowa wards. He knew that as long as they had horses and ammunition and as long as soldiers in great numbers were not readily visible they would slip away to raid in Texas. He resigned in disgust on March 31, 1873, to be replaced by James Haworth, another Quaker who believed that good faith and kind treatment would halt the raids. He was in command, counseling no expeditions by soldiers, when the outbreaks came in 1874.

The immediate cause was the discovery of a new medicine man among the Comanche, Isatai. He supposedly had been visited by the Great Spirit on numerous occasions and had supernatural powers; the Comanche believed he could cure the sick, raise the dead, control the weather, bring cartridges forth from his stomach, and cause the guns of whites to do no harm to Indians. Isatai called for a tribal sun dance, something common to the Kiowa but never performed by the Comanche. Just at this time a group of white thieves raided the Indians' camp and stole forty-three horses. Under the leadership of Quanah Parker, the tribe moved toward total integration, and seven hundred warriors—including Comanche, Kiowa, Cheyenne, and even a few Apache—left the agency bound on attacking a group of buffalo hunters from Kansas who were encamped at Adobe Walls.

On the morning of June 27 they attacked the twenty-eight white men and one woman at the old buildings, which once again had become a trading post (for buffalo hunters). The men inside were armed with new long-range buffalo guns that enabled them to stand off the attackers at a distance; three whites died that day, but so did thirteen Indians and forty-six of their horses. This second battle of Adobe Walls did force the buffalo hunters to return to Kansas in great haste once the Indians retired from the vicinity; it also ended the influence of Isatai, who was accused of making "polecat medicine."[18] The Comanche still thirsted for war and revenge against the whites, but in July, when the Kiowa held their annual sun dance three-quarters of the tribe refused to join the Comanche. Chief Kicking Bird led most of the tribe back to the Fort Sill agency; only Chief Lone Wolf and Chief Swan with their small following joined the militant Comanche, who immediately departed for Texas. There they killed settlers, attacked wagon trains, and left blood in their wake.

General Sherman, when he heard of this outbreak, decided to put an end to Comanche and Kiowa power on the plains forever. President Grant on July 26, 1874, approved placing the Fort Sill Agency under military officers rather than Quakers, and Sherman issued an order for all friendly Indians to be at the agency by August 3 for enrollment; those off the reservation after that time would be pursued, captured, dismounted, disarmed, and held as prisoners of war.[19] At the Fort Sill Agency some Yamparika Comanche under Chief Iron Mountain were enrolled, as were most Kiowa. There was a fight when agents attempted to enroll the Comanche and Kiowa at the Washita Agency (at Anadarko, Oklahoma), but by the second week in August the battle lines had been drawn; the non-hostile Indians had been registered, while the hostiles were on the High Plains of western Texas in the vicinity of Palo Duro Canyon under the leadership of Quanah Parker.

Sherman's strategy for the campaign against the hostiles was the traditional one of converging columns of troops. Major General John Pope ordered three commands into the field: Colonel Nelson A. Miles with eight companies of the 6th Cavalry was to come south from Fort Dodge, Kansas; Major William R. Price was to bring eight companies of the 8th Cavalry down the Canadian River from Fort Union, New Mexico, and join up with Miles; and Lieutenant Colonel Thomas H. Neill was to operate in the vicinity of the Darlington Agency in the western part of the Indian Territory, capturing any hostiles in that vicinity. Meanwhile Major General Augur was dispatching three columns: Colonel Mackenzie was in command of the largest, eight companies of the 4th Cavalry, four from the 10th Cavalry, one from the 11th Infantry, and 30 scouts, which was to move north from Fort Concho; Lieutenant George P. Buell with four companies of the 9th Cavalry, two from the 10th, two from the 11th Infantry, and 30 scouts was to move northwest from Fort Griffin; and Lieutenant Colonel John W. Davidson was to march west from Fort Sill with six companies of the 10th Cavalry, 3 from the 11th Infantry, and forty-four scouts. This six-pronged offensive involved approximately 3,000 soldiers, and their orders were to disregard lines between the various army departments—and even the reservations. Hostiles were to be attacked where found until all surrendered totally. General Augur's instructions to Mackenzie, dated August 28, summed up the situation: "You are at liberty to follow the Indians wherever they go, even to the Agencies."

That summer of 1874 proved one of the hottest ever. Not only did streams and waterholes dry up, but also hordes of locusts descended on the South Plains to eat both grass and leaves. Both Redmen and white, as well as horses, suffered terribly as a result. Nelson A. Miles led his column of 744 men south from Fort Dodge on August 11, marching to the Washita River to establish a supply camp near the Texas-Oklahoma border, and then moving west to Palo Duro Canyon. Twice he came upon bodies of renegades, and in both battles he was victorious, but a shortage of supplies and water prevented his following the Indians onto the plains and defeating them decisively.

Major Price, coming eastward from Fort Union, New Mexico, missed his rendezvous date with Miles, but continued eastward toward Camp Supply, fighting Comanche on Sweetwater Creek and then linking up with Miles in Oklahoma. Colonel Miles thereupon entered the area again, combing the headwaters of the Red River and checking Adobe Walls on the Canadian; finding no concentrations of hostiles, Miles concluded that the war was over and, in December, ordered his troops back to their regular posts.

Meanwhile, Colonel Davidson had departed Fort Sill on September 10, marched up the Washita, turned southwestward to the headwaters of the Red River, and scouted until his supplies ran out. Returning to Fort Sill on September 29, he rested his men and horses almost a month, and then set out again on October 21. Three days later he came upon a party of renegade Comanche, 64 men and 250 women and children, who surrendered to him without a fight. He returned with them to Fort Sill early in November, his campaign over.

These three forces had put sufficient pressure on the Comanche and Kiowa to make several small bands straggle into Fort Sill to surrender. However, it was the work of Buell and Mackenzie that completed the task. Buell late in September left Fort Griffin, marched to the vicinity of the present town of Quanah and there established a supply camp, and then began scouting to the west. His forces destroyed two villages in mid-October, one of eighty-two lodges and the other of some four hundred; in these engagements his men killed only one Indian, but they destroyed so many supplies that the Indians were forced to go to Fort Sill and surrender as winter approached. Buell and his men also were affected by the cold, for in December they retired to Fort Griffin because of rain, snow, icy weather, and bad roads.

On August 23 Colonel Mackenzie and his command of 639 departed from Fort Concho, marched north for a week, and established a supply camp on the Freshwater Fork of the Brazos River. Arriving at last on the High Plains, the column of Blue Coats was greeted by cold winds and rain, and on September 25 they encamped near the head of Tule Canyon. That evening Comanche warriors tried to stampede the soldiers' horses, thereby leaving them afoot, but Mackenzie had anticipated the tactic; all the animals were staked and hobbled, and the Indian effort failed. The next morning Mackenzie learned from his scouts and from a captured Comanchero (who talked about being strung up on a propped-up wagon tongue) that a major Comanche village was in Palo Duro Canyon thirty miles away. Acting as if it knew nothing about this, the column saddled and rode eastward for several hours, then encamped for the night.

Mackenzie's strategy worked, for the Comanche believed he did not know the location of their main camp. However, after dark the colonel ordered his men to saddle, and then under cover of night they rode rapidly to the northwest, and before daybreak they were encamped on the edge of Palo Duro Canyon. The light of day revealed some two hundred lodges far below alongside the tree-lined Prairie Dog Town Fork of the Red River. Single-file, each soldier leading his horse, the troops descended a steep, narrow path. Before they could reach the valley below, however, an Indian sentinel fired a rifle and waved a blanket, signaling their approach, and the renegades fled either up the canyon or into the rocks and crevices of the nearby walls. Only sporadic fire bothered the soldiers as they rounded up 1,424 horses and mules, almost the entire Indian herd, and then set fire to lodges, buffalo robes, blankets, and the winter supply of food.

This accomplished, Mackenzie ordered his men out of the canyon, driving the captured horses and mules with them. Once atop the canyon, he formed his troops into a "living corral" around the animals and returned to his camp at Tule Canyon. There he allowed his scouts to pick what animals they wanted, by way of reward for their finding the Comanche camp, and then Mackenzie had the rest shot; this killing of 1,048 horses and mules consumed the better part of a day (the pile of bones that resulted was for years a reminder of the grisly work). However, the Indians could not stampede and recapture dead animals, nor could they raid without mounts—or eat without food. Mackenzie's strike at this village also demoralized the Comanche, for their medicine men had told them the camp there was safe from the soldiers.

Mackenzie did not quit the field after this engagement. Rather he kept pressuring the Comanche by patrolling the region, following every fresh trail that was found. On one of these scouts near Tule Canyon, Captain Adna R. Chaffee uttered a line that would be quoted in army barracks for half a century and more; by way of encouragement to his troops, he shouted, "Any man who is killed I will promote to corporal." Actually very few Indians or soldiers were killed in the Palo Duro Campaign, and even fewer renegades were captured. What did result was a loss of Indian morale. They saw villages they considered safe attacked, losing food, clothing, and shelter in the dead of winter; and in all they lost more than 7,500 horses and mules (most of these, about 5,500, were sold by the army at auction, the money going into the Indian welfare fund).

The results of these campaigns were dramatic. On February 26 the Kiowa chief Lone Wolf came to Fort Sill and surrendered with 252 followers. Colonel Mackenzie, who had been ordered to Fort Sill to control the Indians there by force, received the surrender in April of Chief Mow-way and 175 Comanche and of Chief White Horse and his followers. And on June 2 Chief Quanah Parker came in with 407 of his Kwahadie Comanche followers. By August that year only an estimated fifty Comanche warriors were still off the reservation. As each group surrendered, it was stripped of its guns and horses.[20] Then the process of separating the guilty leaders from the innocent followers began. This included twenty-five Kiowa, including Chief Lone Wolf, and nine Comanche, including Chief Black Horse. These were sent under Lieutenant R. H. Pratt of the 10th Cavalry for imprisonment in Florida. Later they would be returned to Oklahoma to rejoin their people.

For centuries the Comanche and Kiowa had controlled western Texas, roaming freely, killing buffalo, and terrorizing all other people, white or red, in the area. However, neither the people of Texas nor the federal government was willing to allow a few hundred nomadic tribesmen, even the "lords of the plains," to dominate a region so rich in grass and arable land, a region where hundreds of thousands would eventually live. Decades of captivity and humiliation would follow for these Indians, whose sin was standing in the way of progress by following a wandering existence and practicing an economy based on continual warfare.

6

AMERICANS IN APACHERIA

In 1837 James Johnson, who operated a trading post at Oposura, in the Mexican state of Sonora, demonstrated the high profits that might be made on the Apache of the Southwest. He numbered among his friends the Mimbres Apache, who lived near the Santa Rita Copper Mines (east of the present Silver City, New Mexico), especially Juan José Compa, a respected war leader. Compa had been educated in Mexico, but had turned against Mexicans when his father was murdered; so successful were his raids, for he could read intercepted Mexican dispatches, that the government of Sonora placed a high bounty on his scalp—as it did to a lesser extent on the scalps of all unfriendly Indians in the region. In 1835 that Mexican state's government offered a reward of one hundred pesos (each worth approximately one dollar American money) for the scalp of adult males, fifty pesos for the scalp of squaws, and twenty-five pesos for each child's scalp. Johnson was persuaded by the Sonoran government that, because of his friendship with Juan José Compa, he could kill him and other Apache and collect the reward.

Johnson's method was unique. Onto the back of a donkey he packed a small cannon, known as a mountain howitzer; it had been filled with shot and then its barrel plugged shut. This he concealed beneath a sack of "treats." Entering the Mimbres camp in company with a party of unsuspecting Missouri mule traders, Johnson calmly called the Apache to gather round, touched his cigar to the fuse, and walked away. The explosion killed about a score of Apache, while Johnson himself shot Juan José Compa. He and his men scalped the dead and then escaped with their hairy trophies, but some of the Missourians were not so fortunate.[1] Escaping this massacre—but embittered by it—was Juan José Compa's relative, Mangas Coloradas.

Born sometime during the first half of the 1790s, no doubt in southern New Mexico, Mangas Coloradas eventually gained such fame that Mexicans began saying he was part white, something regularly said about successful Indian leaders by whites eager to explain why "savages" were able to out-maneuver and out-general their own troops. At manhood he stood six feet, six inches tall— and was equally large in his ability to raid in Mexico with impunity. He reportedly had the genius to marry each of his daughters to the chief of a nearby tribe in order to gain allies; however, this worked well only in the case of Cochise, leader of the Chiricahua Apache who lived in nearby southeastern Arizona.[2]

Mexicans were unable to contain the Apache owing to political instability and a callous attitude by national politicians toward the frontier. Mexico City was a steaming cauldron of politics for decades after 1828; revolution followed revolution as *pronuncimientos* were issued regularly by politicians defeated at the ballot box and by generals who aspired to dictatorial or even imperial power. As one New Mexican politician reportedly lamented about his province, "Poor New Mexico. So far from God. So near to the United States." The two Mexican states of Chihauhua and Sonora were particularly hard hit by Apache incursions, and in 1835 Sonora, followed in 1838 by Chihuahua, offered generous bounties for the scalps of dead Apache. Among the leading practitioners of this grisly art were Americans, as well as runaway slaves, Mexicans, and even other Indians.

Prominent among the men practicing this form of "backyard barbering" were Michael James Box, James Kirker, and John Joel Glanton. These men and their followers would go into an Indian village and kill every man, woman, and child there; the bodies would be scalped and the hair turned in to the examining committees in Chihuahua or Sonora for payment. In fact, the scalp bounty hunters quickly ascertained that it was impossible for the examining committees to tell the difference between the hair of a friendly Indian and that of an unfriendly Indian, and soon the whole frontier was aflame; all Indians became unfriendly at the thought of being scalped, and they turned against all whites. Some of these scalp bounty hunters even learned that the examining committees could not tell the difference between Indian hair and Mexican hair, and they began raiding remote Mexican villages, killing the inhabitants, roaching them, and collecting their reward. The conquest of the Southwest by the United States did not end this practice; in fact, it had the opposite effect, for several Forty-niners decided to work their way westward as amateur barbers.[3]

Despite the intense hatreds generated by the scalp bounty system, Mangas Coloradas was still friendly to official parties of Americans at the time of the Mexican War. When Brigadier General Stephen Watts Kearny crossed the region with his dragoons in the fall of 1846, Mangas conferred with him and pledged his friendship for what he called (using the Spanish word) *norteamericanos*. He was fighting Mexicans. They were fighting Mexicans. Hence the two should be allies. Mangas even suggested that if Kearny was in a mood to invade Chihuahua, Sonora, and Durango that the two sides should fight together against the common enemy. Kearny refused the offer, for his orders were to march to California.[4]

The next Americans to enter southern New Mexico on official business were the members of the United States Boundary Commission, whose task it was, in company with the Mexican Boundary Commission, to survey and mark the new international line between their two countries. Arriving at El Paso del Norte (present Juarez, Chihuahua) the first week in December 1850, the American Commission at this time was led by John Russell Bartlett, a Rhode Island Whig of scholarly and artistic inclination. Bartlett had no qualifications for the position he held but had political connections, and he was a firm believer in the "noble savage" concept. He liked to travel in style, for he had a sumptuous carriage fitted out even with fowling pieces and shotguns.

At El Paso Bartlett and the Americans met their Mexican counterparts, and by the following summer the men started westward to the Santa Rita Copper Mines to begin surveying in that area. Guided by John C. Cremony, a Boston newspaperman turned scout and interpreter, Bartlett grew bored with the slow travel of the rest of his party, including the soldiers, and hurried ahead. Advancing into Cooke's Canyon in pursuit of antelope, John Cremony suddenly found himself surrounded by some twenty-five Apache, members of the band of Cuchillo Negro (Black Knife). Knowing that the carriage was right behind him, Cremony drew his revolver and waited. Cuchillo Negro and his warriors advanced on the lone American, whereupon Cremony pointed his pistol at the chief and said that the warriors might kill him but that he would shoot Cuchillo Negro before he died.

Cuchillo Negro thereupon asked what Cremony wanted in that area. The scout replied that he and the many coming behind him were merely passing through the country and that they came in peace. Obviously the Indians thought they had trapped a lone white and that Cremony was lying about others following him, yet they decided to wait before ordering an attack. About fifteen minutes later, just as Cremony's situation was growing tense, the carriage rumbled into view around the point of a mountain—and it was accompanied by troops that had caught up with it. Cuchillo Negro thereupon advanced a short distance toward Cremony, held up his hand, and said, *"Jeunie, jeunie!"* (Friend, friend!). He then wheeled his horse and galloped off.[5]

Once the American members of the Boundary Commission were in camp at Santa Rita, they were visited by many Apache, including members of the bands of Mangas Coloradas, Ponce, and Delgadito. In the days that followed the Apache took advantage of Bartlett's trust to drive off the commission's livestock and to steal everything not heavily guarded. On one occasion the soldiers of the escort had to pursue the Apache—fruitlessly, of course—because the Indians had stolen the army's horses and mules. More would be purchased and herded to the camp, only to be stolen again. Nevertheless, Commissioner Bartlett continued to believe that "kind treatment, a rigid adherence to what is right, and a proper and invariable fulfillment of all promises, would secure the friendship of the Apaches."

About four miles down the canyon from the camp of the Boundary Commission lived a group of miners. Their camp was also raided regularly. On one occasion the Apache stole a herd of cattle at the mining camp, whereupon Lieutenant Amiel Weeks Whipple, a topographical engineer assigned to the boundary survey, led twenty volunteers in pursuit of the raiders and came upon them in a wooded area. The Indians thereupon divided into two parties, one to halt and slow the pursuit and the other to push the stolen cattle on ahead. A lively firefight developed between this rearguard and Whipple's party, during which Delgadito, the chief of the raiding party, began taunting the Americans by exhibiting his posterior and slapping it (a favorite act of ridicule among Apache for anyone they considered an inferior warrior). Delgadito little realized that members of the Boundary Commission had been furnished with the recently perfected Wesson rifle, which could shoot with high accuracy for some four hundred yards, at that time a remarkable distance—and almost exactly the distance Delgadito stood from Whipple's party flaunting his rear end. John C. Cremony took one of the new rifles fitted with special sights and handed it to a man named Wells, a crack shot, pointing at the cavorting Delgadito. Wells took careful aim and fired, hitting the exposed "seat of honor." From the Indian camp came "an unearthly yell and a series of dances and capers that would put a *maitre de ballet* to blush."[6] The Americans then pursued the retreating Apache and came upon the abandoned cattle thirty miles later.

On June 27 Bartlett learned something more about life in New Mexico and among the Apache. That day a party of New Mexican traders, returning from a profitable trip among the Apache, rode into the American camp to secure provisions. Cremony discovered in their midst a young Mexican girl, Inez Gonzales, whom the traders had purchased from the Apache for ransoming to her parents. Cremony informed Bartlett about the girl's presence, whereupon the romantic and chivalrous commissioner had the soldiers forceably remove her to his tent. He found her "quite young, artless, and interesting in appearance, prepossessing in manners, and by her deportment gave evidence that she had been carefully brought up." Bartlett later on a trip into Mexico returned the girl to her family and reported that she grew up to marry a captain in the Mexican

army and lived to a ripe old age.[7] Moreover, Bartlett also rescued
two captive Mexican boys from the Apache and later restored them
to their families.[8]

The Boundary Commission then moved out of Apache country.
However, in 1855, during the course of the boundary survey following the Gadsden Purchase, the new commissioner, Major William
H. Emory of the Corps of Topographical Engineers, had no difficulty with the Apache. Emory had first traversed the Southwest in
company with Stephen Watts Kearny's "Army of the West" in
1846, and he had worked for a time with the boundary surveying
commission following the end of the war with Mexico. His attitude
about the Apache, based on his previous experience with them, was
not to allow them in his camp; about the Indians he said, ". . . I
never trusted them; and during the last year of my experience with
them I gave orders to permit none to come into any camp under
my orders, and to kill them at sight. By taking this harsh but necessary step I was the only person passing through this country who
did not incur difficulty and loss. The Mexican commission was
robbed repeatedly, and on more than one occasion was, in consequence, obliged to suspend its operations."[9]

James S. Calhoun, first superintendent of Indian affairs in New
Mexico, echoed Emory's sentiments, rather than those of Bartlett,
when referring to the Apache. Writing Commissioner of Indian Affairs William Medill on July 22, 1849, shortly after he assumed his
duties, Calhoun said, "The gravest subject with our Indian affairs
in New Mexico relates to the wandering tribes [of Apache and Co-
manche], who have never cultivated the soil, and have supported
themselves by depredations alone. This is the only labor known to
them." In this same letter Calhoun summed up the crux of the
Apache problem: "The thought of annihilating these Indians cannot be entertained by an American public—nor can the Indians
abandon their predatory incursions, and live and learn to support
themselves by the sweat of their own brows. . . ." Less than a
month later Calhoun was complaining to Medill that the Apache
"generally are in a bad temper. The number of troops are not sufficient to keep them in proper check. . . ."[10]

The only solution Calhoun could conceive was twofold: force

and a reservation. He advised his superiors that the only way American citizens could exist in New Mexico and practice their usual economic system would be for the government to use "a strong arm, and a prompt arm, guided by an enlightened patriotism. Expend your million now, if necessary, that you may avoid the expenditure of millions hereafter. . . ." As for the future of the Apache, he said that they and all the "fragments of their tribes, must be penned up, and this should be done at the earliest possible day. . . ."[11]

Colonel Edwin V. Sumner, military commander of the region, was even more pessimistic about New Mexican prospects. His report of May 27, 1852, stated, "So long as we hold this country, as we do now, it must be a heavy burden to us; and there never can be the slightest return for all this outlay. . . . Twenty—fifty years hence—this Territory will be precisely the same it is now. There can never be any inducement for any class of our people to come here whose example will improve this people." Specifically concerning the Apache he declared, "If the Mexicans should act justly by the Indians, I think there would be no difficulty; but if they do not, and war should ensue, the Mexicans would always steal from the Indians quite as much as the Indians would steal from them, and thus there would be no losers in the end."[12]

Because government officials in New Mexico apparently saw no solution to the Apache problem—as well as to the Navajo problem then causing such difficulty—Secretary of War Charles M. Conrad in his annual report of 1852 said:

Would it not be better to induce the inhabitants [of New Mexico] to abandon a country which seems hardly fit for the habitation of civilized man, by remunerating them for their property in money or lands situated in more favorable regions? Even if the government paid for the property quintuple its value, it would still, merely on the score of economy, be largely the gainer by the transaction, and the troops now stationed in New Mexico would be available for the protection of other portions of our own . . . territory. Unless the means I have indicated, or some others, be adopted to relieve the Indians from the necessity of plundering to procure the means of subsistence, their depredations must not only continue, but increase. This would require a corresponding increase in the means of protection.[13]

However, Conrad was determined to act not only to protect travelers on the road to California, but also to honor the American commitment made to Mexico in the Treaty of Guadalupe Hidalgo. Article XI of that agreement had stated, ". . . It is solemnly agreed that all incursions [by Indians raiding into Mexico] shall be forcibly restrained by the Government of the United States, whensoever this may be necessary; and that when they cannot be prevented, they shall be punished by the said Government, and satisfaction for the same shall be exacted; all in the same way, and with equal diligence and energy, as if the same incursions were mediated or committed within its own territory against its own citizens."[14] To accomplish this task in New Mexico was the duty of Colonel Edwin V. Sumner, who arrived to take command of the 9th Department in July 1851.

Sumner first moved the troops out of Santa Fe, which he considered a "sink of vice and extravagance," establishing Fort Union as his supply depot and headquarters. Then that autumn, after contending with the Navajo and establishing a fort in the heart of their country, he considered the Apache problem—and moved rapidly. First he removed the garrisons of soldiers from the towns of El Paso, Doña Ana, and Socorro which to him were as suspect as Santa Fe; the soldiers were put to building Fort Conrad at the north end of the *Jornada del Muerta*, a sixty-mile stretch of barren desert, to slow the raids of the Mescalero and Gila Apache. Also, two other posts became a reality: Fort Fillmore, located at Mesilla to guard pilgrims bound for California, and Fort Webster, situated at the Santa Rita Copper Mines and intended to dampen the enthusiasm of the Mimbres and Warm Springs Apache. Two of the forts proved temporary; in 1854 Fort Conrad was moved and renamed Fort Craig (near the town of Socorro), while Fort Webster was abandoned in 1853. Then in 1855 came the creation of Fort Stanton in the midst of the Mescalero country.

However, the Gadsden Purchase Agreement of December 30, 1853, specifically freed the United States from any financial obligation to halt Indian raids into Mexico—just when the large-scale traffic to California over the Gila Trail was slowing to a trickle. Thereafter the soldiers in New Mexico had little enthusiasm for

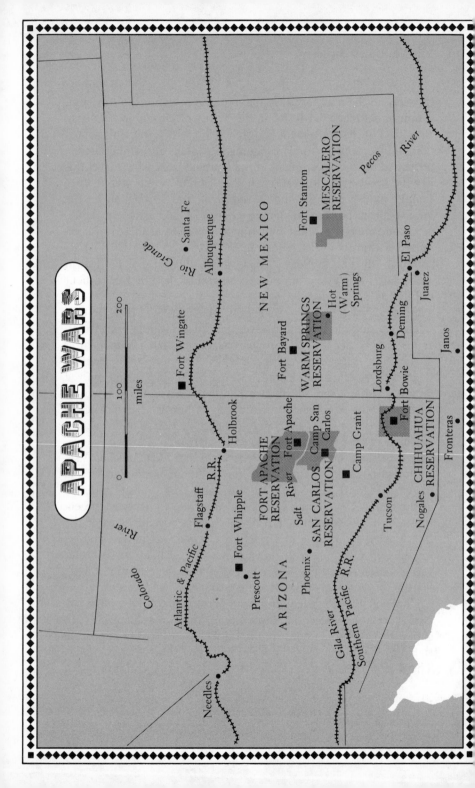

pursuing Apache when their crime was raiding into Mexico.

In what was then the western part of New Mexico, but which eventually would become Arizona, there was no civilian settlement until the Gadsden Purchase was consummated and Tucson became an American town. The Mexicans huddled in the vicinity of this settlement in the Santa Cruz Valley had long suffered at the hands of the various Apache bands nearby: the Chiricahua of south-eastern Arizona, the White Mountain Apache in the region from which they drew their name, and the Pinal and Coyotero Apache of the central and east-central parts of the region. Mexican troops actually stayed at Tucson until March 1856 before withdrawing—which caused loud protests from the American settlers already there, for they were left with no military protection from Apache wrath and raids. Not until November 14, 1856, did Major Enoch Steen with three companies of the 1st Dragoons arrive at Tucson to unfurl the Stars and Stripes—and then leave for the southeastern part of what would become Arizona to establish Fort Buchanan. Four years later another post, Fort Breckinridge, would be established at the junction of the Aravaipa and San Pedro rivers in central Arizona; it was intended as yet another deterrent to parties of raiding Apache. Both these posts were part of the 9th Military Department and controlled from New Mexico.

Among the first American settlers of Arizona was Charles D. Poston, who arrived in 1856 as general manager of the Sonora Exploring and Mining Company. A native of Kentucky, born there in 1825, Poston was a veteran of the California gold rush interested in mining silver in the southern part of the Santa Cruz River Valley; he established his headquarters at the old Spanish presidio of Tubac, and soon he was reporting a silver production of $3,000 a day. Poston in 1859 wrote, "The Apaches have not up to this time given us any trouble; but on the contrary, pass within sight of our herds, going hundreds of miles into Mexico on their forays rather than break their [friendship] . . . with the Americans." Apparently the Indians considered the newcomers to be allies, for the Americans had arrived to fight Mexicans—whom the Apache had been fighting for centuries.

The first note to disturb the harmony of these good relations came in the fall of 1860. Some thirty Mexicans rode into Tubac and told Poston and his men that Apache had raided a ranch in Mexico and were returning to their Arizona haunts by way of a crossing on the Santa Cruz River a few miles downstream from Tubac. The Mexicans asked the men at Tubac to help ambush the Apache, promising them in return half of the three hundred horses and mules which the Indians had stolen and were driving north. Poston refused to allow any of his men to participate in this affair. Thereupon the Mexicans rode a dozen miles north to Canoa, which was the headquarters of a company of lumbermen from Maine; they were whipsawing lumber out of the nearby Santa Rita Mountains, selling it in Tucson for handsome profits, and were always in need of additional horses and mules. The Mexicans made the lumbermen the same offer—half the stock in return for their aid in ambushing the Apache—and the lumbermen accepted. The ambush succeeded admirably. The Apache were caught in a murderous crossfire and abandoned the stock.

"About the next full moon after this event," later wrote Poston, "we had been passing the usual quiet Sunday in Tubac, when a Mexican vaquero came galloping furiously into the plaza crying out, 'Apaches! Apaches! Apaches!'" From him Poston learned that the Apache had attacked the lumbering camp and had exacted a bloody revenge for the recent ambush. The miners rode from Tubac to Canoa and were greeted by a scene of massacre and destruction: "The place looked as if it had been struck by a hurricane," wrote Poston. "The doors and windows were smashed, and the house was a smoking ruin. The former inmates were lying around dead, and three of them had been thrown into the well, head foremost. We buried seven men in a row in front of the burned house." The dragoons at nearby Fort Buchanan were informed of the raid and went in pursuit of the culprits but never caught them.[15]

Apparently the Apache involved were the Chiricahua, followers of Cochise. Born about 1823 or 1824, he was described in 1870 as five feet, nine and one-half inches tall, weighing 164 pounds, with broad shoulders and a stout frame. His eyes and hair were black, his forehead high, and his nose "for an Indian straight." Moreover, his body was scarred all over by buckshot.[16] The son of Nachi, he had succeeded his father as chief of the Chiricahua, who lived by committing depredations and stealing horses, principally from Mexicans. Apparently he liked Americans well enough, for in late 1860 he and his people were under contract to supply wood to the stage station of the Butterfield Overland Mail at Apache Pass.

Cochise's friendship with Americans came to an end in February 1861 as the result of an incident known as the "Bascom Affair." In the Sonoita Valley, some twelve miles from Fort Buchanan lived a rancher named John Ward, who possibly was "a castoff from the Vigilance Committee in San Francisco" and who was described as "a worthless character."[17] With him was his common-law wife, Jesusa Martínez, who had been captured by Pinal Apache and who had borne a son, Felix, during that captivity. Late in 1860 the ranch was raided by Pinal Apache, and the boy Felix, along with some cattle, were taken. Ward was apparently drunk at the time and thought the raiders were Chiricahua Apache led by Cochise. When sober, he went to Fort Buchanan to complain of the theft.

Three months later—and the delay is inexplicable—Lieutenant Colonel Pitcairn Morrison detached Second Lieutenant George N. Bascom, a native of Kentucky and a graduate of West Point in 1858, with approximately sixty men to recover the boy and cattle. Ward accompanied the detachment, whose orders were to use force if necessary.

Bascom led the command eastward to Apache Pass, knowing that Cochise lived in the vicinity. Arriving there on February 4, 1861, Bascom paused at the Butterfield Overland Mail Company's corral in the pass, then went eastward along the road about three-quarters of a mile and made camp; this ruse was designed to give the Indians the impression that the soldiers were on their way to New Mexico—such travel being common—and not pursuing the Chiricahua. And it worked, for Cochise soon came into the camp voluntarily, accompanied by several of his relatives and friends. Bascom invited the Chiricahua chief into his tent, and he and seven followers entered. Thereupon Ward and a group of soldiers surrounded the canvas meeting hall. Lieutenant Bascom bluntly demanded the return of the boy and the cattle stolen from Ward, declaring that Cochise and his party would be held until they were returned.

Cochise protested his innocence, but to no avail. Then, sensing that the lieutenant meant what he had said, Cochise drew his knife and slit an opening in the side of the tent. Through this he plunged, landing outside in the midst of some very startled soldiers. Without pausing, Cochise dashed away, making good his escape. The Indians with Cochise in the tent were not so fortunate, however. One of the warriors followed his chief through the hole in the canvas, but was clubbed by one soldier and bayoneted in the stomach by another. The other six, mostly relatives of Cochise, were seized as hostages.

Cochise quickly rallied his warriors and attacked the unsuspecting employees at the nearby Butterfield Overland Mail station. One was killed and another made prisoner. That evening a wagon train entered Apache Pass on the Butterfield road; on it were two Americans and eight Mexicans. Cochise captured the train, held the two Americans prisoners, and ordered the eight Mexicans tied to the wagon wheels and burned. Then under a flag of truce, he offered to trade his three American captives for the six Apache held by Bascom. This offer was refused.

The army lieutenant realized that his position in the Pass was most precarious, however, for he was surrounded. Somehow the runners he dispatched slipped through the Indian lines and reached Fort Buchanan to ask for aid. On February 14 Lieutenant Isaiah N. Moore and seventy dragoons arrived to find that the Chiricahua had melted away at their approach. During a scout of the vicinity, the bodies of the three Americans held hostage by Cochise were found; they were filled with lance holes and mutilated beyond individual recognition. Bascom's official report told what then transpired: "Finding no fresh sign of Indians, we returned to the [Butterfield] Station and on the next day started for Fort Buchanan; when near the scene of the macsacre [sic] and about three hundred yards from the burnt train, I took the six warriors I had prisoners to the grave of [the] murdered men, explained through the interpreter what had taken place, and my intentions, and bound them securely hand and foot, and hung them to the nearest trees. . . ."[18]

The "Bascom Affair" so enraged Cochise that he launched what would prove a long and bloody war, for he intended no less than

Fort Fillmore, New Mexico, with the Organ Mountains in the background (1852). *Courtesy Library of Congress.*

the total extermination of all Americans in Arizona. Compounding the misery that this engendered was the abandonment of the territory by the army just after the event; the outbreak of Civil War that spring caused the commander of the Department of New Mexico to withdraw all troops to the Rio Grande Valley to protect it from Confederate invasion, leaving southern Arizona without protection. Charles D. Poston was forced to abandon his mines at Tubac; ranchers abandoned their stock; farmers fled their fields. Sylvester Mowry, who was operating a mine for his Arizona Land and Mining Company in the vicinity, alone tried to stay and work his property; but he soon became a virtual prisoner there, even on one occasion suffering the humiliation of seeing Cochise just out of rifle range riding about on Mowry's favorite horse.

That summer of 1861 Colonel John Robert Baylor arrived at Mesilla, New Mexico, at the head of the 258 Confederate soldiers, members of the Second Texas Regiment of Mounted Volunteers. He invaded New Mexico without orders, for he had been sent only to take Fort Bliss at El Paso, but he exceeded his orders and marched an additional forty miles up the Rio Grande to Mesilla. On July 25 Major Isaac Lynde with 300 Union soldiers from Fort Fillmore tried to dislodge the Confederates only to be defeated and then captured. His position secure, Baylor on August 1 issued a proclamation stating that he had taken formal possession of the "Territory of Arizona" (which, according to him, constituted all of the present Arizona and New Mexico south of the 34th parallel). And he volunteered himself as governor of this Confederate territory. Another Confederate force entered the region that December, this one led by Brigadier General Henry Hopkins Sibley, who came to conquer and govern New Mexico itself. Sibley paused at Mesilla to assume command of all Confederate troops operating in West Texas, New Mexico, and Arizona, and to send 200 men west to Tucson under the command of Captain Sherrod Hunter. They arrived in Tucson on February 28, 1862, to be greeted enthusiastically by the local citizens, most of whom were Southern sympathizers and all of whom hoped for protection from Apache raiders. However, this unit mainly concerned itself with scouting in the direction of California.

Fighting the Apache, therefore, was left to the direction of Governor Baylor. And the Chiricahua and Mimbres Apache were making life and property unsafe in almost every part of Baylor's Arizona; only in Tucson and Mesilla was there sufficient safety in numbers for people to sleep safely at night. The governor's answer was a group of volunteers from within Arizona and western Texas, whom he designated the "Arizona Guards" and the "Arizona Rangers." The Rangers were mustered into the service under the command of Captain George M. Frazer and numbered approximately thirty-five men, while the Guards were commanded by Captain Thomas Helm and consisted of about thirty men. These troops were ordered to reopen the road between Mesilla and Tucson and especially to rout the Indians from Apache Pass.

When these measures proved ineffective, Baylor proved himself capable of extreme measures. On March 20, 1862, from his home in Mesilla, he wrote Captain Helm of the Arizona Guards at Tucson: "You will . . . use all means to persuade the Apaches or any tribe to come in for the purpose of making peace, and when

you get them together kill all the grown Indians and take the
children prisoners and sell them to defray the expenses of killing
the Indians." Baylor knew that bait was necessary for the trap he
planned, so he said, "Buy whisky and such other goods as may be
necessary for the Indians and I will order vouchers given to cover
the amount expended." He also realized that surprise and secrecy
were necessary to accomplish this task, for he concluded, "Leave
nothing undone to insure success, and have a sufficient number of
men around to allow no Indian to escape. Say nothing of your
orders until the time arrives. . . ."[19]

Before this plan could be put into effect, the Confederate effort
in New Mexico collapsed, and Baylor was forced to flee. Later,
when his "kill the Indians" policy came under criticism from President Jefferson Davis, Baylor on December 29, 1862, answered his
critics: "Outrages were committed frequently; the mails were
robbed; in one or two instances the passengers were found hanging
up by the heels, their heads within a few inches of a slow fire, and
they thus horribly roasted to death. Others were found tied to the
wheels of the coach, which had been burned. . . ."[20] He commented that "If the [Confederate] Government had the combined
wealth of the world it could not purchase peace with the Indians,
and in my humble opinion it would be far cheaper to board the
savages (were that possible) at first-class hotels than to continue
the reservation, feeding, paint, and blanket system longer. . . ."
He noted that he was enclosing with his letter a shield taken from
an Indian killed by Baylor personally; the shield was decorated, he
wrote, "with a scalp—a woman's fair tresses—those of a Miss Jackson, who had been murdered during one of the frequent raids."

Baylor's methods and attitude were extreme, but probably they
reflected the pioneer attitude prevalent in 1862. When federal
troops occupied the Southwest that year, the frontier was aflame
with hatred, white for red and red for white. Certainly no quick
solution was available, but unfortunately not even an equitable
one was possible.

7

THE FINAL CONQUEST

On September 18, 1862, Brigadier General James Henry Carleton assumed command of the Department of New Mexico—and with it took on the obligation of containing the Apache (as well as the Navajo). He had won this unenviable position by marching the California Column of Volunteers across the Southwest from the Pacific Coast and, in the process, routing the Confederates from Arizona and New Mexico. And on this trek across the Gila Trail, Carleton had received his first taste of Apache warfare.

The California Column had marched through heat and choking dust, drinking foul water and eating bad food, swearing and sweating, to arrive at Tucson early in June of 1862. There Carleton had paused to proclaim himself governor of Arizona, and then on July 4 he had sent Captain Thomas Roberts with 126 men, 22 wagons, and 2 howitzers eastward; they were to follow the old Butterfield stage road to the Rio Grande Valley. Eleven days later, when the column reached Apache Pass, it was attacked by 700 Apache under Cochise; a ten-hour battle followed during which only the howitzers prevented a massacre of the troops. The next day Roberts was able to force his way through Apache Pass and continue eastward. His report stated that 2 of his men had died, but that an estimated 63 Apaches had been killed. An Indian participant later stated that 66 of his fellows had died in this engagement, all but three from artillery shells.[1] One of the Indians wounded in this engagement was Mangas Coloradas, who had brought his Mimbres warriors west to join with Cochise in the fight; his followers took him to Sonora and forced a Mexican doctor, on pain of death, to remove the bullet.[2]

Carleton, following in August, paused at Apache Pass to order the erection of a fort at that strategic site. This post, called Fort Bowie, served both to hold communication open to California and to deny the Indians the use of the strategic pass.[3]

Once in New Mexico General Carleton almost immediately wanted to halt the incursions of the Mimbres. At the time the Apache were disturbing the miners at the southwestern New Mexican community of Pinos Altos, and James Henry Carleton had visions of personal mineral weath. Therefore he sent a small column to this destitute and beleaguered settlement in August 1862. The following January, when he heard that the Apache were raiding there in force, he ordered Brigadier General Joseph R. West to establish Fort West at Pinos Altos; from there West was to take decisive measures. West took with him part of the 1st California Cavalry and the 5th California Infantry, marching at once to the Mimbres River. There he sent Captain E. D. Shirland with the cavalry in advance to scout. Shirland returned on January 18 to a site designated Fort McLane with Mangas Coloradas; Shirland reported that he had "captured" the Apache chief, but Daniel E. Conner, a prospector there, later wrote that Mangas had been lured into the American camp under a flag of truce and then captured.

West later reported that inasmuch as Mangas had voluntarily come in that he could not be executed as he deserved. He therefore informed the Apache that "the remainder of his days would be spent as a prisoner," and that if he tried to escape his life would be "forfeit." According to this report, Mangas that night did make "three efforts to escape and was shot on the third attempt." Conner's version of this incident was quite different. He reported that the guards three times placed heated bayonets against the chief's feet, and that General West told the troops, "Men, that old murderer has got away from every soldier command and has left a trail

Victorio, the Apache chief. *Courtesy U.S. Signal Corps, National Archives.*

of blood for five hundred miles on the old stage line. I want him dead or alive tomorrow morning, do you understand. *I want him dead.*"[4] The next morning Mangas was indeed dead.

The death of this leader did not end the Mimbres menace, however, for his place was quickly taken by a rising warrior named Victorio. This new leader was of uncertain background. Some reports hold that he was Mexican-born, a lad captured and raised by the Mimbres Apache; other reports state that he was a Chiricahua by birth but married into the Mimbres tribe and thereby became a member of it; still a third set of opinions hold that he was Mimbres by birth.[5] Whatever his origins, he proved a charismatic leader, one who rallied the Mimbres in the following decade and a half and whose name came to be synonymous among whites with fear.

Meanwhile, General Carleton was focusing his attention on the Mescalero Apache whose haunts were nearer to the New Mexican settlements. The Mescalero had felt some of the army's ire in 1855 when campaigns had been undertaken against them by Lieutenant Colonel Dixon S. Miles and Captains Richard S. Ewell and Samuel D. Sturgis; at that time they had been so disheartened by this three-pronged attack that they had asked for peace. For the next six years they lived peacefully, if poorly, in their mountain homeland. Since 1861, however, they had been raiding the ranches of their neighbors; according to their agent they killed an estimated forty-six people in 1862 alone and, in addition, carried off many children into captivity. "There is no security for life or property," the agent reported.[6]

Carleton, who was earning the nickname "Mogul" for himself by his high-handed, blunt, domineering ways, decided to put an end to the Mescalero problem, and, as with the Navajo, moved with a dispatch never before seen in New Mexico. Late in September 1862 he sent Colonel Kit Carson with five companies of mounted New Mexican volunteers to reoccupy Fort Stanton in the east-central part of the territory; from there they were to take the field against the Mescalero, as would two companies of California Volunteers under Captain William McCleave, marching east from Mesilla, and two additional companies of Californians under Captain Thomas L. Roberts, who were to move north from El Paso. To all three went "Mogul" Carleton's order: "There is to be no council held with the Indians, nor any talks. The men are to be slain whenever and wherever they can be found. The women and children may be taken as prisoners, but, of course, they are not to be slain." Carleton was equally emphatic that there be no quick granting of peace; should they ask they were to be told "fairly and frankly that you will keep after their people and slay them until you receive orders to desist from these headquarters."[7]

The campaign proved short, for the Mescalero had little heart for fighting. At the outbreak some of the tribe fled south into the

Guadalupe Mountains, while others hastily sought peace. To their astonishment this did not work; when Chiefs Manuelito and José Largo approached the command of Captain William Graydon to discuss terms, the troops opened fire and killed both, along with ten of their followers. By the end of the first week in November more than a hundred of them had come to Fort Stanton to beg Colonel Carson for peace. He sent Chiefs Chato, Cadete, and Estrella to Santa Fe to meet with Carleton; at the territorial capital the three were told about a new reservation which the general had established, Bosque Redondo, a hundred miles northeast of Fort Stanton. That reservation, guarded by Fort Sumner, was the place to go, Carleton told the Mescalero, for there they would be fed and protected; to go anywhere else, he said, meant unrelenting war. Apparently the Mescalero believed him, for by the end of 1862 Carson reported 240 of them at Fort Stanton awaiting transfer to Bosque Redondo and another 100 on their way.[8] The Mescalero war had ended, although about 100 of them would defy all efforts to be conquered and would eventually merge with other hostile branches of the Apache nation.

For the remainder of the Civil War, Carleton would busy himself fighting the Comanche and Navajo—as well as seeking political power and the development of mines that would bring him financial independence. He ordered additional forts built, forts whose purpose was to block Apache war trails out of southwestern and west-central New Mexico into the Rio Grande Valley: Fort McRae on the Rio Grande in the middle of the *Jornada de Muera* and Fort Selden at the southern end of it; these joined Fort Thorn at the northern end as a bulwark of Apache defense, but the Mimbres raiders showed their contempt by stealing horses from the posts. In June 1863 they demonstrated their dominance of the region by catching Captain Albert H. Pfeiffer and his family when they were bathing at the mineral springs near Fort McRae; they slaughtered his wife and a servant and chased the nearly naked captain all the way to the fort. That same month they also killed the detachment bringing the mail to the post and carried off the head of the lieutenant in charge as a trophy.[9] The troops continued to take the field, but ineffectively.

Finally, in the spring of 1865, Chiefs Victorio, Nana, and others sent word to Superintendent of Indian Affairs Michael Steck that they wanted him to come and "make a chain between them and the whites that would never be broken." However, General Carleton, who was at odds with Dr. Steck, refused to allow him to go, insisting that the Indians were exclusively a military concern. Instead he dispatched Lieutenant Colonel Nelson H. Davis, who informed the Mimbres that they could have peace only if they reported to the Bosque Redondo reservation. This the Mimbres Apache refused to do; probably their chiefs recalled the fate of Mangas when he had fallen into the hands of Carleton's men. Therefore the conference came to naught; one reason might be the attitude of Lieutenant Colonel Davis, whose report of the affair contained his thoughts about the Indians: "Death to the Apache, and peace and prosperity to this land, is my motto," he asserted.[10]

The end of the Civil War therefore found the Mimbres Apache still on the warpath. One event that did transpire during this conflict that would have some influence on future events was the creation of the Territory of Arizona on February 24, 1863. The civilians of this region, almost totally neglected by General Carleton and his troops, on occasion took matters into their own hands and fought the Apache—even in treacherous ways. A leader in this movement was King S. Woolsey, who had been born in Alabama in 1832 and who had rushed westward to California in 1850. Arriving in Arizona a decade later, he had joined the Confederate Army but was prevented from active service by illness. He therefore established a ranch on the Agua Fria east of the town of Prescott and made his living by selling hay to the Union soldiers stationed at Fort Whipple, which had been established early in 1864. In January that year, after raids had become too frequent, he gathered thirty Americans and fourteen Indian allies and set out in pursuit of Pinal Apache. In the vicinity of Fish Creek Canyon he came upon his quarry. The Apache agreed to a council at which, on Woolsey's signal, the Americans treacherously opened fire on the unsuspecting enemy and killed five chiefs and fourteen warriors. This incident, labeled the "Massacre at Bloody Tanks," increased Apache hatred of the whites and made a settlement of their dif-

Fort Apache, Arizona, in 1884. *Courtesy U.S. Signal Corps, National Archives.*

ferences more difficult, as did Woolsey's reported practice of giving the Indians *pinole* (corn meal mixed with sugar) loaded with strychnine.[11]

Arizona's first territorial governor, John N. Goodwin, a native of Maine, decided that civilians could bring peace to the land if organized into militia forces; he therefore authorized the raising of a company of "Arizona Volunteers." The men were enlisted for a year, but before they could be organized to take the field, dramatic changes occurred. On January 20, 1865, Arizona was separated from the Department of New Mexico and placed under the military Department of California. Exactly a month later Brevet Brigadier General John S. Mason was appointed to command the "District of Arizona." He arrived in June that year with 2,800 men to re-garrison the old posts and to establish new ones. After a tour of inspection Mason reported, "At the time of my arrival in the district, I believe every ranch had been deserted south of the Gila. The town of Tubac was entirely deserted, and the town of Tucson had

Fort Huachuca, Arizona, a typical Western fort in the 1880s. *Courtesy Western History Collections, University of Oklahoma Library.*

about two hundred souls. North of the Gila, the roads were completely blockaded; the ranches, with one or two exceptions, abandoned, and most of the settlements were threatened with abandonment or annihilation."

Mason spent most of his time constructing forts and building roads between them. His successor, Lieutenant Colonel Thomas C. Devon, who took command early in 1868, vigorously pushed war against the hostiles, but accomplished few positive results. For example, between July 1868 and June 1869 more than fifty people were killed in Pima County alone. Arizonans protested loudly to Washington, but this was the time of the inauguration of the Grant administration, and the peace advocates had his ear. In line with the Grant "Peace Policy," Arizona on April 15, 1870, was separated from the Department of California to become a department itself. In command since 1869 was Brigadier General George Stoneman, who first had seen the Southwest during the Mexican War. Following orders from Washington, Stoneman attempted to persuade the Apache to accept reservations and live there peacefully where they could be taught agricultural pursuits. However, this practice enraged Arizonans who believed that reservations were nothing but feeding stations for Apache and that the Indians regularly slipped away from the enclaves to raid and kill. On April 30, 1871, a citizen army from Tucson, composed of some 50 Americans and almost 100 Papago Indians, attacked a reservation for the Aravaipa Apache near Camp Grant, killing 108 of the Indians— only 8 of them men—and carrying 29 children into captivity. The perpetrators of this "Camp Grant Massacre," as Eastern newspapers headlined it, were arrested and brought to trial in Tucson, but a local jury exonerated them at once; Arizonans simply would not convict a man for killing an Indian, even though the Indian might be a child. "Nits make lice," they said. Beyond this, it was good business for merchants in the Territory when there were Indian troubles. At such times more troops were sent, which meant rations would be bought locally for them and their horses. A group of merchants in Tucson were actively promoting incidents, a group known as the "Tucson Ring"; moreover, they were in collusion with many of the Indian agents to furnish substandard rations at

General Oliver O. Howard. *Courtesy U.S. Signal Corps, Brady Collection, National Archives.*

standard prices, splitting the profits. Sometimes, with the aid of a reservation agent, they furnished no rations at all and pocketed the money.[12]

As a result of the national attention focused on the Apache problem of the Southwest by the Camp Grant Massacre, President Grant sent a peace commission to Arizona. Headed by mild-mannered Quaker Vincent Colyer, this commission was charged with arranging treaties with the various Apache bands and putting them on reservations. Governor A. P. K. Safford reflected public sentiment in the territory when he issued a proclamation asking the people to cooperate with the commission despite its members' "erroneous opinions upon the Indian question and the condition of affairs in the Territory." One local newspaper editor put the matter more bluntly; he asserted that Arizonans "ought, in justice to our murdered dead, to dump the old devil [Colyer] into the shaft of some mine, and pile rocks upon him until he is dead. A rascal who comes here to thwart the efforts of military and civilians to conquer a peace from our savage foe, deserves to be stoned to death, like the treacherous, black-hearted dog that he is." Despite such opposition, engendered by the Tucson Ring and its cohorts, who played on public hatred of the Indians, Colyer proceeded to get some 4,000 Indians onto reservations. In the process he created the Camp Grant Agency for the Pinal Apache and the White Mountain Reservation for the Apache band of that name. When he departed, the only major tribe of Apache in Arizona not on reservations was the Chiricahua, still led by Cochise.

While Colyer was at work, Lieutenant Colonel George Crook had arrived in the territory, and on June 4, 1871, he took command of the department from Stoneman. Before he was allowed to undertake a field campaign, however, yet another peace commission arrived, this one headed by Brigadier General Oliver Otis Howard, a one-armed veteran of the Civil War known to the troops as "Bible-Quoting Howard" or as "The Christian General." He likewise encountered heavy local resistance, but proceeded with his work. He inspected the military posts of the department, arranged conferences with the Pima, Papago, and other sedentary tribes, and

Camp Grant, Arizona, as it appeared in 1871. *Courtesy U.S. Signal Corps, National Archives.*

moved the Camp Grant agency northward to the Gila River, where it was renamed San Carlos. Thereafter this would be the major reservation for Apache.

Finally, with the assistance of Thomas J. Jeffords, a white man who had won the friendship of Cochise, Howard met the aging Chiricahua chief in a dramatic confrontation. Arriving at the meet-

General George Crook. *Courtesy U.S. Signal Corps, National Archives.*

ing unarmed and accompanied only by Jeffords, Howard persuaded
Cochise to accept a reservation approximately fifty-five miles square
in southeastern Arizona, including the Dragoon and Chiricahua
mountains and the Sulphur Springs and San Simon valleys—the
traditional homeland of the Chiricahua. Jeffords would be their
agent. Until three years later when Cochise died, his followers

honored this agreement, despite visits from their New Mexican cousins, the Mimbres Apache, who wanted them to go on the warpath. Cochise, through force of personality, was able to keep all but the most impatient young warriors from raiding into Mexico.

Crook was then free to take the field against the renegades. This forty-three-year-old native of Ohio and graduate of West Point, class of 1852, had risen to prominence during the Civil War, attaining the rank of major general of volunteers. At the end of that conflict he had reverted to his permanent rank of lieutenant colonel. He arrived in Arizona in 1871. At that time he usually wore a canvas suit and a Japanese summer hat, but no military trappings of any sort, not even a symbol of his rank. Because of this and his peculiar whiskers, the Apache dubbed him "Gray Fox." Once he studied the conditions of warfare in the Southwest, he discarded standard army tactics, believing that only an army capable of rapid pursuit could cope with the Indians; therefore he trained his men

Apache Indian scouts at San Carlos, Arizona; note the "Apache Kid" at the far right. *Courtesy U.S. Signal Corps, National Archives.*

to campaign in this fashion, using mules to carry their provisions and operating in extremely mobile, small units. He also decided that the best trackers of Apache were other Apache; he therefore enlisted Indians into units, designated them as Apache Scouts, commanded by his best young officers. They were paid standard army wages for their six-month enlistments.[13]

These theories were tested in the field when General Howard departed the department. During the winter of 1872-1873 Crook and his men took to the field, pressing the hostiles hard during the months when they normally could rest easy, striking them in their winter hideout and demoralizing them. The most spectacular battle of the campaign occurred on December 28, 1872, at Skull Cave, where approximately seventy-five Yavapais were killed. By the following spring all Indians in Arizona, even the Apache, had surrendered, and there was a period of relative peace to the territory. Crook was rewarded for his success by a startling promotion from lieutenant colonel to brigadier general. And when the battles were over, he continued to innovate. On the reservations he issued every Indian a numbered tag so that a quick count could be taken and the reservation-jumpers identified easily. He was hard in battle but just in peace—so much so that the Indians grew to trust him. As long as he remained in Arizona he strongly opposed concentrating all Apache at San Carlos, and he fought to keep the Indian agents honest. In 1875, however, he was transferred north—and trouble developed quickly.

When Cochise died on June 8, 1874, his oldest son, Taza, became the titular head of the Chiricahua Apache. Two years of great hardship, unrest, and disaster followed. Agent Jeffords was openly sympathetic to his charges, but so popular with them that he angered jealous functionaries in the Indian Bureau and the local citizens of Arizona—some of whom coveted the grass-covered parts of the reservation for ranches. Through pressure, the Tucson Ring persuaded officials in Washington first to cut the ration of beef to the Chiricahua, then in February 1876 to halt it entirely. Jeffords thereupon notified the Apache that they would have to supply their own meat by hunting—and Taza, who had never exercised the strong leadership of his father, was unable to prevent a split from developing within the tribe. On a hunting expedition away from the reservation, a fight developed in which shots were fired, killing two men and a young grandson of Cochise. Taza then led most of the tribe back to the reservation, but Skinya and some fifty malcontents remained in the mountains. Four of this group, along with three Coyotero Apache renegades from San Carlos, determined to raid in Mexico, and later returned with about $100 in gold dust and silver. On April 6 the station keeper at Sulphur Springs, named Rogers, sold the renegades whiskey at ten dollars a bottle in exchange for their promise to leave. The next day the Indians demanded more whiskey, but Rogers refused, whereupon they killed him and his cook, stole horses and ammunition, and fled to their camp in the Dragoon Mountains. The next day, April 8, other renegades from Skinya's band killed another white man and stole four horses.

On hearing of these incidents, Jeffords called for soldiers from nearby Fort Bowie and set out in pursuit of the renegades, assuring Taza and his peaceful followers that they would not be harmed. However, Skinya and the malcontents could not be dislodged from the Dragoons, so the troops returned to the fort. Then on June 4 Skinya slipped into Taza's camp and tried to persuade the entire Chiricahua band to go on the warpath under his leadership. They refused, and a fight developed in which Skinya and six of his followers were killed.

The Indian Bureau used these disturbances as an excuse to order the Chiricahua reservation closed and the Indians there moved to the San Carlos Agency. In fact, on May 3, more than a month before, Agent John Philip Clum of San Carlos had received instructions from Washington to go to the Chiricahua reservation, suspend Jeffords, and, if possible, move the Chiricahua to San Carlos. Clum had become agent at San Carlos on August 8, 1874—at that time he was a month short of his twenty-third birthday. Born in Claverack, New York, he had moved to New Mexico in 1871 to organize a meteorological service at Santa Fe. Nominated as an Indian agent by the Dutch Reformed Church, of which he was a member, he was filled with "brass and impudence," according to the Prescott *Arizona Miner*. Within a year after his arrival at San

John P. Clum, youthful agent at the San Carlos Reservation. *Courtesy Arizona Historical Society.*

Carlos, however, he had organized a force of Indian police, had established a court where offenders were tried by an Apache judge and jury, and had ordered the army off the reservation entirely.[14]

Clum's orders to close the Chiricahua Agency came not only because of the activities of Skinya and the renegades, but also because the reservation reportedly had become a refuge for hostiles from both sides of the international boundary. In addition, the Mimbres Apache of New Mexico frequently visited there, usually conducting

The guardhouse at San Carlos Reservation, Arizona, in the 1880s; notice the Apache Scouts serving as guards. *Courtesy Western History Collections, University of Oklahoma Library.*

small raids as they moved east and west. Another reason, however, was Jeffords' steadfast refusal to enter into connivance with the Tucson Ring to cheat his charges, and the Ring in turn had brought pressure to bear in Washington to have it closed.

Clum arrived at the Chiricahua Agency and held a conference with Taza on June 6, during which Taza agreed to remove his followers to San Carlos. On June 12 Clum started on the trip accompanied by Taza and 325 Chiricahua, only 60 of whom were warriors, the rest women and children. Some 400 bronco Chiricahua had refused to move and had fled into Mexico under the leadership of Juh, Nolgee, and a rising war leader named Geronimo. The removal of the Chiricahua to San Carlos and the closing of their separate reservation was a disastrous mistake. The various Apache bands at San Carlos hated each other, and they were living in what seemed to them very cramped quarters—4,000 were crowded onto land that originally had been home to only about 800 Apache. In addition, many of the bands were homesick. Shorted on rations, forced to farm, angry and resentful, these Apache all too often were willing recruits for a warrior promising loot, adventure, and manhood off the reservation. Yet still more Apache continued to be crowded in as more renegades were caught and brought to San Carlos. In fact, on March 20, 1877, Clum received orders from the commissioner of Indian affairs to arrest Geronimo and his followers, who reportedly were at the Ojo Caliente Reservation in New Mexico, as well as to remove Victorio and the Mimbres Apache from the same agency and bring them to San Carlos.

While these events had been transpiring in Arizona, the Mimbres Apache (also known as Mimbreños) under Victorio, Nana, and Loco had finally made their peace. For four years following the end of the Civil War they had held to their old way of life in southwestern and south-central New Mexico. However, the gradual influx of civilians in the area, especially miners, and the increasing pressure of soldiers forced them to seek peace. In 1869 the three chiefs met with army officers and Indian Bureau officials to say that all they wanted was to settle in their traditional homeland, be allowed to plant crops and tend their cattle, and live in peace. By 1871 some 1,200 of them, including members of assorted other bands such as the Gila Apache, had gathered in the vicinity of Ojo Caliente (located thirty-seven miles northwest of the present Truth or Consequences, New Mexico); there they were receiving an irregular ration of food and blankets. However, in 1871 the miners at Pinos Altos began organizing to conduct a repetition of the Camp Grant Massacre. The Mimbres heard of this plan and most fled into the mountains to escape it; the remainder were taken to the Tularosa Agency to be held with the Mescaleros there. This continued until 1874 when Tularosa was abandoned (to be reestablished later for the Mescaleros), at which time all the Mimbres then were returned to Ojo Caliente; this preserve was set aside by executive order on April 9 that year.[15] Inasmuch as *Ojo Caliente* was Spanish for Warm Springs, the Mimbres thereafter were generally referred to by whites as the Warm Springs Apache. Nearby Fort McRae supposedly would protect local whites from the Indians—and the Indians from the whites. However, the nearby miners continued to protest the presence of the Apache, and in 1877, just as Clum was ordered to arrest Geronimo, people in the Indian

Bureau arguing for consolidation of all the Apache tribes at San Carlos won out, and the decision was made to move Victorio and his people westward.

Clum, meanwhile, was reluctant to move against Geronimo without adequate military support, for that Apache leader was known to have several violent followers. They had been stealing horses, mules, and cattle in Mexico during the previous year, driving them north, and selling them to New Mexicans not bothered by the absence of a title. Clum was assured by General August V. Kautz, commander of the Department of Arizona, that his efforts would be coordinated with movements of troops from the 9th Cavalry, the rendezvous to occur on April 21 at Ojo Caliente. The Indian agent thereupon departed San Carlos with a contingent of his Apache police and volunteers from other Apache bands—only to arrive at the designated site and at the appointed hour to find the soldiers not there. Nevertheless, Clum proceeded with the arrest. On April 22 he and his force confronted Geronimo and his 110 followers. Clum's police, who had been hidden, appeared at his signal, and the Apache leader was trapped. "I have seen many looks of hate in my long life," Clum later wrote of that moment, "but never one so vicious, so vengeful. . . . When I took his rifle from him, his lips tightened and [his] . . . sneer was accentuated. The old scar on his right cheek was livid." Before Clum could leave, he was also given custody of Victorio and his followers. Victorio did not resist, and he and 342 members of his band accompanied Geronimo and his followers westward to San Carlos, arriving there on May 20.[16]

The Warm Springs Apache were decidedly unhappy at their new reservation. They viewed their removal west as a breach of faith by the government, for they had been promised they would be allowed to live in their traditional homeland. Moreover, when they were moved, they had to leave behind their half-ripened fields and many of their animals. They were made even more restless by the absence of many of their kinsmen; Loco and Nana, along with most of the warriors, had slipped away before or during the transfer to live in the mountains and raid. Then Agent John Clum resigned his post on August 15, 1877, because of disputes with army

A general view of San Carlos, Arizona. *Courtesy U.S. Signal Corps, National Archives.*

officers and Indian Bureau functionaries. H. L. Hart was appointed to succeed him, and under his direction supplies were insufficient, substandard, or not issued at all.

On the night of September 1 some 310 Warm Springs Apache men, women, and children fled San Carlos toward the east, led by Victorio. Rapid pursuit by the army, guided by White Mountain Apache scouts in government employ, forced the renegades north into the badlands south of Fort Wingate, New Mexico. There they killed a dozen ranchers, stole horses, and created widespread alarm among local civilians. After 56 of their number had been killed, the hostiles agreed to surrender at Fort Wingate; 190 of them came in immediately, to be followed later by another 50. General Edward Hatch, commander of the Department of New Mexico, was indecisive about what to do with these Apache. At length, he determined they could return to Ojo Caliente provided they proved themselves peaceful and no raids occurred in that area.

However, the Indian Bureau refused to accept guardianship of the Warm Springs Apache at Ojo Caliente, and the army was tired of watching over them. Finally the Indian Bureau agreed to take them—only after General William T. Sherman threatened to turn them loose altogether—provided they were delivered to San Carlos. On October 8, 1878, Captain F. T. Bennett arrived at Ojo Caliente with two companies of troops, only to be told by Victorio, "You can take our squaws and children in your wagons, but my men will not go!" Nor did they. He and eighty followers galloped away into the mountains, to be joined shortly by another seventeen. The remainder of the tribe, 169 of them, were loaded onto the wagons and delivered to Fort Apache, Arizona, for internment at San Carlos. That winter in the mountains was so severe that Victorio in the spring approached army officers near Ojo Caliente to plead to be allowed to return to that reservation. He was told that he and his people could go instead to the Mescalero Reservation at Tularosa, and to this he agreed. On June 30, 1879, he surrendered.

Within two months he was back in the mountains, however, for in July he was indicted by a civil grand jury at Silver City. The charges were murder and horse theft. The Warm Springs Apache heard of this indictment and grew worried. Then in September a hunting party of whites rode through the reservation; included in the group were the judge and the prosecuting attorney. Seeing them, Victorio bolted for the hills with his followers. Gathering with him in the mountains of Mexico were renegade Chiricahua and Mescalero Apache. In the year that followed he struck terror into the hearts of Mexicans and Americans alike, killing settlers, cowboys, ranchers, prospectors, and teamsters, stealing livestock and taking booty. American soldiers pursued him relentlessly, along with Texas Rangers and Mexican troops. Time after time as one force or another thought it had him trapped, he eluded them or else caught them in a clever trap. Everywhere in the Southwest the fear was that all renegade Indians of every tribe would join him to form a formidable force. The Silver City *Southwest* declared, "The number of Indians on the warpath cannot be estimated, but Victorio can now certainly command a larger force than General Hatch." Everywhere the local citizens were critical of the army for its failure to corral the renegades; the Tucson *Star* on September 16, 1880, printed a four-column editorial of biting satire headlined, "Victorio's Compliments to President Rutherford B. Hayes."

During this chase American troops began operating legally south of the border. The Mexican government allowed this, for it was equally interested in halting the raids; General Joaquin Terrazas had 1,000 soldiers in the field, and the state of Chihuahua was offering a bounty of $3,000 for Victorio's head. On Ooctober 14 the end came. Victorio and his followers were trapped in a box canyon; knowing this, General Terrazas ordered the American soldiers out of Mexico, then closed in. Apparently the final assault amounted to a massacre rather than a battle, for according to Terrazas seventy-eight Apache, including Victorio, died while only three Mexicans were killed. A Tarahumara Indian scout named Mauricio Corredor fired the shot that killed Victorio, for which he was presented a nickle-plated rifle from the government of Chihuahua. Some thirty Apache managed to escape, among them Nana, and soon this aging chief was ranging far into New Mexico and Chihuahua on his raids.[17] The pitiful remainder of the hostiles eventually straggled in to San Carlos, and there they virtually ceased to exist as a separate tribe; thereafter they became identified with the Chiricahua.

To most New Mexicans and Arizonans, the death of Victorio and the return of his followers to San Carlos seemed to signal the end of Apache hostilities. The year 1881 started peacefully enough. Then in June of 1881, Nakaidoklini (also spelled Noch-ay-del-klinne), a young medicine man part pagan-part Christian mystic, stirred the White Mountain Apache with a new religion. Described as five feet, six inches tall and weighing just 125 pounds, he had attended school in Santa Fe before returning to the Arizona reservation to meditate. Apparently he began preaching a resurrection of the dead and a disappearance of the whites, along with a dance of religious significance. Among the Apache confined on the hated reservation, his promises seemed heaven-sent, and soon there was great excitement among them.[18]

On August 15 J. C. Tiffany, the agent at San Carlos, informed Colonel Eugene A. Carr, commander of the 6th Cavalry and of nearby Fort Apache, that he wished Nakaidoklini "arrested or killed or both." Carr, known as "War Eagle," gathered a force of seventy-nine soldiers, twenty-three Indian scouts he hoped would be loyal, and nine civilians, and on August 29 departed for Cibicu Creek, forty-six miles away from the fort. Carr was extremely worried that his scouts might prove untrustworthy, that they had come under the influence of the Prophet, as Nakaidoklini was called, but he issued them ammunition because he felt he "had to take chances. They were enlisted soldiers of my command for duty; and I could not have found the Medicine man without them." The following day, August 30, he arrived at Cibicu and there arrested the Prophet without incident.

At the encampment that evening, however, the command was attacked by about 300 followers of the new religion. In the fighting the Prophet was killed by his guard. Carr and his soldiers barely reached Fort Apache the next day, pursued by angry Apache—to be welcomed by the news that they had all perished in a Custer-type massacre. Loose bands of Apache renegades were raiding everything in sight, and that same day of September 1 they attacked Fort Apache itself. This was one of the few direct attacks on an army post in the Southwest by Indians since the early days of the Navajo wars in New Mexico. They were driven off, however. Natiotish assumed the mantle of leadership of the White Mountain Apache, and a battle was fought between them and the soldiers at Chevalon Creek on July 17, 1882. Called the Battle of Big Dry Wash, it resulted in the death of twenty-two Apache and the surrender of the rest. This was the last real battle between Indian and soldier fought on Arizona soil.[19]

The Cibicu Incident had several lasting consequences. Brigadier General Orlando B. Willcox, commander of the Department of Arizona, rushed troops into the San Carlos-White Mountain Apache area, and five Apache Scouts accused of mutiny, murder, and desertion were brought to trial at Fort Grant on November 11, 1881. All were found guilty; two were dishonorably discharged and sent to prison at Alcatraz (then an army prison), while the other three were sentenced to death. The three were hanged on March 3, 1882,[20] leading to a continuing debate about the degree of their guilt. Moreover, General Willcox charged Colonel Carr with neglect of duty; Carr demanded a court of inquiry and was granted it. General Hatch came from New Mexico to preside over the

Apache Indian scouts guarding two prisoners to be hanged for the Cibecu
Incident. *Courtesy Western History Collections, University of Oklahoma
Library.*

Geronimo and Nachez (mounted). Geronimo's son Chapo stands at the right.
Courtesy Western History Collections, University of Oklahoma Library.

court. It found Carr's actions did not constitute neglect of duty but that he was guilty of errors of judgment. Later President Chester A. Arthur reviewed the case and directed the commanding general of the army to reprimand Carr.

Moreover, the presence of so many soldiers at San Carlos caused the Chiricahuas to become so nervous that seventy-four of them fled into the mountains and turned south toward Mexico. This outbreak in late September 1881 was under the leadership of the chief of the Chiricahuas, Nachez. Taza, who had succeeded his father Cochise, died on a trip to Washington in June 1876 and was followed by his younger brother Nachez (also spelled Natchez, Nachite, and Naiche). Britton Davis, an army officer in Arizona at this time, later wrote, "Nachite was a good warrior with no peace scruples; but he was fond of the ladies, liked dancing and a good time generally, and was not serious enough for the responsibilities of leadership." Thus this titular head of the Chiricahuas depended for advice on the two leading war chiefs of the tribe, Juh and Geronimo. Juh (also spelled Ju and Woo, and pronounced "ho") was married to Geronimo's favorite sister, and he and Nachez were on good terms. Even though by 1881 he was growing old and fat, he was the most likely successor to Nachez as tribal leader should Nachez die. Geronimo was not related to Chiricahua chieftains and could never become head man of the tribe. Yet it was Geronimo who would gradually exercise all the prerogatives of leadership and who would become the best known of all Chiricahua warriors and chieftains.

According to his own biography, dictated to S. M. Barrett in 1906, Geronimo was born in No-doyohn Canyon, Arizona, in June 1829. His grandfather, Maco, was a chief of the Mimbres Apache, but his father had married outside the tribe and therefore had forfeited his hereditary rights; thus on Maco's death, Mangas Coloradas had become the chief. Of his childhood Geronimo recalled, "I was warmed by the sun, rocked by the winds, and sheltered by the trees as other Indian babes." His mother had taught him the legends of his people, while his father told him "of the brave deeds of warriors, of the pleasures of the chase, and of the glories of the warpath." At age seventeen he was admitted to the council of warriors and took a wife. To them three children were born, "children," said Geronimo, "that played, loitered, and worked as I had done." Then in 1858, when the Chiricahua were on a trading expedition at Janos, Chihuahua, the men went into town to trade while the women and children remained in camp a short distance away; when the men returned, they found that scalp bounty hunters had attacked in their absence, killing, among others, Geronimo's wife, children, and mother. He said of this incident, "I could not call back my loved ones, I could not bring back the dead Apaches, but I could rejoice in . . . revenge." Until that time he apparently had been indolent, even good-natured, for his name had been Goyakla, which means "He Who Yawns." He became a deadly warrior, rising steadily in stature until he became a war chief.[21]

General George Crook with his favorite mule, Apache, and two Indian scouts, Dutchy and Alchise. *Courtesy U.S. Signal Corps, National Archives.*

In the year following the outbreak of September 1881, the renegades had not been caught; in fact, their numbers had grown as more and more young warriors slipped away from San Carlos to join them in their mountain hideouts. Then on September 4, 1882, General George Crook returned to take command of the department from Orlando B. Willcox. Crook's major problem, once back in Arizona, was to regain the confidence the Apache had placed in him earlier. They no longer seemed willing to believe the words of a government official, not even those of the commanding general. To combat this attitude, Crook first sought the removal of several Indian agents who were hampering his work. In this he was successful, replacing them with young army officers of high integrity. Once the Indians still on the reservations began receiving regular rations, they looked upon Crook as a man interested in Indian welfare and one whose word could be trusted. This word, he knew, would filter down to the renegades in Mexico.

This accomplished, he sought to force the hostiles out of Mexico and back to the reservations. To accomplish this, he had to penetrate their mountain hideouts in the Sierra Madre of Sonora; this was made possible by a treaty between Mexico and the United States, signed on July 29, 1882, which allowed soldiers of either nation to cross the international boundary in pursuit of renegades. Then, just as Crook was preparing a campaign in Sonora for March 1883, a small band of hostiles led by Chatto stormed out of Mexico on a raid into Arizona.

Chatto's group came into the southern part of the territory searching for ammunition. Along the way they murdered Judge H. C. McComas and his wife and carried off their six-year-old son Charles; later the boy was found dead. This incident created a national sensation because of the prominence of the judge, and a cry was raised in the newspapers for the punishment of the guilty Indians. One Chiricahua, known as Tso-ay by the Indians and Peaches by the Americans, deserted Chatto's group during this raid, however, and tried to return to the reservation. Captured and taken to Crook for questioning, Peaches agreed to lead the soldiers to the Chiricahua hideout in Sonora. Crook crossed into Sonora with 45 cavalrymen and 193 Apache Scouts, and on May 15 he surprised the renegades at their village high in the Sierra. However, Crook was committed to a policy of negotiation, not extermination, and there, in a region of immense gorges and gloomy mountains seemingly piled one atop another, he talked with them. On May 21 Geronimo, in a tense talk with the general, stated that he wanted peace. Subsequently other chiefs came in, one by one, to talk. On May 23 Crook started home with 285 Apaches who claimed to be tired of war and who wanted only to live at San Carlos in peace. Eventually all the renegades would come in and surrender, so that by January 1884 all were back on the reservation. Peace had been restored, and Crook again was the hero of the hour.[22]

Yet the Apache had never been disarmed or dismounted, and they grew increasingly unhappy at San Carlos—as well they might.

Indian dwellings near the San Carlos Agency, Arizona. *Courtesy National Archives.*

Called "Hell's Forty Acres" by the soldiers stationed there, it was hot, dusty, and barren. Functionaries in the Indian Bureau decreed that the Apache on this reservation should become farmers and sent them harness, plows, two dozen picks and shovels, and a few bags of corn and wheat for seed; but the harness was designed for draught animals twice the size of the small Indian ponies, and even when hitched the horses ran away with peril to the life of those trying to plow, and the point was more frequently above ground than below it. Moreover, the rations promised the Indians by the terms of their agreements to accept reservations were inadequate; despite Crook's efforts, agents again were in charge of this distribution of food—and profiteering. The weekly flour ration "would hardly suffice for a day," said Captain John G. Bourke, General Crook's aide, while the beef delivered contained "not enough fat . . . to fry a jackrabbit." Lieutenant Britton Davis, who was stationed at San Carlos, later stated that some of the cattle delivered to the reservation for rations had to be brought on wagons because they were so old and debilitated.[23]

George Crook was aware that these practices were undermining Apache morale. On October 5, 1882, he had issued General Order No. 43 in which he stated, "Officers and soldiers serving this department are reminded that one of the fundamental principles of the military character is justice to all—Indians as well as white men—and that a disregard of this principle is likely to bring about hostilities, and cause the death of the very persons they are sent here to protect." Yet Crook, in his zeal to uplift the Indians, was one of the causes of their discontent, for he had decreed well-intentioned changes in their social code. He insisted that the Apache not make or drink *tiswin* (a native beer); the Apache responded that officers, soldiers, and civilians regularly drank something "to make them feel good" and wanted to know why they could not. Crook also had forbidden the beating of wives, an ancient Apache custom, just as he also insisted that Apache warriors no longer bite off the nose of an adulterous squaw.

On May 15, 1885, the situation came to a head. That morning a large body of Chiricahua Apache confronted Lieutenant Britton Davis, who had immediate charge of them; to him they said they all drank *tiswin* and asked, "What are you going to do about it? Are you going to put us all in jail? You have no jail big enough even if you could put us all in jail." Davis telegraphed General Crook for instructions, but as the telegram went up through the channels of command it was pigeon-holed by Captain Francis C. Pierce, who failed to recognize its significance.[24] Two days then passed, days in which the Apache waiting in front of Davis' tent grew more and more apprehensive. Then on Sunday, May 17, 132 of them fled into the mountains—while the remaining 400 Chiricahua and Warm Springs Apache remained peacefully at San Carlos. Davis could not report their flight until the next day, for the renegades had cut the telegraph line and then spliced the cut with rawhide so effectively that it was difficult to locate. By that time Geronimo, Nachez, and the hostiles were nearing the Mexican border. Crook later stated, "I am firmly convinced that had I known of the occurrence reported in Lieutenant Davis's telegram . . . the outbreak . . . would not have occurred."[25]

Apache Scouts and soldiers in a posed photograph. *Courtesy Western History Collections, University of Oklahoma Library.*

Governor Luis E. Torres of Sonora was so eager to have American troops come into his state in pursuit of the hostiles that he asked Crook, in a face-to-face meeting that summer, to send them —despite the fact that the treaty of July 29, 1882, had expired. He informed the American general that he would "not interfere with the operations" of troops, and, in fact, issued instructions to the commanders of all prefects to aid the Americans.[26] During that summer and fall, however, no contact could be made that resulted in negotiations; instead there were isolated raids into Arizona and New Mexico by the hostiles, followed by hot pursuit into Mexico.

Then on December 11, 1885, the Apache Scouts took the field under the leadership of Captain Emmet Crawford. Six feet, one inch tall, gray-eyed, untiring, and a man respected by the Apache, Crawford jogged his scouts into Sonora and on January 8, 1886, they found fresh sign. Pushing rapidly ahead during the next forty-eight hours, going without sleep in a desperate drive to make contact, Crawford came upon them an hour before daybreak on January 10 deep inside Sonora. A sharp fight followed, after which Geronimo and the hostiles escaped. That evening, however, a squaw came in as an emissary from the renegades to request a conference the next morning. Crawford agreed readily, for his goal was to persuade the Apache to go north to negotiate with Crook.

Shortly before dawn the next morning, Mexican irregulars—in reality, scalp bounty hunters—came upon the American camp and began firing into it. Captain Crawford jumped atop a rock and shouted in Spanish that his followers were American soldiers; he was shot through the head—reportedly by Mauricio Corredor, the killer of Victorio—and a sharp fight followed between scouts and Mexicans. Geronimo and the hostiles up the canyon heard the shooting and fled. Crawford's chief lieutenant, Marion P. Maus, took command and was able, five days later, to re-establish contact with the hostiles, and from them he secured a promise that they

Apache scouts under the command of Lieutenant Marion P. Maus. This photograph was made at the time of Geronimo's first surrender conference. *Courtesy Western History Collections, University of Oklahoma Library.*

Geronimo's camp just before his surrender conference with General Crook in March 1886. *Courtesy Western History Collections, University of Oklahoma Library.*

would meet General Crook within two months to begin negotiating.[27]

This conference took place at Canon de los Embudos, Sonora (ten miles below the international boundary), on March 25-27. Crook came to the meeting with orders from Washington to get an unconditional surrender from the hostiles with no other promise made "unless it is necessary to secure their surrender." The unconditional surrender proved impossible to secure, but he did get the hostiles to agree to two years' imprisonment in Florida and then a return to their Arizona homeland. Geronimo concluded his speech by stating, "Once I moved about like the wind. Now I surrender to you and that is all." The conference over, Crook immediately returned to Fort Bowie, leaving Lieutenant Maus to escort the surrendered Apache to that post.[28] On the way, however, a wandering whiskey peddler, Bob Tribollet—a known crony of the Tucson ring—sold spirits to the Indians and told them they would be mur-

Geronimo and his warriors at the surrender conference with General Crook.
Courtesy Western History Collections, University of Oklahoma Library.

dered north of the line; that afternoon under cover of a dark, rainy
sky, Geronimo, Nachez, eighteen warriors, thirteen women, and six
children, a total of thirty-nine renegades, decided to return to their
hideout in the Sonoran mountains.

On March 30 Crook wired General Phil Sheridan, commanding
general of the army, of Geronimo's flight. Sheridan responded by
questioning the integrity and honor of the scouts, saying the outbreak could not have occurred without their knowledge. Crook
thereupon tendered his resignation as commander of the department, and on April 2 this was accepted. Moreover, Geronimo's return to the mountains was used by the government as an excuse to
break Crook's promise to those Apache who had surrendered and
had come back to Arizona; they were to be confined in Florida not
for two years but indefinitely.[29]

What Crook could not know at this time was that President
Grover Cleveland had been stung by the nationwide cries of out-
rage stemming from the Apache raids and therefore had determined on a new solution to the problem. As the first Democrat to

occupy the White House in twenty-four years—and facing the off-year elections of 1886 in a nation almost evenly divided between Democrats and Republicans—he wanted the army to win an unconditional surrender from the Apache and then to turn them over to civil juries in Arizona. That Arizona juries probably would hang the Indians promptly bothered him not at all. And the man he person-

Brigadier General Nelson A. Miles. *Courtesy U.S. Signal Corps, Brady Collection, National Archives.*

ally selected to accomplish this task was Brigadier General Nelson A. Miles.

Born in Massachusetts in 1839, Miles had completed high school at age seventeen, then had gone to work in Collomare's Crockery Store in Boston. There at night he studied military tactics with an aging veteran of the Napoleonic wars. At the outbreak of the Civil War he used his savings and borrowed money to raise a company of volunteers and was commissioned a lieutenant; however, he felt he would have been captain of a regiment but for politics and transferred to the 61st New York Volunteers. During the war he rose to prominence; four times he was wounded, and he emerged a major general of volunteers and a recipient of the Medal of Honor. At the conclusion of the conflict he elected to remain in the army, for its uniform and the pomp and ceremony appealed to a young man who had previously led a drab life. Marrying Mary Hoyt Sherman, niece of General William T. Sherman and of Senator John Sherman of Ohio, he managed to secure a colonelcy for himself—much to his disappointment, for he had hoped to retain at least one star. In the next decade and a half he fought in half a dozen Indian campaigns, helping defeat the Nez Perce, the Comanche, and the Cheyenne. He was promoted to brigadier general in 1880, but in 1886 he was smarting under his failure to get a second star. Therefore he came to Arizona determined to secure Geronimo's surrender, for he realized the Indian wars were fast coming to a close.[30]

On April 11 he assumed command of the Department of Arizona, which had been strengthened to 5,000 men by this time—one fifth of the United States Army. His first action was to send the Apache Scouts to the reservation for discharge. Next he began erecting what would prove to be an expensive toy, the heliograph. Finally, he selected 100 of "the best athletes in our service" to pursue Geronimo and the hostiles in the field, men who would hound the hostiles so relentlessly that they would surrender unconditionally. The man chosen to lead this force was Captain Henry Ware Lawton, like Miles a non-West Pointer and veteran of the Civil War. Assigned to Lawton's command at his own request was Leonard Wood, an assistant contract surgeon from Boston then serving in Arizona. On May 9 these men, whom Miles called "the strongest and best soldiers that could be found," took the field—to be led a merry chase; in the next three months they were led a disheartening chase through some of the most rugged country in North America.[31]

Then early in July came a report from Mexico that Geronimo and Nachez were negotiating with the prefect at Bavispe to surrender to Mexican authorities. Such an event would rob Miles of the glory he sought, and he accordingly changed tactics. If his "athletes" could not force a surrender, then he would gain it by Crook's policy of diplomacy and negotiation. He therefore took two steps. To officials in Washington he proposed the removal of all Chiricahua and Warm Springs Apache to Florida—despite the fact that most of these had never fled the reservation and that some of them were still officially enlisted in the army as Apache Scouts. An order to this effect was approved by President Cleveland, however, and the Apache were sent by train on a "trail of tears" to Fort Marion, Florida.[32]

Next, Miles selected two Chiricahua from Fort Apache, Martine and Kayitah, and promised them a liberal reward if they would guide Lieutenant Charles B. Gatewood to the renegade camp. Gatewood, a West Pointer, a native of Maryland, and a former commander of Apache scouts, spoke the language and was known personally by Geronimo and Nachez; his task was to persuade the Apache to meet Miles for a conference to negotiate terms. Guided by the two Apache, Gatewood made his way deep into Sonora, and on August 25 he went alone and unarmed into the renegades' camp to confer with them. He later recalled that he felt "chilly twitching movements" when he came face to face with the Apache leaders. His message from Miles was, "Surrender and be sent to Florida"; Geronimo, after lengthy haggling, responded, "Take us to the reservation or fight." Gatewood was in a quandary; "I couldn't take him to the reservation, and I couldn't fight, neither could I run nor yet feel comfortable," he later recalled.

At this point he had only one other comment to make: why should the Apache want to return to the reservation in Arizona when their relatives were in Florida? Nachez' mother and his daughter, along with Geronimo's family, had been removed eastward. This information stunned the hostiles, for they had not yet learned of the move. After more questions, the Apache went to their camp for the night to discuss their next move, while Gatewood went to the camp of Captain Lawton to await an answer. The next morning, August 26, Geronimo and the renegades came to this camp to tell Gatewood that they would talk with Miles about surrender. At this time Lawton and Wood finally met the men they had been chasing for so long.[33]

As the hostiles marched northward to the international boundary, Miles became increasingly reluctant to meet with them until they had been disarmed and dismounted. Apparently he did not want to suffer Crook's fate should any of the Chiricahua break for the mountains again. To Lawton he telegraphed, "If the Indians give you any guarantee or hostages that they will surrender to me, I will go down, or you can use *any* other means you think available. You will be justified in using *any* measures." Lawton clearly understood the treachery his general was proposing, but he wanted no part of it; in reply he telegraphed, "They [the Apache] are unusually alert and watchful, and to surprise them is simply impossible. I could by treachery perhaps kill one or two of them, but it would only make everything much worse than before." Moreover, Lawton understood the danger to his own career, for he concluded that telegram, "I would be glad to have an officer directly from yourself come out and take command."[34]

Miles approached the conference nervously, as did the Apache, both for different reasons, but the meeting did take place on September 3-4 at Skeleton Canyon, Arizona. At this time Miles promised the Apache that they would be reunited with their families in Florida, that all would be held there for two years, and then all would be returned to Arizona. On this basis the hostiles surrendered, to be marched north and on September 8 put aboard a train for the east.

The President and his advisers were astonished to learn that the Apache hostiles, whom he wanted captured on the basis of unconditional surrender, were on their way to Florida. Hot telegrams to General Miles produced only evasive double-talk, whereupon the President had the train carrying the Apache halted at San Antonio.

A few of the Chiricahua Apache who surrendered to General Miles in September 1886. This photograph was made at San Antonio. Chapo, son of Geronimo, is at the extreme right. *Courtesy Western History Collections, University of Oklahoma Library.*

There General D. S. Stanley questioned Geronimo about the terms under which he had surrendered. When finally aware of the terms granted these hostiles, President Cleveland immediately broke them by ordering those on the train sent to Fort Pickens, Florida, not to Fort Marion where the other Chiricahua and Warm Springs Apache were being held. Nor were they returned to Arizona in two years. Instead they were transferred to Mount Vernon Barracks, Alabama, in 1888, and six years later were taken to Fort Sill, Oklahoma. There they were held as prisoners of war until 1915.[35]

The "Geronimo Campaign," as it came to be known, brought the Indian wars of the Southwest to a close. No longer would troops be called to chase hostiles in the region. Instead the Indian would be an administrative problem, one to be handled by bureaucrats who were sometimes well-intentioned, sometimes do-gooders, sometimes downright stupid, sometimes evil.

CONCLUSION

The voices are still now, voices that once preached death and destruction. The contest on the field of battle ended almost nine decades ago, and the participants in those events are gone almost without exception. After 1886 the Indian had become an administrative problem, not a military one. The reservations became a policing system whereby the Indians were to be fed and where half-hearted attempts would be made to teach them to farm. Good intentions were the vehicle for the passage of the Dawes Act of 1887. According to the do-gooders who motivated this act—most of them self-appointed—the best way to make the Indians become farmers was to encourage them to take up 160 acres under the homestead provisions that had been established in 1862. In short, the intent was to break up the Indian tribes, to dissolve the reservations, to force each Indian head-of-family to accept 160 acres and to send his children to a white school, and to cause the Indians to forget their tribal heritage.

Yet the tears of the living mingled with the blood of the dead and formed a strong fertilizer, one that grew an enduring crop of hatred and misunderstanding. Despite the efforts of men of reason —red and white—the wars still continue in a broad sense. The Indians would be given citizenship in 1924, but even today a debate continues as to what type of citizens they should be. The fundamental cause of this war, as of the battles fought between 1846 and 1886, was two philosophies of life directly in opposition. The Indians involved in that four-decade struggle in the Southwest—Apache, Comanche, and Navajo—had a life style based on aggression and the raw use of force. Their social, economic, and political systems demanded raiding and, as a concomitant, killing and the abduction of women and children. Today their descendants argue that the land of their fathers was taken from them by force, forgetting that their ancestors took the same land by force from an earlier owner who either was killed or else driven so far away that he did not remain to complain.

Their opponents in this contest for the Southwest were American frontiersmen unwilling to allow a few tribes of "uncivilized" natives to have domain over a land containing fertile acres, good grass, and mineral wealth. These newcomers felt they had a right to the land because of a superior civilization and that the old order had to give way. Yet these Americans brought with them the intellectual baggage of their own ancestors, who had come to the New World believing in the Anglo-Saxon common law and the Christian ethic; both of these stressed the sacredness of life and the sanctity of property. To salve his conscience and prove that it was ethical to kill the Indians and take their land, this white man had to convince himself somehow that the Christian ethic and the Anglo-Saxon common law pertained only to "humans" and that the natives were something less (this has been a problem in every American war: to change young men into killers when they have been taught since birth to respect life and property). This change in attitude toward the Indian was wrought by propaganda of an enduring sort.

From the time of Jamestown and Plymouth Rock forward to the third quarter of the nineteenth century, a quarter of a millennium, whites told each other that the Indians were murderers of men, rapers of women, kidnappers of children, and thieves without peer. William Tecumseh Sherman capsuled this attitude in his famous comment, "The only good Indian is a dead Indian," which at once became a justification and an inspiration for killing. General John Pope, commanding the Division of the Missouri, wrote in January

1880, "Everybody knows beyond the probability of dispute that the Indians on this reservation (like all the Apaches) are a miserable, brutal race, cruel, deceitful and wholly irreclaimable—although for years they have been fed by the government and 'civilized' by their agent, they are in no respect different from what they were when the process began."

With officials in high places expressing such sentiment, little wonder that it filtered down to the common man, especially on the frontier. Benjamin Butler Harris, bound for the gold fields of California in the spring of 1849, was told by a settler on the banks of the Brazos River in Texas, "Shoot at every Indian you see and save them a life of misery in subsisting on snakes, lizards, skunks, and other disgusting objects."[1] Ambrose Bierce, the angry young man of the post-Civil War era who compiled his acidic view of life in *The Devil's Dictionary*, defined "Aborigines" as "Persons of little worth found cumbering the soil of a newly discovered country. They soon cease to cumber; they fertilize." Many frontier Americans agreed with this definition and did their best to make it come true.

Simultaneously the Indians needed no propaganda to ready themselves to kill. Their view of humanity was limited, for they felt it all was contained within their immediate tribe. Killing was murder only when done within the tribe. The one who did it outside the tribe gained social and political standing, as well as material wealth through taking the goods of the deceased. Such had been their attitude long before the coming of the whites. The Navajo and other tribes had captured slaves, while the Comanche and Apache practiced the most terrible cruelties by torturing warriors captured in battle. Even the names which these tribes called themselves translate as "the people," implying most strongly that they saw themselves as human and everyone else as something less.

Thus at the time whites and Indians met each other in the Southwest for the first time, they already looked upon each other as less than human. Therefore each felt it was not only right but even a positive good to kill the other and to take from him. Murder had been dignified, bringing with it honor and standing and somehow equating with "manhood." For the Indian it was the route to political power as a war chief, while for the white it meant standing and respect in his community. War between two such cultures was inevitable. And because the whites were numerically superior and more advanced technologically, their ultimate victory was predictable.

Yet at the end of these wars in 1886, when the tribes had been forced to accept permanent reservations, they did not disappear. True the physical threat they posed was gone; no longer did the lonely frontiersmen fear the sounds of the night, thinking the hoot of an owl or the howl of a coyote might presage a crimsoned tomahawk. Therefore his image of the Indian began to change. He did at last concede that the native Americans were human, but not adults. By law the Indians became wards of the government, which implied a child-parent relationship. The Indian was seen as a child —and a drunken, lazy one at that, for on the reservations frustration and lack of jobs caused some Indians to turn to alcohol.

To a large extent this image still pertains. The white too often sees the Indian as not yet a true adult, while the Indians see whites as oppressors who have stolen their land and imprisoned them. There has never been a concerted effort on either side to see the other as adult humans. Recent books, some of them on the bestseller list for months, have been propaganda of the old type, wretched as history and biased in attitude, making no attempt to achieve a balance between the two races. Many recent works have depicted the Indian as human and the whites as inhuman, just as earlier works portrayed the white as human and the Indian as inhuman. Pronouncements by militant Indians have carried this same theme—that the whites are villainous ogres who have degraded the noble Redman. Simultaneously, however, many of the practices of the Bureau of Indian Affairs are designed to perpetuate the status of the Indian as a child. Neither side yet is able wholly to concede the other the status of adult humans. The sins of our fathers have plagued us the Biblical seven generations and more.

And in these cross-currents of prejudice and hatred, democracy has lost. The melting pot has not worked. In fact, some insist violently that it should not work; however, the fabric of the country should be strong enough to withstand variant cultures and ethnic groups under the same umbrella of representative government. If indeed the American people believe in the credo of the Founding Fathers that "All men are created equal; that they are endowed by their Creator with certain unalienable rights; that among these are life, liberty, and the pursuit of happiness," then what is needed today to solve the enduring Indian-white problem is men of reason, not men of rage; men of humanity; not men of hate; and men of breadth of spirit and understanding, not men who preach meanness and misunderstanding.

To the extent that both Indian and white have denied one another their humanity, then to that extent both have demeaned democracy and the republican ideal. To the extent that hatred and war have prevailed, to that extent we have belittled the ideals and concepts of the Founding Fathers—and demeaned our own humanity. Every blow, physical and verbal, red and white, has diminished us and damaged the fabric of ourselves. To continue pointing to the sins of the past three centuries—and the sins are on both sides of the racial barrier—is to continue to fight in the future.

The great chief of the Sioux, Crazy Horse, might well have been speaking for both sides when he stated, "The war will end when the Indian is treated as any other American."

NOTES

Chapter 1

1 Elsie Clews Parsons, *Pueblo Indian Religion* (2 vols., Chicago: University of Chicago Press, 1939); Edgar Lee Hewett, *The Pueblo Indian World* (Albuquerque: University of New Mexico and School of American Research, 1945).

2 Edward F. Castetter and Willis H. Bell, *Pima and Papago Indian Agriculture* (Albuquerque: University of New Mexico Press, 1942); for the Maricopa, Leslie Spier, *Yuman Tribes of the Gila River* (Chicago: University of Chicago Press, 1933).

3 For the Yuma and the Mohave, see Jack D. Forbes, *Warriors of the Colorado* (Norman: University of Oklahoma Press, 1960).

4 Frank C. Lockwood, *The Apache Indians* (New York, 1938); Gordon Baldwin, *The Warrior Apaches* (Tucson: Dale S. King, 1966); Morris E. Opler, *An Apache Life-Way* (Chicago: University of Chicago Press, 1941); Will C. Barnes, *Apaches and Longhorns* (Los Angeles: Ward Ritchie Press, 1941).

5 Frances E. Watkins, *The Navajos* (Los Angeles: The Southwest Museum, 1945); Ruth M. Underhill, *The Navajos* (Norman: University of Oklahoma Press, 1956).

6 Ernest Wallace and E. Adamson Hoebel, *The Comanches: Lords of the South Plains* (Norman: University of Oklahoma Press, 1952).

7 For a look at Indian life through this period in the Southwest, see Edward H. Spicer, *Cycles of Conquest: The Impact of Spain, Mexico, and the United States on the Indians of the Southwest* (Tucson: University of Arizona Press, 1962).

8 For a brief overview of Spanish relations with some of these Indians, see Jack D. Forbes, *Apache, Navajo, and Spaniard* (Norman:
University of Oklahoma Press, 1960).

9 Robert M. Utley, *Frontiersmen in Blue: The United States Army
and the Indian, 1848-1865* (New York, 1967); Don Rickey, Jr., *Forty
Miles a Day on Beans and Hay: The Enlisted Soldier Fighting the
Indian Wars* (Norman: University of Oklahoma Press, 1963).

Chapter 2

1 Edward Sapir and Harry Joijer, *Navajo Texts* (Iowa City: Linguistic Society of America, University of Iowa Press, 1942), 331.

2 D. C. Allen, *Col. Alexander W. Doniphan: His Life and Character*,
in William E. Connelley, *Doniphan's Expedition* . . . (Topeka,
Kansas: Crane & Co., 1907), 27.

3 Quoted in Connelley, *Doniphan's Expedition*, 266; see also Philip
St. George Cooke, *The Conquest of New Mexico and California in
1846-1848* (New York, 1878), 75.

4 Quoted in Frank McNitt, *Navajo Wars: Military Campaigns, Slave
Raids, and Reprisals* (Albuquerque: University of New Mexico Press,
1972), 101.

5 Marcellus Ball Edwards, Diary, quoted in *Marching with the Army
of the West*, edited by Ralph P. Bieber (Vol. 4 of Southwest Historical Series, Glendale: Arthur H. Clark, 1936), 32.

6 John Taylor Hughes, *Doniphan's Expedition* (Cincinnati: U. P.
James, 1847).

7 Quoted in Hughes, *Doniphan's Expedition*, 307.

8 *Ibid.*, 275.

9 Edwards, Diary, quoted in *Marching with the Army of the West*,
212-13.

10 See the Diary of Philip Gooch Ferguson in *Marching with the
Army of the West*, 320-21, and *Santa Fe Republican*, September 10,
1847.

11 *Santa Fe Republican*, April 2, 1848.

12 *Ibid.*, May 21, 1848.

13 *Ibid.*, July 8, 1848.

14 For the text of the treaty signed on September 9, 1849, see James H. Simpson, *Journal of a Military Reconnaissance from Santa Fe, New Mexico, to the Navajo Country made in 1849*, in *Senate Executive Document 64*, 31 Cong., 2 Sess. (reprinted as *Navajo Expedition*, edited by Frank McNitt, Norman: University of Oklahoma Press, 1964, 258-61).

15 Annie H. Abel (comp. and ed.), *Official Correspondence of James S. Calhoun while Indian Agent at Santa Fe and Superintendent of Indian Affairs in New Mexico* (Washington, D.C.: Government Printing Office, 1915).

16 J. Manuel Espinosa, ed., "Memoir of a Kentuckian in New Mexico," *New Mexico Historical Review*, XIII (January 1938), 7.

17 Proclamation of James S. Calhoun, quoted in Abel, *Official Correspondence*, 302.

18 Abel, *Official Correspondence*, 305-6.

19 *Ibid.*, 383-84.

20 For accounts of this foray, see Richard H. Dillon, ed., *A Cannoneer in Navajo Country: The Journal of Josiah M. Rice* (Denver: Old West Publishing Company, 1970); Clinton E. Brooks and Frank D. Reeve, eds., "A Dragoon in New Mexico, 1850-1856," *New Mexico Historical Review*, XXII (January 1947), 79-81.

21 Abel, *Official Correspondence*, 433-34.

22 Henry L. Dodge file, Arizona Historical Society, Tucson.

23 For a study of the silver work of the Navajo, especially as it was reflected in their horse trappings, see Laverne S. Clark, *They Sang for Horses: The Impact of the Horse on Navajo and Apache Folklore* (Tucson: University of Arizona Press, 1966).

24 A copy of this treaty is in McNitt, *Navajo Wars*, 436-40.

25 See Washington Irving, *The Adventures of Captain Bonneville, U.S.A., in the Far West . . .*, edited by Edgeley W. Todd (Norman: University of Oklahoma Press, 1961).

26 Details of these events are in McNitt, *Navajo Wars*, 341-429, and Lynn R. Bailey, *The Long Walk: A History of the Navajo Wars, 1846-68* (Los Angeles: Westernlore Press, 1964), 93-122. Both of these books are excellent on the plight of the Navajo during this time.

Chapter 3

1 For details on this treaty, as well as on the life of Colonel Canby, see Max L. Heyman, *Prudent Soldier: A Biography of Major General E. R. S. Canby, 1817-1873* (Glendale: Arthur H. Clarke, 1959).

2 Marc Simmons, "A Horse Race at Fort Fauntleroy: An Incident of the Navajo Wars," *La Gaceta*, V (No. 1, 1970), quotes one anonymous account of this affair; other testimony is in "Condition of the Indian Tribes," *Senate Executive Document 156*, 39 Cong., 2 Sess.

3 For a history of the Civil War in this region, see Robert L. Kerby, *The Confederate Invasion of New Mexico, 1861-1862* (Los Angeles: Westernlore Press, 1958); George W. Baylor, *John Robert Baylor: Confederate Governor of Arizona* (edited by Odie B. Faulk, Tucson: Arizona Pioneers' Historical Society, 1966).

4 For details on his life, see Aurora Hunt, *Major General James Henry Carleton, 1814-1873: Western Frontier Dragoon* (Glendale: Arthur H. Clark, 1958).

5 Lincoln's approval for this reservation is noted in *House Executive Document 1*, 38 Cong., 2 Sess.; see also *Report on the Condition of the Tribes, 1867* (Washington, D.C.: Government Printing Office, 1867), 238.

6 Santa Fe *Gazette*, January 21, 1865.

7 *Ibid.*

8 *Report on Condition of Tribes*, 108.

9 Quoted in M. Morgan Estergreen, *Kit Carson: A Portrait in Courage* (Norman: University of Oklahoma Press, 1962), 24-25. For additional biographical details, see Harvey L. Carter, *Dear Old Kit: The Historical Christopher Carson* (Norman: University of Oklahoma Press, 1968).

10 For a copy of this, see Milo M. Quaife, *Kit Carson's Autobiography* (Chicago: Lakeside Classics, 1935, and reprint).

11 *Report on Condition of Tribes*, 114.

12 *Ibid.*, 128.

13 *Ibid.*, 124.

14 *The War of the Rebellion: A Compilation of the Official Records of the Union and Confederate Armies* (128 vols., Washington, D.C.:

Government Printing Office, 1880-1901), Series 1, XXVI, part 1, 235. Hereafter cited as *Official Records*.

15 *Ibid.*, XXXIV, part 1, 34.

16 *Report on Condition of Tribes*, 132.

17 *Official Records*, Series 1, XLVIII, part 1, 899.

18 *Ibid.*, XXVI, part 1, 255-56.

19 Quoted in Estergreen, *Kit Carson*, 250.

20 *Report on Condition of Tribes*, 161.

21 *Official Records*, Series 1, XLI, part 3, 261.

22 *House Executive Document 70*, 38 Cong., 1 Sess.

23 *Official Records*, Series 1, XLI, part 2, 898-900, and XV, part 1, 665-66.

24 *Report on Condition of Tribes*, 161.

25 *Official Records*, Series 1, XLI, part 2, 192; Santa Fe *Gazette*, October 8, 1864.

26 Santa Fe *Gazette*, January 26, 1867.

27 *House Executive Document 308*, 40 Cong., 2 Sess., 677-79, contains a copy of Sherman's telegram.

Chapter 4

1 Cabello to Croix, No. 186, February 12, 1780, Bexar Archives (Austin: University of Texas Archives); Croix, "General Report of 1781," translated and quoted in A. B. Thomas, *Teodoro de Croix and the Northern Frontier of New Spain, 1776-1783* (Norman: University of Oklahoma Press, 1941), 74, 77.

2 Mattie A. Hatcher, *The Opening of Texas to Foreign Settlement* (Austin: University of Texas Bulletin 2714, 1927), 224-25.

3 Hugh McLeod to M. B. Lamar, March 20, 1840, quoted in *Richmond* (Texas) *Telescope and Texas Register*, April 4, 1840; see also *Journals of the House of Representatives of the Republic of Texas*, 5 Cong., 1 Sess., Appendix, 133ff.

4 For an eyewitness account, see Houston (Texas) *Telegraph and Texas Register*, September 3, 1840.

5   For Felix Huston's report of this battle, see *Journals of the House of Representatives of the Republic of Texas*, 5 Cong., 1 Sess., Appendix, 141ff; for other accounts, see Houston *Telegraph and Texas Register*, August 19 and 26, September 3, 1840.

6   For Moore's report, see Houston *Telegraph and Texas Register*, November 18, 1840.

7   The standard history of this unique organization is Walter P. Webb, *The Texas Rangers* (Boston, 1935).

8   Walter P. Webb, ed., *The Handbook of Texas* (2 vols., Austin: Texas State Historical Association, 1952), II, 335.

9   For details about this era, see Martin L. Crimmins, "Colonel Robert E. Lee's Report on Indian Combats in Texas," *Southwestern Historical Quarterly*, XXXIX (July 1935), 21-32; Lena C. Koch, "Federal Indian Policy in Texas, 1845-1860," *Southwestern Historical Quarterly*, XXVIII (1924), 223-24; XXIX (1925), 19-35, 98-127; Rupert N. Richardson, *The Comanche Barrier to South Plains Settlement* (Glendale: Arthur H. Clark, 1933), 222-58.

10   Abel, ed., *Official Correspondence*, 105, 106, 161.

11   Nollie Mumey, ed., *March of the First Dragoons to the Rocky Mountains in 1835: The Diaries and Maps of Lemuel Ford* (Denver: Eames Brothers Press, 1957), 72; and Elliott Coues, ed., *The Journal of Jacob Fowler* (New York, 1898), 72-73.

12   "Report of Major Ruff, July 3, 1860," quoted in *Annual Report of the Secretary of War, 1860*, in *Senate Executive Document 1*, 36 Cong., 2 Sess., 58.

13   See Santa Fe *Weekly Gazette*, November 3, 1860, for details.

14   *Ibid.*, June 8, 1861.

15   For additional information about events in New Mexico during this period, see the Annual Reports of the Commissioner of Indian Affairs, 1857, 1858, 1859, and 1860. The best secondary account of the Comanchero traffic is in Charles L. Kenner, *A History of New Mexican-Plains Indian Relations* (Norman: University of Oklahoma Press, 1969), 78-97, 115-37.

Chapter 5

1   Lieutenant A. L. Anderson to Lieutenant Colonel William Chapman, June 19, 1861, *Official Records of the War of the Rebellion*, Series I, IV, 36.

2   Albuquerque *Rio Abajo Weekly Press,* August 26, 1863.

3   Statement of Robert North, November 10, 1863, *Official Records of the War of the Rebellion,* Series I, XXXIV, Part 4, 100.

4   See Santa Fe *Weekly New Mexican,* April 7, 1865.

5   For Carson's report, see *Official Record of the War of the Rebellion,* Series I, XLI, Part 1, 939-42. See also George H. Pettis, "Kit Carson's Fight with the Comanche and Kiowa Indians," *Publications of the Historical Society of New Mexico,* XII (1908), 7-35.

6   For details on this continuing traffic, see Kenner, *New Mexican-Plains Indians Relations,* 155-200.

7   For the record of Indian depredations in Texas during this war, see Dorman H. Winfrey, ed., *Texas Indian Papers, 1825-1916* (4 vols., Austin: Texas State Library, 1959-1961), IV, 1-90.

8   *Annual Report of the Commissioner of Indian Affairs for the Year 1867* (Washington, D.C.: Government Printing Office, 1867), 2.

9   Winfrey, ed., *Texas Indian Papers,* IV, 95-105, 235-36; *Senate Executive Document 74,* 40 Cong., 2 Sess., 20.

10 *Annual Report of the Commissioner of Indian Affairs for the Year 1866,* 280.

11 *Annual Report of the Secretary of War for the Year 1867,* 36-37.

12 *Senate Report 156,* 39 Cong., 2 Sess., 3-8.

13 Quoted in Henry M. Stanley, *Early Travels and Adventures in America and Asia* (New York, 1905), 252-53; and in Ernest Wallace and David M. Vigness, eds., *Documents of Texas History* (Austin: Steck Company, 1963), 206.

14 Charles J. Kappler, *Indian Affairs: Laws and Treaties* (3 vols., Washington, D.C.: Government Printing Office, 1903), 980-89.

15 For details on Mackenzie's life, see Ernest Wallace, *Ranald S. Mackenzie on the Texas Frontier* (Lubbock: West Texas Museum Association, 1964); Robert G. Carter, *On the Border with Mackenzie* (Washington, D.C.: Eynon Printing Company, 1935).

16 *Senate Miscellaneous Document 37,* 42 Cong., 1 Sess., 1-2.

17 *Annual Report of the Commissioner of Indian Affairs for the Year 1874,* 272; James Mooney, "Calendar History of the Kiowa," *Seventeenth Annual Report of the Bureau of American Ethnology, 1895-1896* (Washington, D.C.: Government Printing Office, 1898), 210.

18 *Annual Report of the Commissioner of Indian Affairs for the Year 1875,* 220; George Bird Grinnell, *The Fighting Cheyennes* (New York, 1915), 313; Olive K. Dixon, *Life of "Billy" Dixon* (Dallas: P. L. Turner Company, 1914), 170-77; William Sturtevant Nye, *Bad Medicine & Good: Tales of the Kiowa* (Norman: University of Oklahoma Press, 1962), 182.

19 *House Executive Document 1,* 43 Cong., 2 Sess., 26; *Annual Report of the Secretary of War for the Year 1874,* 4.

20 Details of this long, involved campaign may be found in *Annual Report of the Secretary of War for the Year 1875; Annual Report of the Commissioner of Indian Affairs for the Year 1875;* Carter, *On the Border with Mackenzie;* Nelson A. Miles, *Personal Recollections of General Nelson A. Miles* (Chicago: Werner Company, 1896). The best secondary source is William H. Leckie, *The Military Conquest of the Southern Plains* (Norman: University of Oklahoma Press, 1963). For the role of the 9th and 10th Cavalry in this campaign, see William H. Leckie, *The Buffalo Soldiers* (Norman: University of Oklahoma Press, 1967). Also extremely helpful in understanding the campaign is J. Evetts Haley, *Fort Concho and the Texas Frontier* (Kansas City: H. C. Revercomb-Americana, 1953).

Chapter 6

1 John C. Cremony, *Life Among the Apaches* (San Francisco: A. Roman and Company, 1868, and reprint), 31, calls Jackson an Englishman. However, Benjamin D. Wilson, who was camped nearby when the incident occurred, said Johnson was American; see Arthur Woodward, ed., "Benjamin David Wilson's Observations on Early Days in California and New Mexico," *Historical Society of Southern California Quarterly* (no volume, 1934), 74-150. See also J. P. Dunn, Jr., *Massacres of the Mountains* (New York, n.p., n.d.), 315.

2 Details about his early life are scant. See James H. McClintock, *Arizona: Prehistoric, Aboriginal, Pioneer, Modern* (3 vols., Chicago: S. J. Clarke, 1916), I, 176; and Will Levington Comfort, *Apache* (New York, 1931).

3 For further information about the scalp bounty system, see Ralph A. Smith, "The Scalp Hunter in the Borderlands, 1835-1850," *Arizona and the West,* VI (Spring 1964), 5-22; Smith, "Apache 'Ranching' Below the Gila, 1841-1845," *Arizoniana,* III (Winter 1962), 1-17; Smith, "Apache Plunder Trails Southward," *New Mexico Historical Review,* XXXVII (January 1962), 20-42; and Smith, "John

Joel Glanton: Lord of the Scalp Range," *The Smoke Signal* of the Tucson Corral of Westerners (No. 6, Fall 1962), 9-16.

4   Dwight L. Clarke, *Stephen Watts Kearny: Soldier of the West* (Norman: University of Oklahoma Press, 1961), 183-84.

5   Cremony, *Life Among the Apaches*, 23.

6   *Ibid.*, 82-85; John Russell Bartlett, *Personal Narrative of Exploration and Incidents* . . . (2 vols., New York, 1854, and reprint), I, 346-53.

7   Cremony, *Life Among the Apaches*, 52-57; Bartlett, *Personal Narrative*, I, 303-18.

8   *Senate Executive Document 119*, 32 Cong., 1 Sess., 258-61.

9   William H. Emory, "Report of the United States and Mexican Boundary Commission," *Senate Executive Document 108*, 34 Cong., 1 Sess. (3 vols. in 2), 88.

10   These letters are quoted in William A. Keleher, *Turmoil in New Mexico, 1846-1868* (Santa Fe: The Rydall Press, 1952), 45-46.

11   *Ibid.*, 54.

12   Edwin V. Sumner, "Reports from the Ninth Military Department, New Mexico," Santa Fe, May 27, 1852, *Senate Executive Document 1*, 32 Cong., 2 Sess., Part II, 25.

13   "Report of the Secretary of War," *ibid.*, 6.

14   William M. Malloy, comp. and ed., *Treaties, Conventions, International Acts, Protocols and Agreements Between the United States of America and Other Powers, 1776-1909* (2 vols., Washington, D.C.: Government Printing Office, 1910), I, 1110.

15   For details about this raid, as well as about Poston, see his *Apache Land* (San Francisco, 1868), and *Building A State in Apache Land* (Tempe, Arizona, 1963).

16   Tucson *Weekly Arizonian*, September 17, 1870, reprinted in *Arizoniana*, I (Fall 1960), 24. See also Barbara Tyler, "Cochise: Apache War Leader," *Journal of Arizona History*, VI (Spring 1965), 1-10.

17   Thomas E. Farish, *History of Arizona* (8 vols., San Francisco: The Filmer Brothers Electrotype Company, 1915-1918), II, 30.

18   Robert M. Utley, "The Bascom Affair: A Reconstruction," *Arizona and the West*, III (Spring 1961), 59-68; and B. Sacks, "New Evidence on the Bascom Affair," *Arizona and the West*, IV (Autumn 1962), 261-78.

19   *Official Records of the War of the Rebellion*, Series I, L, Part 1, 942.

20   *Ibid.*, Series I, XV, 914-18.

Chapter 7

1   For Roberts' report, see *Official Record of the War of the Rebellion*, Series 1, L, Part 1, 128-32. See also Cremony, *Life Among the Apaches*, 164.

2   Cremony, *Life Among the Apaches*, 175-76.

3   *Official Record of the War of the Rebellion*, Series 1, L, Part 1, 100-105.

4   West's report is in *ibid.*, Series 1, L, Part 2, 296-97. Conner's version is in Daniel E. Conner, *Joseph Reddeford Walker and the Arizona Adventure*, edited by Donald J. Berthrong and Odessa Davenport (Norman: University of Oklahoma Press, 1956), 34-42.

5   See C. L. Sonnichsen, *The Mescalero Apaches* (Norman: University of Oklahoma Press, 1958), 159; Frederick Webb Hodge, *Handbook of American Indians North of Mexico* (2 vols., Washington, D.C.: Government Printing Office, 1907), I, 64, 282; Ralph H. Ogle, *Federal Control of the Western Apaches, 1848-1886* (Albuquerque: University of New Mexico Press, 1940), 56.

6   *Annual Report of the Commissioner of Indian Affairs for the Year 1862*, 248.

7   *Official Records*, Series 1, XV, 579-80.

8   *Senate Report 156*, 39 Cong., 2 Sess., 101-4.

9   For depredations in the years 1863-1864, see *Senate Report 156*, 39 Cong., 2 Sess., 247-64.

10   *Ibid.*, 220-21, 244, 304-7.

11   Conner, *Joseph Reddeford Walker*, 171-76; Clara T. Woody, "The Woolsey Expeditions of 1864," *Arizona and the West*, IV (Summer 1962), 157-76. See also Woolsey File, Carl Hayden Collection, Arizona Historical Society, Tucson.

12   For an example of their propaganda, see *Memorial and Affidavits Showing Outrages Perpetrated by Apache Indians in the Territory of Arizona for the Years 1869-1870* (San Francisco: Francis & Valentine, 1871).

13   For biographical details, see George Crook, *General George Crook: His Autobiography*, edited by Martin F. Schmidt (Norman: University of Oklahoma Press, 1946); John G. Bourke, *On the Border with Crook* (New York, 1891, and reprint). See also Crook File, Arizona Historical Society.

14   For biographical details, see Clum File, Arizona Historical Society; Wentworth Clum, *Apache Agent* (Boston, 1936).

15   See *Annual Report of the Commissioner of Indian Affairs for the Year 1874*, 310-11; and *Executive Orders Relating to Indian Reservations from May 14, 1855, to July 1, 1912*, 120-21.

16   John Clum, "The Capture of Geronimo," *San Dimas* (California) *Press*, April 21, 1927 (copy in Gatewood Collection, Arizona Historical Society). See also Clum, "Apache Misrule," *New Mexico Historical Review*, V (April, July 1930); and Clum, "Geronimo," *New Mexico Historical Review*, III (January, April, July 1928).

17   James B. Gillett, *Six Years with the Texas Rangers* (New Haven: Yale University Press, 1925, and reprint), 142-87; and Webb, *The Texas Rangers*, 395-406. The best general account of this event is in Dan L. Thrapp, *The Conquest of Apacheria* (Norman: University of Oklahoma Press, 1967), 182-210.

18   See Thomas Cruse, *Apache Days and After* (Caldwell, Idaho: The Caxton Press, 1941), 93-94; and James Mooney, "The Ghost Dance Religion," *Fourteenth Annual Report* of the Bureau of American Ethnology (Washington, D.C.: Government Printing Office, 1896), 704-5.

19   For details of the Cibicu affair, see Cruse, *Apache Days*, 93-133; Cruse was a participant in these events. See also James T. King, *War Eagle: A Life of General Eugene A. Carr* (Lincoln: University of Nebraska Press, 1963), 193-226.

20   Tucson *Star*, March 3 and 4, 1882.

21   See S. M. Barrett, ed., *Geronimo's Story of His Life* (New York, 1906), for biographical details.

22   For the events of this campaign, see Dan L. Thrapp, *General Crook and the Sierra Madre Adventure* (Norman: University of Oklahoma Press, 1971); and John G. Bourke, An Apache Campaign in the Sierra Madre (New York, 1886).

23   Bourke, *On the Border with Crook*, and Britton Davis, *The Truth About Geronimo* (New Haven: Yale University Press, 1929), detail the cheating and mistreatment accorded the Apache at San Carlos.

24 Copies of this telegram are in the Gatewood Collection, Arizona Historical Society, and in Thrapp, *Conquest of Apacheria*, 313. See also Dan L. Thrapp, *Al Sieber: Chief of Scouts* (Norman: University of Oklahoma Press, 1964), 294.

25 Quoted in Frank C. Lockwood, *The Apache Indians* (New York, 1938), 280.

26 Torres, Decree to all Prefects, October 2, 1885, "Apache Folder, 1856-1886," Archives of Sonora (microfilm copy in Arizona Historical Society, Tucson). The treaty of July 29, 1882, allowing American troops into Mexico had expired after two years; thus in 1885 Crook had to make his own arrangement with Governor Torres.

27 Ed Arhelger to C. B. Gatewood, Jr., Maywood, California, May 5, 1928, Letter No. 661, Gatewood Collection. Maus' report and other documents are in the Maus Collection, Special Collections Division, Library, University of Arizona, and the Maus File, Arizona Historical Society. See also Bernard C. Nalty and Truman R. Strobridge, "Captain Emmet Crawford: Commander of Apache Scouts," *Arizona and the West*, VI (Spring 1964), 30-40; "The killing of Captain Crawford," Prescott *Morning Courier*, March 24, 1886; and W. E. Shipp, "Captain Crawford's Last Expedition," *Journal of the United States Cavalry Association*, XIX (October 1905), 280 et seq.

28 Bourke, *On the Border with Crook*, 474-75; his account of the surrender proceedings are on pages 474-79. Davis, *The Truth About Geronimo*, 196-212, contain a complete transcript of the conference, along with copies of Crook's letters regarding it.

29 For details of these events, see Davis, *The Truth About Geronimo*, 214-17. Crook's comments on these events are contained in George Crook, *Resumé of Operations Against Apache Indians, 1882-1886* (n.p. privately printed, 1886).

30 Virginia W. Johnson, *The Unregimented General: A Biography of Nelson A. Miles* (Boston, 1962). See also Newton F. Tolman, *The Search for General Miles* (New York, 1968), and Miles' two autobiographical efforts, *Personal Recollections and Observations* (Chicago: The Werner Company, 1897), and *Serving the Republic* (New York, 1911).

31 H. C. Benson, "The Geronimo Campaign," *Army and Navy Journal* (July 3, 1909); copy in the Gatewood Collection. See also William Stover, "Uprising of Apaches Under Geronimo," *Washington National Tribune*, April 23, 1925.

32 For copies of this correspondence, see *Senate Executive Document 117*, 49 Cong., 2 Sess., Part III, 49-77.

33   Charles B. Gatewood, "An Account of the Surrender of Geronimo," Gatewood Collection; this reminiscence was written about 1895. An abbreviated version of this paper, edited by Gatewood's son, appeared as "The Surrender of Geronimo," in *Proceedings of the Annual Meeting and Dinner of the Order of Indian Wars of the United States* (Washington, D.C., 1929).

34   These telegrams were copies from the originals at the headquarters, Division of the Pacific, San Francisco, by C. B. Gatewood, Jr., and are in the Gatewood Collection, Arizona Historical Society.

35   For additional details about events following Geronimo's surrender, see Odie B. Faulk, *The Geronimo Campaign* (New York, 1969), 176-221.

Chapter 8

1   Benjamin Butler Harris, *The Gila Trail: The Texas Argonauts and the California Gold Rush,* edited by Richard H. Dillon (Norman: University of Oklahoma Press, 1960), 31.

BIBLIOGRAPHY

The literature of the Indian wars of the Southwest is extensive, running to hundreds of volumes and a far larger number of articles. Beyond the items listed below and the works that are obvious, I recommend that the serious student of the period look at the articles in the *Southwestern Historical Quarterly*, *West Texas Historical Association Yearbook*, *Texana*, *Panhandle-Plains Historical Review*, *Museum Journal* of the West Texas Association, *Password*, *New Mexico Historical Review*, *Journal of Arizona History*, *Arizona and the West*, *The American West*, *Journal of the West*, *Southern California Quarterly*, and *California Historical Society Quarterly*.

Original Sources

Apache Folder, 1856-1886, Sonoran Archives. Microfilm copy at the Arizona Historical Society, Tucson.

Bartlett, John Russell. *Personal Narrative of Exploration and Incidents.* . . . 2 vols. New York, 1854.

John Robert Baylor File, Arizona Historical Society, Tucson.

Benson, H. C. "The Geronimo Campaign," *Army and Navy Journal*, July 3, 1909.

Béxar Archives. Austin: University of Texas Archives.

Bourke, John G. *An Apache Campaign in the Sierra Madre.* New York, 1886.

————. *On the Border with Crook.* New York, 1891.

Brooks, Clinton E., and Frank D. Reeve, eds. "A Dragoon in New Mexico, 1850-1856," *New Mexico Historical Review,* XXII (January 1947), 51-97.

Carter, Robert G. *On the Border with Mackenzie.* Washington, D.C.: Eynon Printing Company, 1935.

John Clum File, Arizona Historical Society, Tucson.

Clum, John. "Apache Misrule," *New Mexico Historical Review,* V (April, July, 1930).

————. "The Capture of Geronimo," *San Dimas* (California) *Press,* April 21, 1927. Copy in Gatewood Collection, Arizona Historical Society, Tucson.

————. "Geronimo," *New Mexico Historical Review,* III (January, April, July 1928).

Cochise File, Arizona Historical Society, Tucson.

Conner, Daniel E. *Joseph Reddeford Walker and the Arizona Adventure,* edited by Donald J. Berthrong and Odessa Davenport. Norman, Oklahoma, 1956.

Cooke, Philip St. George. *The Conquest of New Mexico and California in 1846-1848.* New York, 1878.

Coues, Elliott, ed. *The Journal of Jacob Fowler.* New York, 1898.

Cremony, John C. *Life Among the Apaches.* San Francisco: A. Roman and Company, 1868.

Croix, Teodoro de. "Report," in A. B. Thomas, *Teodoro de Croix and the Northern Frontier of New Spain, 1776-1783.* Norman, Oklahoma, 1941.

George Crook File, Arizona Historical Society, Tucson.

Crook, George. *George Crook: His Autobiography,* edited by Martin F. Schmitt. Norman, Oklahoma, 1946.

————. *Resumé of Operations Against Apache Indians, 1882-1886.* N.p., privately printed, 1886.

Cruse, Thomas. *Apache Days and After.* Caldwell, Idaho, 1941.

Davis, Britton. *The Truth About Geronimo.* New Haven, Connecticut, 1929.

Dillon, Richard H., ed. *A Cannoneer in Navajo Country: The Journal of Josiah M. Rice.* Denver: Old West Publishing Company, 1970.

Dunn, J. P. *Massacres of the Mountains.* New York, n.d.

Edwards, Marcellus Ball. "Diary," in *Marching with the Army of the West,* edited by Ralph P. Bieber. Vol. 4 of Southwest Historical Series. Glendale, California, 1936.

Espinosa, J. Manuel, ed. "Memoirs of a Kentuckian in New Mexico," *New Mexico Historical Review,* XIII (January 1938), 1-13.

Ferguson, Philip Gooch. "Diary," in *Marching with the Army of the West,* edited by Ralph P. Bieber. Vol. 4 of Southwest Historical Series. Glendale, California, 1936.

Gatewood, Charles B., Jr. "The Surrender of Geronimo," in *Proceedings of the Annual Meeting and Dinner of the Order of Indian Wars of the United States.* Washington, D.C., 1929.

Gatewood Collection. Arizona Historical Society, Tucson.

Geronimo. *Geronimo's Story of His Life*, edited by S. M. Barrett. New York, 1906.

Gillett, James B. *Six Years with the Texas Rangers*. New Haven, Connecticut, 1925.

Harris, Benjamin B. *The Gila Trail: The Texas Argonauts and the Gila Trail*, edited by Richard H. Dillon. Norman, Oklahoma, 1960.

Hughes, John Taylor. *Doniphan's Expedition*. Cincinnati: U. P. James, 1847.

Maus Collection. Special Collections Division, Library, University of Arizona, Tucson.

Memorial and Affidavits Showing Outrages Perpetrated by Apache Indians in the Territory of Arizona for the Years 1869-1870. San Francisco: Francis & Valentine, 1871.

Nelson A. Miles File. Arizona Historical Society, Tucson.

Miles, Nelson A. *Personal Recollections and Observations*. Chicago: The Werner Company, 1897.

———. *Serving the Republic*. New York, 1911.

Mumey, Nollie, ed. *March of the First Dragoons to the Rocky Mountains in 1835: The Diaries and Maps of Lemuel Ford*. Denver: Eames Brothers Press, 1957.

Poston, Charles D. *Apache Land*. San Francisco, 1868.

———. *Building a State in Apache Land*. Tempe, Arizona, 1963.

Quaife, Milo M., ed. *Kit Carson's Autobiography*. Chicago: Lakeside Classics, 1935.

Shipp, W. E. "Captain Crawford's Last Expedition," *Journal of the United States Cavalry Association*, XIX (October 1905), 280 et seq.

Stanley, Henry M. *Early Travels and Adventures in America and Asia*. New York, 1905.

Wallace, Ernest, and David M. Vigness. *Documents of Texas History*. Austin, 1963.

Winfrey, Dorman H., ed. *Texas Indian Papers, 1825-1916*. 4 vols. Austin: Texas State Library, 1959-1961.

Woodward, Arthur, ed. "Benjamin David Wilson's Observations on Early Days in California and New Mexico," *Historical Society of Southern California Quarterly* (1934), 74-150.

Woolsey File. Hayden Collection, Arizona Historical Society, Tucson.

Government Documents

Abel, Annie H., comp. and ed. *Official Correspondence of James S. Calhoun While Indian Agent at Santa Fe and Superintendent of Indian Affairs in New Mexico*. 1915.

Annual Report of the Commissioner of Indian Affairs for the Year 1857. And for the years 1858, 1859, 1860, 1862, 1866, 1867, 1874, and 1875.

Annual Report of the Secretary of War for the Year 1867. And for the years 1874 and 1875.

Emory, William H. "Report of the United States and Mexican Boundary Commission," *Senate Executive Document* 108, 34 Cong., 1 Sess. 2 vols.

Executive Orders Relating to Indian Reservations from May 14, 1855, to July 1, 1912.

Hodge, Frederick Webb. *Handbook of American Indians North of Mexico.* 2 vols., 1907.

House Executive Document 70, 38 Cong., 1 Sess.

House Executive Document 1, 38 Cong., 2 Sess.

House Executive Document 308, 40 Cong., 2 Sess.

House Executive Document 1, 43 Cong., 2 Sess.

Journals of the House of Representatives of the Republic of Texas. 5 Cong., 1 Sess. (Texas).

Kappler, Charles J., comp. and ed. *Indian Affairs: Laws and Treaties.* 3 vols. 1903.

Malloy, William M., comp. and ed. *Treaties, Conventions, International Acts, Protocols and Agreements Between the United States of America and Other Powers, 1776-1909.* 2 vols. 1910.

Mooney, James. "Calendar History of the Kiowas," *Seventeenth Annual Report of the Bureau of American Ethnology.* 1898.

————. "The Ghost Dance Religion," *Fourteenth Annual Report of the Bureau of American Ethnology.* 1896.

Report on the Condition of the Tribes, 1867. 1867.

Senate Executive Document 64, 31 Cong., 2 Sess.

Senate Executive Document 119, 32 Cong., 1 Sess.

Senate Executive Document 1, 32 Cong., 2 Sess.

Senate Executive Document 108, 34 Cong., 1 Sess., 2 vols.

Senate Executive Document 1, 36 Cong., 2 Sess.

Senate Executive Document 156, 39 Cong., 2 Sess.

Senate Executive Document 74, 40 Cong., 2 Sess.

Senate Executive Document 117, 49 Cong., 2 Sess.

Senate Miscellaneous Document 37, 42 Cong., 1 Sess.

Senate Report 156, 39 Cong., 2 Sess.

Simpson, James H. "Journal of a Military Reconnaissance from Santa Fe, New Mexico, to the Navajo Country in 1849," in *Senate Executive Document 64,* 31 Cong., 2 Sess.

The War of the Rebellion: A Compilation of the Official Records of the Union and Confederate Armies. 128 vols. 1880-1901.

Newspapers

Albuquerque *Rio Abajo Weekly Press*
Houston *Telegraph and Texas Register*

Prescott *Arizona Miner*
Prescott *Morning Courier*
Richmond (Texas) *Telescope and Texas Register*
Santa Fe *Gazette*
Santa Fe *New Mexican*
Santa Fe *Republican*
Santa Fe *Weekly Gazette*
Santa Fe *Weekly New Mexican*
Silver City (New Mexico) *Southwest*
Tucson *Star*
Tucson *Weekly Arizonian*
Washington *National Tribune*

Secondary Sources

Bailey, Lynn R. *The Long Walk: A History of the Navajo Wars, 1846-48.* Los Angeles, 1964.

Baldwin, Gordon. *The Warrior Apaches.* Tucson: Dale S. King, 1966.

Barnes, Will C. *Apaches and Longhorns.* Los Angeles: Ward Ritchie Press, 1941.

Baylor, George W. *John Robert Baylor: Confederate Governor of Arizona,* edited by Odie B. Faulk. Tucson: Arizona Pioneers' Historical Society, 1966.

Bieber, Ralph P. *Marching with the Army of the West.* Vol. 4 of Southwest Historical Series. Glendale, California, 1936.

Carter, Harvey L. *Dear Old Kit: The Historical Christopher Carson.* Norman, Oklahoma, 1968.

Castetter, Edward F., and Willis H. Bell. *Pima and Papago Indian Agriculture.* Albuquerque, 1942.

Clark, Laverne H. *They Sang for Horses: The Impact of the Horse on Navajo and Apache Folklore.* Tucson, 1966.

Clarke, Dwight L. *Stephen Watts Kearny: Soldier of the West.* Norman, Oklahoma, 1961.

Clum, Wentworth. *Apache Agent.* Boston, 1936.

Comfort, Will Levington. *Apache.* New York, 1931.

Connelley, William E. *Doniphan's Expedition.* . . . Topeka, Kansas: Crane & Co., 1907.

Crimmins, Martin L. "Colonel Robert E. Lee's Report on Indian Combats in Texas," *Southwestern Historical Quarterly,* XXXIX (July 1935), 21-32.

Dixon, Olive K. *Life of "Billy" Dixon.* Dallas: P. L. Turner Company, 1914.

Estergreen, M. Morgan. *Kit Carson: A Portrait in Courage.* Norman, Oklahoma, 1962.

Farish, Thomas E. *History of Arizona.* 8 vols. San Francisco: The Filmer Brothers Electrotype Company, 1915-1918.

Faulk, Odie B. *The Geronimo Campaign.* New York, 1969.

Forbes, Jack D. *Apache, Navajo, and Spaniard.* Norman, Oklahoma, 1960.

———. *Warriors of the Colorado.* Norman, Oklahoma, 1965.

Grinnell, George Bird. *The Fighting Cheyennes.* New York, 1915.

Haley, J. Evetts. *Fort Concho and the Texas Frontier.* Kansas City: H. C. Revercomb-Americana, 1953.

Hatcher, Mattie A. *The Opening of Texas to Foreign Settlement.* Austin: University of Texas Bulletin 2714, 1927.

Hewett, Edgar Lee. *The Pueblo Indian World.* Albuquerque, 1945.

Heyman, Max L. *Prudent Soldier: A Biography of Major General E. R. S. Canby, 1817-1873.* Glendale, California, 1959.

Hunt, Aurora. *Major General James Henry Carleton, 1814-1874: Western Frontier Dragoon.* Glendale, California, 1958.

Irving, Washington. *The Adventures of Captain Bonneville, U.S.A., in the Far West . . . ,* edited by Edgeley W. Todd. Norman, Oklahoma, 1961.

Johnson, Virginia W. *The Unregimented General: A Biography of Nelson A. Miles.* Boston, 1962.

Keleher, William A. *Turmoil in New Mexico, 1846-1868.* Santa Fe: The Rydall Press, 1952.

Kenner, Charles L. *A History of New Mexican-Plains Indian Relations.* Norman, Oklahoma, 1969.

Kerby, Robert L. *The Confederate Invasion of New Mexico, 1861-1862.* Los Angeles, 1958.

King, James T. *War Eagle: A Life of General Eugene A. Carr.* Lincoln, Nebraska, 1963.

Koch, Lena C. "Federal Indian Policy in Texas, 1845-1860," *Southwestern Historical Quarterly,* XXVII (1924), 223-234; (1925), 19-35, 98-127.

Leckie, William H. *The Buffalo Soldiers.* Norman, Oklahoma, 1967.

———. *The Military Conquest of the Southern Plains.* Norman, Oklahoma, 1963.

Lockwood, Frank C. *The Apache Indians.* New York, 1938.

McClintock, James H. *Arizona: Prehistoric, Aboriginal, Pioneer, Modern.* 3 vols. Chicago: S. J. Clarke, 1916.

McNitt, Frank, ed. *Navajo Expedition.* Norman, Oklahoma, 1964.

———. *Navajo Wars: Military Campaigns, Slave Raids, and Reprisals.* Albuquerque, 1972.

Nalty, Bernard C., and Truman R. Strobridge, "Captain Emmet Crawford: Commander of Apache Scouts," *Arizona and the West,* VI (Spring 1964), 30-40.

Nye, William Sturtevant. *Bad Medicine and Good: Tales of the Kiowa.* Norman, Oklahoma, 1962.

Ogle, Ralph H. *Federal Control of the Western Apaches, 1848-1886.* Albuquerque, 1940.

Opler, Morris E. *An Apache Life-Way.* Chicago, 1941.

Parsons, Elsie Clews. *Pueblo Indian Religion*. 2 vols. Chicago, 1939.

Pettis, George H. "Kit Carson's Fight with the Comanche and Kiowa Indians," *Publications of the Historical Society of New Mexico*, XII (1908), 7-35.

Richardson, Rupert N. *The Comanche Barrier to South Plains Settlement*. Glendale, California, 1933.

Rickey, Don, Jr. *Forty Miles a Day on Beans and Hay: The Enlisted Soldier Fighting the Indian Wars*. Norman, Oklahoma, 1963.

Sacks, B. "New Evidence on the Bascom Affair," *Arizona and the West*, IV (Autumn 1962), 261-278.

Sapir, Edward, and Harry Joijer. *Navajo Texts*. Iowa City: Linguistic Society of America, University of Iowa Press, 1942.

Simmons, Mar. "A Horse Race at Fort Fauntleroy: An Incident of the Navajo Wars," *La Gaceta*, V (No. 1, 1970).

Smith, Ralph A. "Apache Plunder Trails Southward," *New Mexico Historical Review*, XXXVII (January 1962), 20-42.

———. "Apache 'Ranching' Below the Gila, 1841-1845," *Arizoniana*, III (Winter 1962), 1-17.

———. "John Joel Glanton: Lord of the Scalp Range," *The Smoke Signal* of the Tucson Corral of Westerners (No. 6, Fall 1962), 9-16.

———. "The Scalp Hunter in the Borderlands, 1835-1850," *Arizona and the West*, VI (Spring 1964), 5-22.

Sonnichsen, C. L. *The Mescalero Apaches*. Norman, Oklahoma, 1958.

Spicer, Edward H. *Cycles of Conquest: The Impact of Spain, Mexico, and the United States on the Indians of the Southwest*. Tucson, 1962.

Spier, Leslie. *Yuman Tribes of the Gila River*. Chicago, 1933.

Stover, William. "Uprising of Apaches Under Geronimo," Washington *National Tribune*, April 23, 1925.

Thomas, Alfred B. *Teodoro de Croix and the Northern Frontier of New Spain, 1776-1783*. Norman, Oklahoma, 1941.

Thrapp, Dan L. *Al Sieber: Chief of Scouts*. Norman, Oklahoma, 1964.

———. *The Conquest of Apacheria*. Norman, Oklahoma, 1967.

———. *General Crook and the Sierra Madre Campaign*. Norman, Oklahoma, 1971.

Thrapp, Dan S. *General Crook and the Sierra Madre Adventure*. Norman: University of Oklahoma Press, 1971.

Tolman, Newton F. *The Search for General Miles*. New York, 1968.

Tyler, Barbara. "Cochise: Apache War Leader," *Journal of Arizona History*, VI (Spring 1965), 1-10.

Utley, Robert M. "The Bascom Affair: A Reconstruction," *Arizona and the West*, III (Spring 1961), 59-68.

———. *Frontiersmen in Blue: The United States Army and the Indian, 1848-1865*. New York, 1967.

Wallace, Ernest. *Ranald S. Mackenzie on the Texas Frontier*. Lubbock: West Texas Museum Association, 1964.

———— and E. Adamson Hoebel. *The Comanches: Lords of the South Plains.*
    Norman, Oklahoma, 1952.
Webb, Walter P., ed. *The Handbook of Texas.* 2 vols. Austin: Texas State
    Historical Association, 1952.
————. *The Texas Rangers.* Boston, 1935.
Woody, Clara T. "The Woolsey Expeditions of 1864," *Arizona and the
    West,* IV (Summer 1962), 157-76.

INDEX

Adobe Walls, 122, 136-37, 138; battle of, 121

Agua Chiquita, Navajo chief, 67, 70

Anea, Juan, Mexican silversmith, 59

Anza, Juan Bautista de, visits Yumas, 14, 108

Apache Indians, 199, 200; origin and location of, 18-19; religion and culture, 19, 18-23, 28, 31, 35, 53, 76, 80, 136, 142-97; final conquest of, 158; move to San Carlos contemplated, 173; picture of, 197

Apache Indian police, 174, 177

Apache Pass, 153, 154, 156, 158, 159

Aravaipa Apache, attacked by Tucsonians, 166

Arizona Land and Mining Company, 155

Arizona Rangers, mustered to fight Indians, 156

Arthur, President Chester A., reprimands Carr, 183

Athagascan, linguistic group, 18

Augur, General C. C., commander of Department of Texas, 134, 138

Austin, Stephen F., leads American colonists, 91, 97

Backus, Major Electus, begins fort construction, 54, 64

Backus, Captain William H., constructs fort, 118

Baird, Samuel M., Navajo agent, 56; replaced as agent, 57

Barboncito, Navajo chief, 80

Barrett, S. M., 184

Bartlett, John Russell: visits Pima Indians, 10; boundary commissioner, 144-45, 146, 147

Bascom, George N., 153, 154

Bascom Affair, 153